THE ABRAHAMIC ARCHETYPE

The

Abrahamic Archetype

Conceptual and Historical Relationships
between Judaism, Christianity and Islam

by

Samuel Zinner

This first edition published in 2011 by
Archetype
Chetwynd House
Bartlow, Cambridge
CB21 4PP
UK
www.archetypebooks.com

in association with The Matheson Trust

ISBN 978 1 901383 41 6

A full CIP record for this book is available from The British Library
A full CIP record for this book is available from the Library of Congress

Designed and Typeset by Ian Abdallateef Whiteman
Printed and bound in Great Britain

CONTENTS

PREFACE

THE AUTHOR'S MAIN burden in this monograph is to argue for a rapprochement on the part of the church towards the ancient theology of Jewish Christianity, and by extension towards Islam, and to demonstrate that such a rapprochement would be neither unreasonable nor without precedent in ecclesiastical history. If such a rapprochement were to be undertaken, the church would be in a far better position to understand Islam more sympathetically, since the latter parallels to a significant degree much of the essential ethos and theological heritage of Jewish Christianity, which to varying degrees constitutes in turn the historical matrix of later eastern and western Christianity.

The increased contact between cultures, as well as the tragedies of inter-religious strife which mark our time, underscore for the church the urgency of the question regarding Islam's status as a world religion and as a heavenly revelation. At the very least, mutual understanding may lead to toleration and peaceful societal coexistence of peoples of diverse religious affiliation. But beyond this, we may hope that a mutual understanding and shared theological exploration among Jews, Christians and Muslims may lead to a genuine respect and the sharing of ever-deepening spiritual and philosophical insights.

The first part of the monograph is predominantly concerned with historical matters, detailing rivalries between ancient Gentile and Jewish Christianity and the latter's subsequent archetypal reflection in Islam. This is, of course, not to imply that every Islamic parallel to Jewish Christianity was borrowed historically from the early Jerusalem church under James, the 'brother' of Jesus. Such a historicist view would not sufficiently take into account the possibility of similar ideas and rites arising independently in two separate religious variants, issuing forth from a single transcendent archetype underlying the Abrahamic faiths. The second part of the monograph is mainly theological and metaphysical, and concentrates on such controversial questions as christology, trinity and crucifixion. Yet in both parts one finds historical, theological, philosophical, and mystical or metaphysical themes, some of which are at times repeated in varying forms throughout the course of the work. With this method we hope to acquaint the reader gradually with some of our more involved, and perhaps somewhat less familiar arguments and evidence.

Though in our work we refer to a widely eclectic body of authors, our frequent allusion to two modern metaphysicians in particular, Frithjof Schuon and Seyyed Hossein Nasr, is owing to the monograph's special emphasis on Sufi speculative theology and metaphysics. Schuon's and Nasr's body of work on the essential commonalities and formal disjunctions existing between the various world religions is especially applicable to our own investigation of the Abrahamic religious archetype and its varying formal manifestations on the plane of world history.

It would not be out of place here for the author to refer to the relatively recent controversial Vatican document, *Dominus Iesus,* according to which the precise nature and status of the non-Christian religions is left as an open question for Catholic experts to research. The church has by no means definitively pronounced upon or fully clarified the question at hand. This monograph is presented as a contribution to the debate, and the exploration of the nature of the relationship existing between the three Abrahamic religions of Judaism, Christianity and Islam. Both continuities and discontinuities in the three groups must be admitted in order to arrive simultaneously at a principled or 'inward' ecumenism of the heart and to avoid an unprincipled or 'extrinsic' syncretism.

Regarding commonalities and disjunctions existing between the world religions, we may note that, just as a northern view of a point in the distance cannot be reduced to or identified with a southern view of the same point, so the basic spiritual points of view of Christianity and Islam cannot be reduced to each other through any sort of forced or artificial religious eclecticism. Judaism, Islam and the church rightly remain distinct religious systems. To acknowledge and preserve such distinctions, we upon occasion italicize or place quotation marks around certain words or expressions. This serves to indicate that such formulations must be understood in a qualified or restricted sense. We therefore ask the reader to keep this editorial practice in mind while reading the monograph in order to avoid misunderstanding the author's intentions.

Yet there are undeniable similarities and overlapping realities of a transcendent order in the content of the various religions; parallels which can be explored and which indeed constitute the main burden of this monograph. If we employ a *pia interpretatio* along with dialectical reasoning, we will find that the three Abrahamic religions have much more in common than is often conceded. Additionally, Thomas Aquinas's teaching on analogical predication reminds us of the relativity of all dogma, and of its inability to completely circumscribe the truths to which such verbal articulations point, though dogma admittedly can adequately serve the relative purpose for which it is formulated. While by no means denying the plenary character of any divinely inspired prophet's teaching — a teaching which would in any case constitute not dogma, but revelation — analogical predication nevertheless reminds us of the cognitive limitations and barriers faced by anyone seeking to understand an inspired prophet's revealed message. In short, revelation is sent from heaven, whereas dogma is not, even if, in a certain sense and to some extent, heaven assists the human reflection necessary to formulate dogma. If dogmas are not to be taken 'literally' and exhaustively, then the extent to which apparently contradictory doctrines of different religions may overlap and be reconciled through dialectical synthesis increases considerably.

As a general rule, polemics usually interfere with a logical and fair presentation of evidence and argumentation. We have therefore avoided polemic other than in a few isolated cases, where we feel it may be justified. The various extreme and even outrageous views current in today's religious climate, reflecting prejudice or bigotry against Judaism, Christianity or Islam, certainly deserve sharp criticism and justify an occasional spirited remark, for Justice is, after all, one of the divine attributes.

Since this book is in large measure a survey study, it should be self-evident that when we allude to or cite the work of various modern Christian theologians, this by no means necessarily implies an endorsement of their work in general or as a whole. Several of these contemporary theologians currently wield immense influence in the world of ideas among popular and scholarly audiences. It is therefore our intention to offer guidance both to a general readership and to scholars concerning which theological or historical opinions of such authorities may be trusted, and on what points they should be critically questioned or even rejected with regard to the main topics of our study. This critical sifting is all the more necessary given the regrettable lack of knowledge certain Christian scholars sometimes exhibit concerning both Jewish and Islamic traditions. Naturally also regrettable are the sometimes distorted views concerning Christian and Jewish beliefs and rituals which one at times encounters among some Muslims, both in past literature and in current popular beliefs.

Unless otherwise noted, citations from the Qur'an are given according to Marmaduke Pickthall's version with occasional modifications, especially with regard to spelling (e.g., 'wherein' instead of the older orthographic form 'wherin'). Translational modifications of Pickthall have been undertaken with reference to the standard Arabic text of the Qur'an and to several modern English language translations of commentaries on Islam's sacred book in various languages. Transliteration of foreign language texts is almost always a special problem in theological and philosophical works. Because of the widely diverging variety of transcription systems, we have on the whole sought to avoid in particular Arabic diacritics, not only in our own original text, but also in the works of other authors quoted in the monograph. Regarding quotations, material in brackets belongs to the author of this monograph; remarks in parentheses are those of the author/s being cited.

SAMUEL ZINNER
Casablanca, Morocco, 2011

CHAPTER ONE

Jewish Christianity and Islam: Historical and Archetypal Convergences

HISTORICALLY VIEWED, CHRISTIANITY was not originally a separate religion in an absolute sense apart from Judaism. Early in its history, Christianity constituted, so to speak, a 'reform' branch[1] within Judaism, which retained the latter's requirements for Gentile converts, the so-called Noachide laws (see *Acts* 15). These 'Messianists', who have been called Jewish Christians, seem to have come principally from among the Pharisees and Essenes,[2] and their first leader after Christ was his 'brother', James the Just. What has traditionally been called Judaism after the destruction of the Second Temple is basically constituted by the descendants of the ancient Pharisee branch, whereas after Jewish Christianity experienced an historical eclipse on account of first- and second-century CE Roman persecutions, the Gentile sector of the church, or what has been called the Great Church, formed originally under the impetus of St. Paul's mission to the Gentiles, gained ascendancy in ecclesiastical history. Jewish Christians lived for the most part in peace with their Jewish compatriots; it was Gentile Christianity, which was to dominate nearly all of church history and much of the world's affairs for two millennia, that early on fell into severe and heated conflict with Judaism.

Viewed from the plane of history, the schism, as David Flusser has called it,[3] between Judaism and Christianity (in essence, the Gentile 'Great Church'), and the heated bitterness resulting from it, led to a bifurcation and then separation in group identity, a process well known to sociologists as a dynamic related to group formation and crystallization; yet the perspective of faith would suggest a providential process operative in at least certain aspects of this development. In the Catholic Church, the beginning of a rapprochement with Judaism emerged in the early 20th century, when various Popes began emphasizing that Christians are spiritual 'Semites', or 'Hebrews'; an admittedly somewhat problematic formulation, since 'Semite' is principally a 'racial' or 'ethnic' category, rather than a religious label. In any case, already in the early 20th century, one saw Catholic books with imprimaturs bearing titles such as *How Christ Said the First Mass*, by Fr. James L. Meagher, D.D. (New York: Christian Press Association Publishing Co., 1906), which argued in favour of the theological truth and validity of Catholic beliefs and practices by pointing to their historical Jewish roots, or at least to their Jewish archetypal parallels and analogues. A genuine interest in Judaism shows through such argumentation, which was certainly not exclusively an apologetic defence in favour of the antiquity of Catholic ritual leveled against Protestants, who claimed 'popish' faith and praxis were merely 'pagan' inventions or degradations dating only from the 'Dark Ages'.

In fact, the example of the medieval Catholic kabbalists presents us with a much earlier manifestation of a lively interest in Judaism within Christianity. It is sometimes asserted that the Christian kabbalists were interested in the Kabbalah for exclusively anti-Jewish polemical and pro-Catholic apologetical reasons. But when one reads, for example, John Reuchlin (1455–1522) or Petrus Galatinus (c. 1460–1540), the impression grows that these authors, despite their traditional anti-Jewish rhetoric, were nevertheless genuinely enchanted by and enamoured of the Jewish Kabbalah, and that in order to justify their interest in it to certain ecclesiastical authorities, they more or less consciously felt compelled to add to their presentation of Jewish theosophy a pro-Catholic apologetical and anti-Jewish polemical thrust.

Historically viewed, Christianity is not a 'departure' from Judaism; it is a providential transformational development of ancient Jewish ideas assimilated to Greco-Roman and Germanic thought and expression. Jewish Christianity is that branch of the church which saw little need of 'translating' Hebrew-based biblical theology into Greek philosophical categories. As Daniel Boyarin explains, Rabbinic Judaism was a 'nativist attempt to separate itself' from Hellenism and from what it labelled a '"Christian" logos theology' that was in fact a first-century Jewish development.[4] The church's traditional anti-Jewish diatribe, sometimes still employed by parish priests in homilies, about Judaism being a 'legalistic' religion on account of its 613 'talmudic' religious commandments as opposed to only 10 biblical commandments, is self-defeating, for the legal prescriptions in the Catholic code of canon law run literally into the thousands. Ultimately, what is going on between modern Judaism and Christianity is in several respects the survival of an ancient family conflict between Pharisee, Sadducee, Essene and 'Messianist' groups. The two-millennia-long conflict between Judaism and Christianity can be seen essentially as an internecine familial affair involving two different formal branches emanating from a single Abrahamic religious archetype.

The fact of Christianity's emergence as a separate religion apart from Judaism, at least from the perspective of historical comparative religious studies, requires at this point an explication of the ideas of religious abrogation and supersession. The terms may be allowed as theologically valid only if we view them as 'symbolic truth' and not as 'objective truth', as Frithjof Schuon has proposed.[5] As this author clarifies, abrogation is '"symbolically true," in the sense that the rejected forms are considered not in themselves and from the standpoint of their intrinsic truth but solely in certain contingent and negative aspects ... .'[6] For concerning Christianity in relation to Judaism, 'the Mosaic religion, insofar as it is the Word of God, cannot by any means be annulled, since "our Torah is for all eternity ..." (Maimonides).'[7] Abrogation is therefore 'relative, whereas the intrinsic reality of the Mosaic religion is absolute, because Divine.'[8] Schuon further explicates the matter dialectically, by explaining that the Messiah's 'abrogation' of Judaism is of a less intrinsic order than is the 'permanence' of Judaism, since the latter 'derives from the Divine Essence itself', so that Christ abrogated 'only a particular mode' of Judaism 'and not its "eternal" quality ... .'[9]

The Schuonian paradigm enables us to define that all religions are 'superior' to others only at the level of various 'aspects' of their 'manifestation', and not in the 'essence' of the religions, for at the level of the latter all religions are equally 'superior'.[10] The central event that led to the historical separation of Christianity from Judaism was that an 'exclusive and absolute value' was attributed, in a quite legitimate way of course, to a particular aspect of Judaism that coincides with Christianity.[11] We may say that such an emphasis demonstrates that Christianity cannot constitute an essential or universal abrogation of the religion of Moses, for the church is founded upon a spiritual element emanating from within Judaism itself. We refer to the Jewish prophetic teaching concerning a new, or more precisely stated, a *renewed* covenant, in the sense of a renewal of the one original or ancient covenant, not in the sense of a *replacement* or *supersession* of the primordial covenant. Indeed, the import of Paul's teaching in the eleventh chapter of *Romans*[12] is that Christians are saved by their union with the church because the latter is the mystical Body of Christ, the same Christ who mediates salvation specifically by means of his historical and 'mystical' participation in Judaism, the salvific covenant of God. In other words, the church participates in salvation because Christ mediates to it the salvation inherent in the *Jewish* covenant. That Christian theologians later excluded Jews from salvation because of their perceived lack of union with the church is not only ironic, it is anti-scriptural, contradicting as it does St. Paul's teaching that the church participates in salvation through the Jewish covenant, *and not vice versa*.

The abrogation of divine revelations in an absolute sense is denied in Qur'an 2:106: 'None of Our revelations do We abrogate or cause to be forgotten, but

3

We substitute something better or similar: Knowest thou not that God hath power over all things?' Abdullah Yusuf Ali, whose translation we have just cited, draws out the verse's implications in the following commentary:

> God's Message from age to age is always the same, but ... its form may differ according to the needs and exigencies of the time. That form was different as given to Moses and then to Jesus and then to Muhammad ... . There is nothing derogatory in this if we believe in progressive revelation ... . This does not mean that eternal principles change. It is only a sign of God's infinite Power that His creation should take so many forms and shapes not only in the material world but in the world of man's thought and expression.[13]

Each varying religious form serves the purpose of emphasizing certain doctrinal and ritual emphases that the other forms are not designed to embody and convey in the same manner or to the same degree. Thus the various religious forms would seem to differ only in a complementary sense by way of particular emphasis rather than by essentially contradictory content.

Every historian and theologian knows that Christ and his earliest followers were Torah-observing Jews. Before Christ's ascension, according to solid ecclesiastical tradition, James the Just was appointed head of the church, which was at first centered in Jerusalem. We know from Josephus and Hegesippus that James was revered by non-Christian Jewish Pharisee leaders up to the time of his death, which would have been impossible had James and his brother Jesus's movement advocated abandoning the Torah.[14] The following standard outline of ancient Jewish-Christian history will help illumine the earliest phases of Christian history: after the martyrdom of James (c.62 CE), the Jerusalem church, that is, the Jewish Christians, soon fled to the Pella region, east of Jordan. After the fall of Jerusalem (70 CE), some returned to the holy city, where the Jewish Christians thrived under bishops, successors of James, all of whom were most likely the closest physical relatives of Jesus, until the expulsion of the Jews from Jerusalem in 135 CE.[15] Thereafter, the Gentile section of the church gained predominance, and focus shifted away from James and Jerusalem to Peter's successors in Rome. Although ecclesiastical tradition documents James's appointment as head of the church by Christ himself, the Just One, as James was called, is mentioned only three times in the *Acts of the Apostles*, and only eight other times in the remainder of the New Testament, as opposed to nearly 170 biblical references to Paul.[16]

Such an apparent de-emphasis of James would most naturally have been the result of the early divisions felt between Paul's Gentile Christian churches and the Jerusalem Jewish-Christian community. But their respective theologies are only dialectically divergent, not essentially irreconcilable, for the two positions' mutual compatibility can be deduced from various facts which we explore below. At first, the sole area of contention between the two Christian variants, Jacobean and Pauline, was the question of Torah observance, not the question of christological dogma, since at the beginning of Christianity the Jerusalem church's christology was the only available model. But regarding the later christological crises, the Gentile Christians' demand that Jewish Christians adopt Greek philosophical concepts and terminology to express the nature of Christ and the trinity proved disastrous from the point of view of ecclesiastical history. It was to a large extent an attempt to impose an outward theological uniformity upon a question that in the New Testament itself was formulated with theological diversity and non-conformity. The New Testament contains a rich variety of christologies, so that one can concede the validity of distinct theological languages, one Hellenistic and abstractly philosophical, the other Semitic, biblical, and metaphorically concrete.

The main objection from Gentile Christians to Jewish-Christian christology was the latter's apparent denial of Jesus's pre-existence as the Logos and a refusal to assign to Jesus the title 'God'. Ironically, the Jewish Christians were, in certain fundamental respects, more correct in their christology than some of the early Gentile Christians, at least from the perspective of later Catholic theology, for according to the latter, as we will explore below, Jesus is not to be identified simplistically with the Logos. Furthermore, the Jewish Christians, like Jesus, James, and the early Jerusalem church, used the word 'God' strictly in the biblical sense of 'the Father', and their refusal to apply the term 'God' to Christ can be seen as analogously equivalent to the Gentile Christians' refusal to equate 'God the Father' with 'God the Son'.

The fact of the matter is that the Gentile Church's christological and trinitarian conciliar dogmas are not to be found *as such* in the New Testament, but were extrapolated from subsequent interpretations of biblical texts. The dogmas exist explicitly at the conciliar, not at the biblical level. In other words, we cannot attribute a fully developed Nicene level of knowledge to the biblical authors. The explicit teachings of the incarnation (in the sense of hypostatic union) and trinity as later formulated at councils were naturally unknown to the biblical authors, including the Jewish Christians under James. Indeed, the Gentile Christian de-emphasis on the humanity of Christ in favour of his divinity probably explains why 'Son of Man' as a formal christological title died out in the Great Church early on, and is in fact never once found in the Pauline writings. Outside the New Testament, it most likely would have survived as a living title only among Jewish Christians. In the church fathers it survived only as a quotation from the canonical gospels.

Though there are a few places of refuge where it seems that Jewish Christianity may have survived into modern times, especially in Ethiopia, there is another place where, to the surprise if not shock of Christian theologians, parallels to much of the heritage of early Jerusalem Christianity have maintained themselves to the present day: within Islam. As Hans Joachim Schoeps established in his groundbreaking German-language study, *Theologie und Geschichte des Judenchristentums* (*Theology and History of Jewish Christianity*),[17] there exist certain historical and theological affinities between ancient Ebionite Jewish-Christianity and Islam.[18] The historical links and archetypal parallels shared by Ebionitism and early Islam are extensive. As Schoeps observes, in Arabia the Prophet Muhammad would not have encountered representatives of the Great Church, but Ebionite and Monophysite faiths; the claim is then advanced that from these faiths various Jewish-Christian 'beliefs flowed in an unbroken stream of tradition into the proclamation of Muhammad'.[19] A balanced assimilation of Schoeps' ideas must guard against his historicist proclivities; however, it cannot be denied that every heavenly revelation avails itself of previous cultural data and experience.[20]

In Islamic theology we find, in accord with Ebionite doctrine, a series of seven True Prophets,[21] followed by an eighth 'definitive' Prophet, that is, Jesus or Muhammad, in Ebionitism and Islam respectively.[22] Schoeps emphasizes: 'The True Prophet concept of Ebionitism resurfaces in Islam as a dogma of reincarnation ... .'[23] As evidence, Schoeps cites the following *hadith* from Ibn Saʿd: 'I was sent [by God] repeatedly from age to age from the best generations of humanity, until I was finally sent in the age in which I now live.'[24] This *hadith* may, of course, be interpreted in other than a reincarnational sense, for as Schoeps clarifies, we have here an idea of a 'metamorphosis of the Shekhinah or the True Prophet, which we find in the *Pseudo-Clementines* (*verus propheta ab initio mundi per saeculum currens*), "the True Prophet, from the beginning of the world hastening through the age," *Rec.* 2:22)[25] ... .' The Holy Spirit, the *Shekhinah*, according to this paradigm, was passed down from Adam through the 'succession' of the Prophets.[26] Mohammad Ali Amir-Moezzi similarly prefers to interpret the transmission of the divine Light from Adam to the Prophet Muhammad and then to the Imams, not as involving metempsychosis, but rather what he calls 'metemphotosis', or the 'displacement of light'.[27] We read in *Clementine Recognitions* III, chapter 20, that the Holy Spirit is possessed by Christ, and 'that he alone has it, who has changed his forms and his names from the beginning of the world, and so reappeared again and again in the world, until coming upon his own times, and being anointed with mercy for the works of God, he shall enjoy rest for ever. His honour it is to bear rule and lordship over all things ... .'[28] As Schoeps reminds us, the Ebionite 'cyclical' doctrine of the sinless True Prophet beginning with Adam can be traced 'from Elkesai, the Mandeans, Mani, and Muhammad, to the Shiitish Imam-doctrine of the *Hadith*'.[29]

We may here make the observation that the *Genesis* account of Adam's 'transgression' may be reconciled with the Islamic idea of Adam's retention of moral integrity, for St. Paul writes in *Romans* 8:20-21: 'For the creature was made subject to vanity, not willingly, but by reason of him that made it subject in hope: Because the creature also itself shall be delivered from the servitude of corruption, into the liberty of the glory of the children of God.' Despite all the convoluted reasoning of certain Christian exegetes who have wrestled with this passage, the most natural interpretation would seem to be that Adam provisionally subjected the world to 'vanity' in the hope of setting in motion a providential plan for the world's redemption that would result in beatitude to a degree that otherwise may not, or perhaps even could not, have occurred, were it not for the 'fall'. In Pauline language, 'where sin abounded, grace did more abound' (*Romans* 5:20); in this spirit, the Catholic Church's liturgy has traditionally celebrated Adam's 'transgression' as a 'blessed fault'.

Frithjof Schuon reflects on the mystery of evil in relation to the 'fall' of Adam as follows: '[T]he fall of Adam is nothing other than the actualizing ... of the separative principle of existence.'[30] After noting how Judaism, Christianity and Islam assign responsibility for the 'fall' variously to Adam, Eve, or Satan, Schuon offers the following conclusion: 'Metaphysically one could, if one went beyond the level at which the notion of "sin" has a meaning, attribute the negative cause to God himself,' because evil cannot arise out of any cosmic randomness.[31] The same author adds that Adam 'could not not fall, since God "could not not create." ... Creation requires limitation and diversity. These in turn require ... evil.'[32]

The 'fault' of Adam does not necessarily contradict the Islamic doctrine of the sinlessness of the prophets, of whom the first was Adam. Indeed, in support of the Islamic 'exoneration' of Adam is an entire school of theology in Catholicism that lays the principal fault for the fall on Eve, not Adam, so that the Virgin Mary as the typological New Eve restores fallen humanity, in union, of course, with the New Adam. *1 Timothy* 2:14: 'And Adam was not seduced; but the woman being seduced, was in the transgression.' *Sirach* 25:33: 'From the woman came the beginning of sin, and by her we all die.' *2 Enoch* teaches the same doctrine, with the specification that the sinless Adam was indirectly affected by Eve's ignorant action: 31:6-7: 'And he [Satanail] understood his condemnation and the sin which he had sinned before; therefore he conceived thought against Adam, and in such a form he entered and seduced Eve, but Adam he did not touch. For her ignorance I cursed them both.' This shifting of responsibility, however, merely avoids the question of the providential plan of evil's role, for no matter who was responsible for the primordial 'transgression', the question of the problem of evil as such remains.

According to a quite remarkable text, *Wisdom* 10:1, personified Wisdom 'prevented' Adam from falling into any personal sin. Jean Daniélou comments on the verse: 'This certainly seems to be an example of a speculation on *Genesis*, showing an archetypal Man, unique and a stranger to sin.'[33] Daniélou, on the same page, gives his own rather literal translation of the Greek text of *Wisdom* 10:1-2: 'She (Wisdom) guarded to the end the first formed father of the world that was created alone, And preserved him from all personal sin, and gave him strength to get dominion over all things.'

We may note that the Clementine literature does not locate the entrance of sin into the world in *Genesis* 3's account of Adam and Eve, but in *Genesis* 6's account of the descent to earth of the 'sons of God' (widely interpreted as 'angels'; in Islam one would consider them jinn) to the 'daughters of men'. The 'angels' are commonly interpreted as the righteous descendents of Seth, who at the time of the deluge mated with the 'daughters of men', identified in later patristics and in some parts of the *Zohar* with the wicked descendents of Cain. Similarly, the *Book of Wisdom*, which does not speak of an Adamic transgression, first mentions sin in relation to Cain and the deluge. *Wisdom* 10:3-4a: 'But when the unjust [Cain] went away from her [Wisdom] in his anger, he perished by the fury wherewith he murdered his brother [Abel]. For whose [Abel's] cause, when water destroyed the earth, Wisdom healed it again... .' Such a linking of Cain and the deluge is indeed intriguing. In light of *Wisdom* 10:1's view of a sinless Adam, we may argue that *Wisdom* 2:23-24 does not refer to the *Genesis* 3 account of Adam's 'transgression', but to the sin of Cain: 'For God created man incorruptible, and to the image of his own likeness he made him. But by the envy of the devil, death came into the world.' We would maintain that 'death' here refers more specifically to the 'murder' of Abel by Cain, motivated by 'envy'. Support for our interpretation may be found in *1 John* 3:12: 'Not as Cain, who was of the wicked one, and killed his brother. And wherefore did he kill him? Because his own works were wicked: and his brother's just.' Cain, motivated by envy at the instigation of the devil, introduced death, through murder, into the world, and thus, as *Wisdom* 2:24 phrases it, 'by the envy of the devil, death came into the world.' In *John* 8:44, Christ, in line with *Wisdom* 2:24, assimilates Cain to Satan, for Christ in *John* says of 'the devil': 'He was a *murderer* from the beginning,' an obvious reference to Cain's murder of Abel 'in the beginning',[34] that is, as recorded in the *Book of Genesis*. As Frithjof Schuon reminds us: 'For Islam Adam could not sin... . According to this way of seeing things it is only through Cain that sin came into the world.'[35]

That *Wisdom* 10 calls Adam the 'father of the world', or 'father of the cosmos' (πατηρ κοσμου), is quite startling, for as Jarl Fossum observes, this 'was a well-known title of the demiurge in the Hellenistic age' and in effect 'ascribes *pre-existence* to the Man' Adam.[36] May not the phrase 'father of the world' in *Wisdom* 10:1 also be an allusion to the Hebrew text of *Isaiah* 6:9, where the promised Davidic Messiah is given the title 'father of eternity'? The Vulgate quite legitimately interprets the Hebrew word *olam*, which can mean 'eternity', as 'world' (= 'age') and interestingly adds in Jewish targumic fashion the concept of futurity to the title: *Pater futuri saeculi*, i.e., 'father of the world to come'. As the first Adam was father of the world, so the second, or last Adam, is father of the world to come.

Regarding the Pauline teaching on Adam referred to above, if one views *Romans* 5's portrayal of Adam's 'transgression' in the ameliorating light of *Romans* 8:20-21, then one may still interpret Paul's general teaching on Adam as dialectically reconcilable with the Islamic doctrine of Adam's essential sinlessness. That there was a providential plan to work out despite, or even by means of, human suffering, as indicated by *Romans* 8:20-21, might also be suggested in Qur'an 2:30: 'And when thy Lord said unto the angels: Lo! I am about to place a viceroy in the earth, they said: Wilt Thou place therein one who will do harm therein and will shed blood, while we, we hymn Thy praise and sanctify Thee? He said: *Surely I know that which ye know not.*'

To return to the various archetypal correspondences between Islam and Ebionitism, we may note regarding Muhammad's teaching that he was merely reaffirming the primordial religion of Abraham, reaching back before the Jewish Torah and Christian Gospel, and that he was but proclaiming the essential message of all previous prophets and religions, which according to Ibn al-'Arabi retain truth and validity even after the appearance of Muhammad; we cite the following lines of verse to illustrate Ibn al-'Arabi's position:

> My heart has become capable of every form: it is a pasture for gazelles and a convent for Christian monks,
> And a temple for idols, and the pilgrim's Ka'ba, and the tables of the Torah and the book of the Koran.
> I follow the religion of Love, whichever way his camels take. My religion and my faith is the true religion.[37]

We cite a prose passage from the same author to emphasize his universal religious outlook:

> Do not attach yourself to any particular creed exclusively, so that you disbelieve in all the rest; otherwise you will lose much good, nay, you will fail to recognize the real truth of the matter. God, the omnipresent and omnipotent, is not limited by any one creed, for He says (Kor. 2. 109), 'Wheresoever ye turn, there is the face of Allah.'[38]

The basic orientation of interreligious toleration and respect in these lines agrees in principle with standard Ebionite theology.[39] Schoeps correctly expounds: 'Muhammad's revelatory share in the *kitab* (heavenly book) merely establishes the earlier revealed parts of the heavenly book and on account of precisely this makes him the prophet of religious tolerance,'[40] and all this is in striking agreement with the Ebionite perspective of religious inclusiveness as described by Schoeps, when he explains that for the Ebionites the religions of Moses and Jesus were but two manifestations of 'a primordial religion (*Ur-religion*)' and that both religions are divine 'covenants', and consequently 'God accepts everyone who believes in either of them (*Hom.* 8:6) ... .'[41]

Here we quote the relevant section on the coexistence of the two covenants from the *Clementine Homilies* 8, chapters 4-7, which, because of its central importance for our subject will be given *in extenso*:

IV

Then Peter, wondering at the eagerness of the multitudes, answered, 'You see, brethren, how the words of our Lord are manifestly fulfilled. For I remember his saying, "Many shall come from the east and from the west, the north and the south, and shall recline on the bosoms of Abraham, and Isaac, and Jacob." "But many", said he also, "are called, but few chosen." The coming, therefore, of these called ones is fulfilled. But inasmuch as it is not of themselves, but of God who has called them and caused them to come, on this account alone they have no reward, since it is not of themselves but of him who has wrought in them. But if, after being called, they do things that are excellent, for this is of themselves, then for this they shall have a reward.

V

For even the Hebrews who believe Moses, and do not observe the things spoken by him, are not saved, unless they observe the things that were spoken to them. For their believing Moses was not of their own will, but of God, who said to Moses, "Behold, I come to thee in a pillar of cloud, that the people may hear me speaking to thee, and may believe thee for ever." Since, therefore, both to the Hebrews and to those who are called from the Gentiles, believing in the teachers of truth is of God, while excellent actions are left to every one to do by his own judgment, the reward is righteously bestowed upon those who do well. For there would have been no need of Moses, or of the coming of Jesus, if of themselves they would have understood what is reasonable. Neither is there salvation in believing in teachers and calling them lords.[42]

VI

For on this account Jesus is concealed from the Jews, who have taken Moses as their teacher, and Moses is hidden from those who have believed Jesus. For, there being one teaching by both, God accepts him who has believed either of these. But believing a teacher is for the sake of doing the things spoken by God. And that this is so our Lord himself says, "I thank thee, Father of heaven and earth, because Thou hast concealed these things from the wise and elder, and hast revealed them to sucking babes." Thus God Himself has concealed a teacher from some, as foreknowing what they ought to do, and has revealed him to others, who are ignorant of what they ought to do.

VII

Neither, therefore, are the Hebrews condemned on account of their ignorance of Jesus, by reason of Him who has concealed him, if, doing the things commanded by Moses, they do not hate him whom they do not know. Neither are those from among the Gentiles condemned, who know not Moses on account of Him who hath concealed him, provided that these also, doing the things spoken by Jesus, do not hate him whom they do not know. And some will not be profited by calling the teachers lords, but not doing the works of servants. For on this account our Jesus himself said to one who often called him Lord, but did none of the things which he prescribed, "Why call ye me Lord, Lord, and do not the things which I say?" For it is not saying that will profit any one, but doing. By all means, therefore, is there need of good works. Moreover, if any one has been thought worthy to recognize both as preaching one doctrine, that man has been counted rich in God, understanding both the old things as new in time, and the new things as old.'[43]

Ebionite theology is therefore far removed from the standard Protestant 'evangelical' or 'fundamentalist' interpretation of the general damnation of Jews who do not accept Jesus as Messiah.[44] This is not to say that the Ebionites watered down the importance of accepting, as is also emphasized in the Qur'an, all of God's messengers, but the contrast with the nuance of the Great Church's theology, at least as historically articulated, remains striking. The Ebionite inclusive salvific doctrine is admirably paralleled in Qur'an 2:62 and 5:69, both of which are nearly identical in import and phraseology:

2:62: Lo! Those who believe (in that which is revealed unto thee, Muhammad,) and those who are Jews, and Christians, and Sabaeans – whoever believeth in Allah and the Last Day and doeth right – surely their reward is with their Lord, and there shall no fear come upon them neither shall they grieve.

5:69: Lo! Those who believe, and those who are Jews, and Sabaeans, and Christians – Whosoever believeth in Allah and the Last Day and doeth right – there shall no fear come upon them neither shall they grieve.

Abdullah Yusuf Ali, in his 1934/1938 commentary on 2:62, writes that the label, 'People of the Book', conceded in this verse to the Sabaeans, 'can be extended by analogy to cover earnest followers of Zoroaster, the Vedas, Buddha, Confucius and other Teachers of the moral law,'[45] a liberal and generous application curiously lacking from the revised edition of the A. Y. Ali Qur'an translation published in 1991 by the Amana Corporation (Brentwood, Maryland).[46]

Another unique parallel between Ebionite Jewish Christianity and Islam is the labelling as 'falsified' those sections of the Jewish scriptures which narrate 'unworthy or immoral deeds concerning the Old Testament worthies recognized by the Ebionites, such as Abraham, Isaac, Jacob, and Moses',[47] and not excluding Adam.[48] Agreeing perfectly with Islamic dogma, the Ebionite 'basis for this puristic attitude must be that the individuals who manifest the True Prophet must be completely unblemished'.[49] Of course, the Ebionite rejection of certain passages from the Jewish scriptures was an extrinsic, not an essential or intrinsic, position. This can be supported by the fact that the Ebionites included all the offensive sections in their biblical canon.[50] Similarly in Islam, the rejection of certain passages from the Torah and Gospel is at the Qur'anic level strictly extrinsic, since the statements about scriptural falsity can be interpreted as criticisms merely of incorrect theological interpretations of the true scriptures. That the Torah and Gospel are still preserved in an inspired form is presupposed in the writings of several medieval and modern Islamic authorities. Frithjof Schuon reconciles the unfavourable Jewish accounts of David and Solomon with Islamic doctrine by employing analogical and dialectical reasoning.[51] But in light of the Ebionite doctrine of falsified scriptures, and given the genetic relationship archetypally between Ebionitism and Islam, it would seem that the Qur'anic criticisms of certain Jewish and Christian exegetical interpretations would to some extent encompass an at least extrinsic questioning of certain scriptural passages.[52] Perhaps here we should speak of differing 'degrees' or 'categories' of scriptural inspiration, or perhaps better, of the varying *purposes* of inspiration, an idea reconcilable with traditional Catholic theology, since the latter recognizes that the teachings of certain scriptural passages sometimes have only a limited or temporary application for a concrete given historical situation within or relating to a particular community of faith.[53]

Schoeps writes that Islam 'labels as *Qur'an* the heavenly book (28:46; 32:2; 34:43), which is preexistent like the Jewish Torah ... from which derives the revelations of all earlier prophets'.[54] According to traditional Islamic theology, as we have surveyed above, through the course of time passages from these books have been falsified,[55] either in faulty manuscripts or in oral exegesis and preaching. In each generation prophets are sent to correct the falsification of the scriptures and false preaching.[56] These prophets include, lastly, the Seal of the Prophets, Muhammad.

As Schoeps also writes, the Islamic confession of faith, 'There is no god but God, and Muhammad is His Messenger,' is strikingly paralleled in the Ebionite *Clementine Homilies* 7:8: 'This is religion, to fear him [God] alone and to believe only the Prophet of Truth.'[57] The same scholar concludes that the many parallels shared by Jewish Christianity and Islam shed light on the rapid spread of Islam near Arabia.[58]

Schoeps delineates additional parallels shared by Ebionitism and Islam, such as ritual ablutions, the initial facing toward Jerusalem during prayer (*qibla*), dietary restrictions, and anti-Paulinism,[59] though the latter is admittedly a later development in Islamic thought, for Muhammad himself did not oppose Paul, and the 'Apostle to the Gentiles' is simply never mentioned in the Qur'an.[60] We could also recall that the Islamic rule against drinking wine is paralleled by the absence of wine at the Ebionite Eucharist.[61] Muhammad's central title of 'Seal of the Prophets' is found earlier in Manichaeism, but the underlying meaning is equivalent to the Jewish-Christian True Prophet concept, for according to the Jewish-Christian *Gospel of the Hebrews*,[62] Jesus is the last in a series of prophets, and, as the last of a particular cycle at that time, the Spirit rests in him in its fullness. Schoep's conclusion, however, that because the Ebionites saw Jesus as the cessation of prophethood, there were therefore no charismatic activities in Jewish Christianity,[63] has been invalidated by the more recent research of Michael Goulder.[64] Neither did the Islamic belief in Muhammad as the Seal of the Prophets exclude a charismatic and mystical dimension from Islam from its very inception; on the contrary, the mystical dimensions of the Qur'an and the account of Muhammad's Night Journey and Heavenly Ascent made the presence of the esoteric within Islam inevitable.

At the exoteric level at least, the Qur'an's non-divine Jesus ('Isa in Arabic) and its stress on divine unity rather than trinitarian union agrees eminently with Jewish-Christian dogma.[65] The Qur'an's general avoidance of anthropomorphic descriptions of God is also an essential Ebionite trait.[66] Jewish Christian in flavour is also the Qur'anic 'argument that the dietary laws were laid upon the Jews as a restriction on account of their sins'.[67] The latter is clearly reminiscent of Christ's teaching that divorce was allowed by Moses only on account of his followers' 'hardness of heart', and that the divorce dispensation, though encoded in the Torah, did not agree with the spirit of the primordial covenant as witnessed in the *Genesis* Eden account. This principle was utilized by the Ebionites in their argumentation and is certainly related to the concept of 'falsified scriptures', and seems to suggest that the latter concept has more to do with identifying temporary injunctions, dispensations and abrogations than with any intrinsic condemnation of certain scriptural passages in themselves.

The Qur'anic version (61:6) of Christ's sayings that stand behind *John* 14-16 interprets the promised Paraclete as a future prophet, just as did the Christian Montanus and Mani, in agreement with standard Islamic exegisis. Below in our section on Frithjof Schuon's thesis of the ternary nature of monotheism, we will investigate in depth the Islamic claim of Muhammad as promised Paraclete. Additionally, the Islamic caliphate amd Imamate are structurally paralleled by the Jerusalem monarchial bishopric of James and his successors, who appear to have constituted for the most part a family dynasty of Jesus's closest relatives.[68]

Among Schoeps' concluding remarks, he stresses that, 'If it was possible for Jewish Christianity to have a new law in addition to the ancient law, there was certainly "also room for something still newer after the new."'[69] By noting in this context that Muhammad, like Jewish-Christian theology before him, saw his 'new law' as merely a reaffirmation of 'the oldest law of all', that is, the primordial law, then we can conclude that Islam in this respect offers no contradiction at all to the traditional Christian claim that Christ embodies the 'final' revelation of God to humanity. Muhammad may be 'final' in the temporal or chronological sense, but Muhammad does not 'supersede' or 'replace' Christ in any essential sense, insofar as he *confirms* the message of the Messiah. Muhammad never claimed to bring a new religion in an absolute or even sociological sense (though concrete effects in society were inevitable): 'The pre-Mosaic revelation is identical with the teaching of Islam.'[70] However, to be complete, one must acknowledge that each Abrahamic religion providentially 'shattered the forms that preceded it'.[71] Schoeps concludes by stating: 'And thus we have a paradox of world-historical proportions, viz., the fact that Jewish Christianity indeed disappeared within the Christian church, but was preserved in Islam and thereby extended some of its basic ideas to our own day.'[72]

Confronted by the fact of the historical schism between Judaism and Christianity, we must attempt to reconstruct the events and the underlying ideologies that led to the unfortunate, yet providential and understandable, bifurcation in question. In the end, we will discover that the division between the two Abrahamic variants in question was the result of a previous fissure within Christianity itself. We refer here to the split between Jewish Christianity and Gentile Christianity. The parting of the ways between these two paradigmatic manifestations of belief in Christ has been interpreted variously by historians and theologians throughout the centuries. One interpretation of the events under discussion was presented in the early eighteenth century by John Toland, who argued that St. Paul, in perfect accord with St. Peter and St. James the Just, the 'brother' of Jesus, intended for Jewish Christians to continue observing the Torah (dietary *kashrut* rules, circumcision, etc.), but for Gentile Christians to observe only the Noachide laws, in accord with the rules promulgated at the first church council, as recorded in *Acts* 15. Thus Jewish and Gentile Christians were to coexist peacefully, the one group observing the Jewish Torah, the other group observing the Jewish Noachide laws.

John Toland has left us with a study of primitive Jewish Christianity published in 1718 under the title *Nazarenus*,[73] which has attracted the attention of modern scholars of Judaism and Jewish Christianity.[74] Here we will focus on summarizing those sections wherein Toland argues that the first-century Torah-observing Jewish Christians and the Gentile Christians observing only the minimal Noachide requirements were by providence to coexist within the church, and that the abrogation of the Torah for Jewish converts to Christianity was not sanctioned by St. Paul, nor had such been intended by Christ.

According to Toland, for Paul the abrogation of Jewish Christianity would have made as little sense as the abrogation of the human sexes: 'In comparison of the New Creature, Circumcision and Uncircumcision are as nothing; which yet no more takes away the distinction of Jewish and Gentile Christianity, than the distinction of sexes; since it is likewise said in the same sense, and in the same place [*Galatians* 3:8], that in Christ there is neither Male nor Female.... . [T]his Union without Uniformity, between Jew and Gentile, is the admirable Economy of the Gospel.'[75] The continuance of the Torah in the church is grounded in Christ's will, for ' ... Jesus did not take away or cancel the Jewish Law in any sense whatsoever, Sacrifices only excepted ... .'[76]

Much could be said concerning sacrifices, but in this context we will make only a few provisional observations. Judaism never required animal sacrifices of Gentiles, whose sins were expiated merely by following the universal Noachide laws. Yet the principle of sacrifice for expiation of sins also has a universal aspect, and it is the latter which justified St. Paul's understanding of the cross as an atonement for Gentiles. But that Mosaic sacrifices remain valid for Jews and Jewish Christians after the ascension of Christ is demonstrated by at least two facts. Firstly, the Jewish prophecies concerning the eschatological kingdom of the Messiah clearly indicate that sacrifices will once again be offered, with divine sanction and effectiveness, in Judaism (see *Zechariah* 14:21 for a typical example). Secondly, according to *Acts* 21:23-26, St. Paul, years after his conversion to Christ, still practiced Mosaic vows, purifications, and sacrifices for sin in the temple; the vow described in *Acts* 21 which Paul took upon himself required, according to *Numbers* 6:13-15, both animal sacrifices and grain offerings. The *Letter to the Hebrews'* argument against animal sacrifices after the time of Christ is therefore applicable to Gentiles, not to Jews or Jewish Christians. The apostolic letter's argument possesses a limited and therefore partially extrinsic dimension. Already in pre-Christian Judaism, *4 Maccabees* proclaims that the death of Jewish martyrs brings forgiveness of sins and purification for the nation of Israel, but this in no way was understood to cancel the need for the Mosaic sacrifices for sin and purification. Jewish Christianity naturally would have inherited this traditional theological posture and applied it to Jesus's earthly end; Jewish Christianity therefore saw no contradiction between the Mosaic sacrifices and the forgiveness of sins effected through

Christ's earthly end. Only with Paul, whose mission was solely to the Gentiles, does one encounter a 'gospel of the cross'; in the New Testament, the strictly Jewish-Christian writings never mention the cross or even the death of Jesus (e.g., the *Epistle of James* and the *Epistle of Jude*).

To return to Toland, he observes that the coexistence of Jewish and Gentile Christianity 'shows a perfect accord between the Old Testament and the New; and proves that God did not give two Laws, wherof the one was to cancel the other... .'[77] Toland therefore rightly interprets *John* 1:17 in a progressive manifestational sense, not in an oppositional sense: 'The Law was given by Moses, but Grace and Truth came by Jesus, who has confirm'd that Law.'[78] As Toland argues, ' ... Jesus did not, as tis universally believ'd, abolish the Law of Moses, neither in whole nor in part, not in the letter no more than in the spirit... .'[79] Furthermore, '[S]ome of the fundamental doctrines of Mahometanism [had] their rise, not from Sergius the Nestorian monk ... but from the earliest monuments of the Christian religion.'[80] Toland then quotes an excerpt from a Petrine speech preserved in the Clementine literature regarding a proposed abrogation of the Torah: 'For this were to act against the Law of God spoken by Moses, and which has the testimony of our Lord for its perpetual duration, since he thus has said: heaven and earth shall pass away, yet one jot or one tittle shall not pass from the Law.'[81] Toland asserts that this charge of abrogation of the Law was lodged, unjustly, against Paul by some of the earliest Jewish converts to Christianity, a position we can reconstruct from the New Testament and other early Christian writings. As Toland observes, not all the Jewish Christians were opposed to Paul, for some understood that he was not arguing for the abrogation of the Torah for Jewish converts, but only for Gentile converts.[82]

Galatians 2 reveals that the Apostolic College agreed with Paul that there was a gospel of the circumcision and a gospel of the uncircumcision.[83] *Acts* 21:20 says there were thousands of Jews who converted to the church, who were all zealous for the Law. When Paul came into their presence, they confronted him with the necessity of publicly denying the charges that had been unjustly brought against him, namely, that he was preaching against the Law, and that he should publicly make it known that as a Jew he still observed the Torah, and that he demanded of Gentile converts the observance of the Noachide laws, that is, 'that they keep themselves from things offer'd to Idols, and from blood, and from things strangl'd, and from fornication'.[84] Toland comments on the Noachide rules: 'By the way, here is no restriction made as to time or place, either in the abstinence of the Gentile Christians from these four heads, or in the keeping of the Law by the Jewish Christians.'[85] Paul obeyed the Jewish Christians on both counts publicly: 'It follows therfore irrefragably, that Paul contended onely for the liberty of the Gentiles from Circumcision and the rest of the Law, but not by any means of the Jewish Christians... .'[86]

This is the clear and natural interpretation of *Acts* 21: Paul was in agreement with the Jewish Christians on both matters of Torah for Jews and Noachide laws for Gentiles. Toland comments on the tortured logic exegetes have used to escape the obvious implications of *Acts* 21: 'Abstruse and multiform are the windings of error; but the clew of truth is uniform and easy.'[87] The same Pauline stance is confirmed in *1 Corinthians* 7: 'Is any man call'd being circumcis'd? Let him not become uncircumcis'd; is any man call'd in uncircumcision? Let him not become circumcis'd. Circumcision is nothing, and uncircumcision is nothing, but the keeping of the commandments of God. Let every man abide in the calling wherin he was called.'[88]

Toland refers to copious verses from the Hebrew scriptures which clearly state that the Jewish covenant, along with circumcision, Levitical rites, etc., would endure as long as 'the days of heaven and earth' (see *Genesis* 17:7, 10, 13; *Exodus* 31:16, 17, 29:9, 40:15; *Leviticus* 7:36; *Deuteronomy* 4:40, 6:2, 11:21).[89] In view of the clarity of the Hebrew scriptures on the impossibility of the abrogation of the Mosaic Law for all 'the days of heaven and earth', and Christ's solemn declaration that 'till heaven and earth pass, one jot, or one tittle shall not pass of the law, till all be fulfilled' (see *Matthew* 5:17-18),[90] it is understandable why St. Justin Martyr, as Toland records, was 'farr from damning or excommunicating' the Jewish Christians for their Torah observance. Justin, though not fully sympathizing with them, nevertheless 'acknowledges them for brethren, and teaches communion with them in all things else ... : "I think they ought not onely to be receiv'd, but likewise to be admitted to a communion of all things, as those of the same bowels and brethren."'[91] The evidence shows that early on Augustine was even more sympathetic than Justin in this regard. Augustine 'maintain'd for some time ... that the Christian Jews shou'd ever observe their own Laws, without imposing the Levitical ceremonies on the Gentiles.'[92]

According to Toland, in the account of *Acts* 10, although 'there is not one word of Peter's subjecting those converted Gentiles to the Mosaic Law,' neither does it speak of any 'exemting the Jewish Christians from the observation of it: and tho he did eat with Cornelius, it does not appear that he ate any thing prohibited by the Law... .'[93] Regarding the prohibitions of *Acts* 15, they were universally observed until Augustine's time, and still retain force in the Eastern Orthodox Church, 'but, even till the eleventh century, in most parts of the Western Church'. The *Acts* 15 decrees were 'commanded in an assembly of the *Apostles*, without limitation of time'.[94]

Toland clarifies that, since some of the 'dietary' restrictions of *Acts* 15 are allowed by *Deuteronomy* 14:21 'to travelling strangers and aliens', that is, non-Jews, the restriction here must not be 'grounded on the Law of nature'.[95] But even this concession in the Torah is not granted to Jews. The paradigm of Torah for Jews and Noachide laws for Gentile converts is therefore of enduring force. Thus Toland opines as follows concerning some moderns who would force upon Gentile Christians certain Torah requirements: 'Here I wou'd desire those among us, who press the necessity of observing the Jewish Sabbath (for which reason they are call'd *Sabbatarians*, or *Seventh-day-sabbath-men*) to consider, that they were not the Christians from among the Gentiles, but the Nazarens from among the Jews, that antiently observ'd, or rather were onely bound to observe, the Jewish Sabbath: for we of the Gentile stock are not oblig'd *to observe days, or months, or times, or years*; we are to be *judg'd by no man in meat or in drink, or in respect of a holy day, or of the new moon, or of the Sabbaths.*'[96] Even in the Catholic Church it is understood that the non-Jewish Sunday sabbath Mass observance is not a commandment of God, nor one required by natural law, but a commandment of the church, a commandment which under certain circumstances may be dispensed with, and which theoretically could be abrogated by the church. Inclement weather, for example, can relieve one of Sunday Mass obligation.

Toland surveys a debate on Jewish Christianity between Augustine and Jerome which had far-reaching repercussions, and which helped seal the fate of the Ebionites in the eyes of the Gentile Great Church. For Jerome, the Jewish Christians were 'neither Jews nor Christians'.[97] Toland refers to and quotes from Jerome: 'Jerom roundly tells us, *that the Cerinthians and Ebionites, who were the Jews that believ'd in Christ, were anathematiz'd by the Fathers for this onely thing, that they intermixt the ceremonies of the Law with the Gospel of Christ... .*'[98] Toland retorts: 'Here you see the antiquity of pressing *Uniformity*, and the effects of it too: and I am entirely satisfy'd, that, were it not for this execrable treatment of them (so contrary to the practice of Jesus, and the doctrine of the Gospel) not a Jew, but, many ages since, had been likewise a Christian; as it must be on this foot alone, that their conversion to Christianity can ever be reasonably expected. Thus then the poor Jews were expell'd at once, and none of 'em to be ever receiv'd again, according to the mind of the Fathers, without a particular abjuration not only of their Judaism, but I may say of their Christianity too.'[99]

As Toland reminds us, Augustine was scandalized by Jerome's argument that Paul, in accusing Peter to his face (see *Galatians* 2), was deliberately engaging in deception, 'for the sake of a good end'. Augustine responded 'smartly' to Jerome 'and justify'd Paul by saying ... that when he speaks against the Law as dangerous or useless, he means this of the Gentiles: and that all passages spoken by him or others in favour of the Law, or enjoining the observation of it, relate purely to the Jewish Christians... .'[100] Jerome, incensed, wrote back to Augustine saying of the latter's argument: 'This in short is the sense [of what you say]; that Peter did not err, in thinking the Law shou'd be observ'd by those, who believ'd among the Jews: but that he declin'd from the right way, in forcing the Gentiles to Judaize... . The sum of your ... judgment, is this; that, even after the Gospel, the Jews who believe, do well to observe the ordinances of the Law: that is to say, if they offer sacrifices as Paul did, if they circumcise their children, if they keep the sabbath, etc.'[101]

Toland comments on Jerome's anti-Augustinian stance: 'This he's so farr from approving, that he utterly detests it: tis turning Christianity into Judaism. *If we must ly*, says he, *under the necessity of receiving Jews together with their observations of the Law; and that they may perform in the Churches of Christ, what they exercis'd in the Synagogues of Satan: I'll tell you my opinion freely, they will not become Christians, but make us Jews.*'[102] Toland rejoins that it obviously escaped Jerome that no such intermingling would have occurred, for in the ancient and medieval church different liturgical rites were always celebrated separately, as they are to this day in Christianity in general. The Jewish Christians would have performed 'their peculiar ceremonies in their own Churches, which he [Jerome] blasphemously calls the synagogues of Satan'.[103] Jerome continues his overly dogmatic diatribe and vitriol against Augustine, Judaism, and the Jewish Christians: 'I must speak to the contrary ... and, tho the whole world shou'd be of another mind, pronounce with a loud voice, that the ceremonies of the Jews are pernicious and damnable to Christians; and that whoever will observe them, be he of the Jewish or Gentile race, is plung'd into the gulf of the Devil.'[104]

Toland then turns to a survey of a more ancient question, namely, the theological contentions surrounding the debate on justification by faith or works as embodied in Paul's writings and in the *Letter of James*. Toland commences by noting 'that the Apostle James does not in his Epistle mean by "works" the moral Law, nor by "faith" a merit in believing.... . "Works" there signify the Levitical Law, as Faith is put for Christianity. This likewise is apparently Paul's meaning, whenever he uses the same expressions... .' Toland continues his explication:

James writes expressly to the scatter'd tribes of the Jews, and therefore tells them that Faith (i.e. Christianity) *can neither profit nor save them without Works* (i.e. the Levitical rites) as being oblig'd by an eternal and national covenant to the Law of Moses: but Paul, writing of the Gentile converts to the Romans, tells them that *a man is justify'd by Faith without the Works of the Law*, the Gentiles not being at all concern'd in the Mosaic rites or ceremonies. James says, that the Faith of a Jew (for to such onely he writes) *without the Works of the Law is dead*: and Paul says, that the Gentiles (for such he himself calls the Romans) *are dead to the Law by the body of Christ....* . Thus *that the Law was our Schoolmaster to bring us unto Christ*, and that *its ordinances were blotted out and nail'd to Christ's cross*, are phrases to be understood onely of us Gentiles.[105]

19

Therefore, 'there is no such abrogating or obrogating according to the original plan of Christianity. The Religion that was true yesterday is not false to day; neither can it ever be false, if it was once true.'[106]

Regarding the Ebionite, or Nazorean theology of the two covenants, 'all this is very intelligible, easy, and consistent, according to the Nazaren System; wheras nothing in the world is more intricate, difficult, or incoherent, than the controversies between the Protestants and the Papists, about the Merit of Works and Justification by Faith, occasion'd by the seeming contradiction of James and Paul.'[107]

Indeed, as Toland surmises, for the Gentile Great Church to consign all of Jewish Christianity to the status of a heresy, as did the church fathers after Justin, makes little sense historically: 'Since the Nazarens or Ebionites are by all Church-historians unanimously acknowledg'd to have been the first Christians, or those who believ'd in Christ among the Jews, with which his own people he liv'd and dy'd, they having been the witnesses of his actions, and of whom were all the Apostles: considering this, I say,' continues Toland, 'how it was possible for them to be the first of all others (for they are made to be the first Heretics) who shou'd form wrong conceptions of the doctrine and designs of Jesus? and how came the Gentiles, who believ'd on him after his death, by the preaching of persons that never knew him, to have truer notions of these things; or whence they cou'd have their information, but from the believing Jews?'[108]

Toland concludes his study by offering various historical data on the *Hebrew*, or *Jewish Gospel*,[109] the written source and heritage of faith for the Jewish Christians: 'This Gospel was publickly read in their Churches as authentic, for above 300 years... . [I]t was written before the Gospels now receiv'd for Canonical, as being collected by the eye and ear-witnesses of Christ, or by such as were familiarly acquainted with the Apostles, and ... it was one of the many mention'd by Luke ... as written before his own; and which he does not reject as false, or erroneous, or for any other reason.'[110] As for the ancient authority of the *Jewish Gospel* even in the Great Church, Toland records the following facts on page 79 of his monograph:

It was translated into Greec and Latin by Jerome, who very often makes use of it, as likewise did Origen and Eusebius; not rejecting it as Apocryphal, nor receiving it as Canonical, but placeing it among what they call'd the Ecclesiastical books: that is, books whose antiquity they were not able to deny, but whose authority they were not willing to acknowledge. Long before these the *Gospel of the Hebrews* was by Papias, Ignatius, Clemens Alexandrinus, and others, alleg'd as a true Gospel. So it seems to have been by Justin Martyr ... , so was it by Hegesippus, who was himself a Jew, and the father of Ecclesiastical, as Herodotus of Civil history.

Toland amplifies on Hegesippus: 'In his list of the first Heresies, preserv'd in his own words by Eusebius, he is far from reckoning the Nazarens or Ebionites among 'em: as good a proof that he was one himself, as that he delighted to quote their Gospel.'[111] In his book's final pages, Toland once again reminds the reader that the theology of the Jewish Gospel eminently agrees with Islam's understanding of Jesus Christ.[112]

Toland's thesis that the Jewish and Gentile Christians were to coexist within the church is quite valid and unassailable as far as it goes, as *Acts* 15 and 21 make clear enough. But Toland's belief that there was perfect accord in every respect between Paul and the twelve apostles is not tenable if left unqualified. Paul's *Letter to the Galatians* explicitly records the fact that the accord between James and Paul won by the compromise agreed to at the Jerusalem meeting, referred to in *Galatians* 2:9, soon collapsed.[113] When Peter visited Antioch (*Galatians* 2:11), he ate with Gentiles (of course abstaining from non-kosher foods); but James was concerned about such praxis, as the delegation from him makes abundantly clear (*Galatians* 2:12). Paul's reference to James's delegation in 2:12 demonstrates that he is referring to James and his official emissaries also in 1:7, where he accuses them of wanting 'to pervert the gospel'; they are 'false brethren' (2:4); in 2:2, 6, 9, Paul refers to the emissaries, and indeed to James, Cephas and John, as '*reputed* pillars', implying that the claim was in some sense exaggerated. 2:6, speaking of the three pillars of Jerusalem, sounds even more striking: 'And from those who were reputed to be something (what they were makes no difference to me).... '[114]

As we will soon discover, though James and his emissaries conceded Paul's calling, they do not seem to have accorded the same category of apostolic status to him which they themselves enjoyed, specifically because he had not been with Christ in the flesh during his earthly ministry, a perspective agreeing with the conditions for apostleship legislated by Peter in *Acts* 1:21-22.[115] This is why Paul in *Galatians* 1:11-12, 16 stresses that the gospel was taught to him directly by the 'revelation' of Christ, God's Son, and not by 'flesh and blood'. The perceptive reader, as Paul intended, will notice that the Apostle to the Gentiles is actually alluding to the saying of Christ preserved in the *Gospel of Matthew* 16:16-17, addressed to Peter, proclaiming that Peter's declaration concerning Christ as 'the Son of God' was 'not revealed by flesh and blood', but directly unveiled to Cephas by God. Then follows the promise of Christ to build the church, in some sense, on the foundation of Peter (*Matthew* 16:18). Paul's reference to 'building' and 'tearing down' in *Galatians* 2:18 may also be an intentional allusion to *Matthew* 16:18. Paul is polemicizing against Peter by using Christ's very words of promise to Cephas as the foundation stone. Paul's point is that although Peter is the foundation stone of the church, he is so only in a relative sense, for he is not the 'corner stone', and the other apostles also function as foundations of the church, as *Ephesians* 2:20 states: 'Built upon the foundation of the apostles and prophets, Jesus Christ himself being the chief corner stone.'

Our contention of a certain extrinsic enmity or tension between Paul and James can be strengthened by a comparison of *Galatians* with Paul's two letters to the Corinthians. In *1 Corinthians*, we learn that there was at Corinth a party who claimed loyalty to Peter. Paul had been away from Corinth, and apparently a Jerusalem delegation had visited Paul's church, disturbed by rumours of disorder and lack of respect for the Torah. Paul resents the intervention and, as in *Galatians* 2:18, so in *1 Corinthians* 3:11, he alludes to Christ's saying in *Matthew* 16:18 regarding Peter as the foundation of the church, and turns the dominical logion on its head, as it were, by claiming that only Christ can be the foundation of the church, again in agreement with *Ephesians* 2:20. Moreover, *1 Corinthians* 3:15, 17's use of the images of building and destroying reminds us of the themes of building and tearing down in *Galatians* 2:18. As Paul in *Galatians* refers to James and his emissaries and fellow apostles as 'false brethren' and '*reputed* pillars', in *2 Corinthians* he similarly refers to 'false apostles' (11:13) and to 'super-apostles', or more literally, 'hyper-apostles' (11:5; 12:11).

Paul is naturally employing hyperbole in the heat of the moment, but he is also, according to Christian theology, speaking by inspiration. But not everything spoken under inspiration must be interpreted in a literal sense. An inspired hyperbolic statement remains hyperbole. Ultimately for Paul, James and his emissaries could only have been 'false' in a limited, extrinsic sense, that is, 'false' in only certain relative areas of dogma and praxis. The delegation referred to in *2 Corinthians* 3:1 must have been from Jerusalem and authorized by Peter and James. In *2 Corinthians*, the delegates arrived with plenipotentiary letters of authorization (3:1); they claim Paul appointed himself an apostle (3:5), and that he, unlike them, was not taught by Christ in the flesh; a claim responded to by Paul in *2 Corinthians* 5:16. As in *Galatians* 1:8, where Paul charged the James delegation with 'preaching a different gospel', so in *2 Corinthians* 11:4, the 'super-apostles' are charged by Paul with 'preaching a different gospel'. And as Paul calls his opponents in *Galatians* 2:4 'false brethren', and in *2 Corinthians* 11:13 'false apostles' who 'pervert the gospel' (*Galatians* 1:7), so Paul's opponents level the same charge against him, namely, of falsifying the word of God (*2 Corinthians* 4:2). As Paul anathematizes his opponents as 'Judaizers' in *Galatians* 1:8-9, in like manner he does so again in *1 Corinthians* 16:22.

2 Corinthians 11:22 proves that Paul's opponents in Corinth were Jews, that is, 'Judaizing', or Jewish Christians requiring Torah observance, and not 'pneumatical' Greek antinomian proto-Gnostics.[116] Again, there is no *absolute* contradiction between the emissaries of James and Paul, so that each is labelled 'false' in a strictly hyperbolic and exaggerative sense. We may say that the bitter rivalries at times experienced among the apostles during Christ's earthly ministry (see *Matthew* 20:17-28) seem to have also erupted between the apostolic college and Paul in the era of the early church. We can perhaps more fully understand some of the tensions that existed between James and Paul by comparing their case with that of the divergences which erupted between the Companions of the Prophet Muhammad, divergences which led to the Islamic split between Sunnis and Shi'a. Not only were extrinsic political factors at work in this 'schism', but also intrinsic aspects issuing forth from the sacred personality of the Prophet Muhammad, so that one could say that the split was ultimately the result of necessary manifestations of archetypal possibilities and realities.[117]

An identification of Paul's opponents with the Jerusalem apostolic authorities should not be interpreted as unprecedented or without historical or even patristic support. As Schoeps notes, Ambrosiaster numbers James the Just among the opponents of St. Paul. Victorinus writes in his *Commentary on Galatians*: 'But clearly Paul was not able to learn anything from James, for the latter possessed a different view of the Gospel... . James was not an apostle, and he may even have been in heresy. Now Paul does record that he saw James: "I saw the novelty that James was spreading around and preaching, but because I knew and spurned his blasphemy, you Galatians should also reject it."' Ambrosiaster and Victorinus both name James the Just as the ultimate source of the Ebionite followers of Symmachus.[118] The Christian Pharisees of *Acts* 15:5, identified by the church fathers as the first Ebionites, are interpreted by Oekumenius and Theophylakt as the individuals referred to by Paul in *Galatians* 1:17, where he writes of 'those who were apostles before me'.[119] The church fathers in turn generally identify the Christian Pharisees of *Acts* 15:5, who were respected and entirely legitimate representatives at the first apostolic council, with the 'false brethren' attacked by Paul in *Galatians* 2:4.[120] What settles the question of the identity of the Galatian and Corinthian 'hyper-apostles', however, is the fact that, if they had not been emissaries of the Jerusalem apostolic college, or if they had been so but had merely overstepped their orders from James or Peter, then Paul's bitter conflicts with the emissaries – conflicts which endured for years – could and would have been settled with a mere request sent to Jerusalem to denounce the intruders as not reflecting the will of the reigning apostles.

Frithjof Schuon theologically justifies the existence of Jewish Christianity, and suggests that it is related archetypally to Islam in the following statements: ' ... a Judaizing Christianity is possible... .'; 'Mosaism had the right to survive – the advent of Islam is, paradoxically, an indirect proof of this... .'; 'Saint Paul inaugurated the "de-Judaization" of Christianity; now one could conceive of a Christianity faithful to at least the fundamental prescriptions of Moses, and this Christianity has existed in fact... .'; 'The excessively unilateral interpretation of the "Old Law" ... derive[s] from the Epistles and not from the Gospel.'[121]

We may therefore conclude that there were serious divisions, even though of a chiefly extrinsic nature, among the apostles from the earliest times of the church. Early on, the desire for uniformity began to assert itself, leading to mutual recriminations such as accusations of 'false apostles', 'perverting the gospel' and the like. Diversity in unity, not unity in uniformity, was the original Christian ideal, which unfortunately was not always realized in the apostolic church, though the Christian scriptures do reveal that such divinely sanctioned diversity did manage to manifest itself concretely in several respects. The trajectory of forced uniformity emerging from the discord of the era, carefully toned down (though not essentially distorted) by Luke in *Acts* 15, a discord quite evident enough in Paul's letters, was fated to prove paradigmatic throughout much of later ecclesiastical history.

The New Testament, whose canon was chosen by the Great Church composed of Gentile Christians, presents Christly and apostolic teaching in mainly Pauline categories. The Jewish-Christian version of Christ's and the Jerusalem apostolic college's teaching was not included in the New Testament canon for two reasons. Jewish-Christian literature largely perished early on, and such literature, along with Jewish Christianity in general, was later shortsightedly condemned as heretical by the Gentile Christians of the Great Church, alienated from and ignorant of the Jewish religion of Christianity's founders. Thus we see the first-century paradigm of rivalry between Pauline and Jerusalem factions, reflected above all in *Galatians* and *2 Corinthians*, playing itself out in later centuries, both in the selection of the New Testament canon and in christological and trinitarian dogmatic conciliar formulations. What often were originally merely dialectical contrarieties came to be unnecessarily perceived as absolutely irreconcilable contradictions.

Here we may note some further points of contact between primitive Jewish Christianity and Islam overlooked by Schoeps, but discussed in various works by Hans Küng. First of all, not only is the term 'seal of the prophets' (applied to Jesus of course), found in Tertullian's treatise, *Adversus Judaeos*, but we read in Sozomen's ecclesiastical history (*ca.*439–450) of 'Jewish Christians who legitimated themselves by descent from Ishmael and his mother (Hagar)'.[122] Küng does not mention, however, that pre-Islamic Samaritan theology assigns both Muhammadan titles of 'Apostle' (or 'Messenger') and 'Seal of the Prophets' to Moses. In the fourth-century Samaritan work *Memar Marqa* ('The Teaching of Marqa') 5:3, we read of Moses: 'By your life, O Apostle of God, remain with us a little longer! By your life, O Seal of the prophets, stay with us a little longer!'[123] The Qur'anic christology agrees with the main categories of Jewish-Christian christology, namely, a pneumatic christology (Jesus is the Word and Spirit of God), and a Servant christology according to which 'Servant of God' functions as a christological title. The Qur'anic angelic pneumatology, that is, Gabriel as identified in some sense with the Holy Spirit, is also typical of primitive Jewish Christianity, which applied angelic imagery to the Spirit as well as to Christ.[124] Küng quotes from Claus Schedl, 'When Muhammad puts the title "servant" at the center of his preaching about 'Isa (Jesus), he is adopting a scheme from earliest Christianity, purging it of contemporary misinterpretations, but avoiding ontological precision – of the kind one would expect from Hellenistic Eastern thought... .' Based upon these observations, 'it should no longer be said that Muhammad had only a defective knowledge of Christianity.'[125]

Even if there had been Arabic translations of at least portions of the New Testament already in Muhammad's lifetime, he almost certainly was acquainted with the story of Christ in the form of oral traditions circulating in Arabia. It is not impossible there were also already existing Arabic translations of the originally Greek apocryphal gospels concerning Mary and Christ. But again, these apocryphal gospels were not the sources of the various and rather striking parallels of their contents found in the Qur'an. John Toland's observations on this subject remain as valid today as when he first penned them in 1718, when he commented on the 'grave assertion' that Muslims had merely derived their traditions about Christ from ancient Christian apocryphal texts: '[A]s if they had kept these with more care than the Christians, and without ever naming or producing any of the Apocryphal books they cou'd' so easily suppose.'[126]

Toland's conclusion concerning the historicity of Islamic beliefs regarding Christian realities as laid out in his 1718 work is essentially supported by modern disinterested scholars: '[W]hat the Mahometans believe concerning Christ and his doctrine, were neither the inventions of Mahomet, nor yet of those Monks who are said to have assisted him in the framing of his *Alcoran*; ... they are as old as the time of the Apostles, having been the sentiments of whole Sects or Churches....'[127]

Surprising from a history of religions perspective is that, despite the primitive Ebionite parallels found in the Qur'an, its statements on Jesus include a so-called 'high' Logos christology, and its verses on Mary presuppose the dogma of her immaculate conception and the virginal conception of her son Jesus. Though Schoeps demonstrates the primitive Jewish-Christian character of the Qur'anic christology, he fails to mention its teaching on the virginal conception of Christ. This would not seem to fit well with his contention that the original Ebionites universally denied the virginal conception of Christ. We are faced with the possibility that the beliefs found in the Qur'an paralleling the Christian Logos christology (albeit in a modified sense) and virginal conception, and other Qur'anic parallels to the Christian apocrypha, formed a part of primitive Jewish-Christian traditions which migrated to Arabia along with the general Ebionite heritage. These beliefs do not seem to reflect later, so-called 'Hellenistic', theological developments, but appear to have formed a part of the belief of the descendants of the original Jerusalem community headed by Jesus's brother James.

Certain Catholic traditions presently viewed by scholarship as anti-historical may from a renewed ecumenical Qur'anic-Christian perspective be legitimately maintained as valid, at the very least if understood as theological statements, if not as actual historical events. One example would be the stay of Mary in the temple, known from the *Protevangelium Jacobi* and the Qur'an. The feast of Mary's stay in the temple is still fervently celebrated in the Orthodox Church, but is spurned by modern Roman Catholic historians and theologians as anti-historical. Catholic theologians have ironically overlooked the story's potential ecumenical significance in the dialogue with Islam. If we admit that at least the symbolism of Mary's stay in the temple retains theological profundity, and thus is worthy of use in theology and liturgy, then the ecumenical dialogue with Islam can be seen as potentially enriching for Catholic theology, liturgy and popular belief.

To return to the question of the Qur'an's Logos christology, many modern theologians miss the mark when they claim that John's 'Logos' concept is 'Hellenistic' in origin, and would therefore have been unacceptable to the early Jewish Christians. Such experts overlook the fact that in the Johannine literary corpus at least, the Logos concept is Jewish.[128] Still operative in many Christian scholars' reasoning is a concept concerning early Christian literature which argues that 'Hebrew' or 'Jewish' thought implies an 'early' text, and that conversely, 'Greek' or 'Hellenistic' traits imply a 'late' text. As a whole modern generation of New Testament exegesis and theology has revealed, Hellenistic and Hebraic elements coexisted from the very beginning in Christianity, because they already coexisted in pre-Christian Judaism.[129]

In Islamic thought, Christ is unique in several respects, just as each prophet naturally is unique in his own nature and mission. In the Qur'an the prophets are not identical in all respects. As Frithjof Schuon explains, for Ibn 'Arabi 'each Prophet is superior to the others by reason of a particularity that is peculiar to him, and therefore in a certain respect.'[130] Thus, each prophet possesses a 'relative superiority'.[131] The Sufis consider Jesus to be the 'Seal of Sanctity' (*khatam al-wilaya*) and the 'Seal of the Saints' (*khatam al-awliya'*), though this implies neither any denigration whatsoever of the Prophet Muhammad nor any invalid exaltation of the created human nature of Jesus to the uncreated level, an idea which would have been rejected by even the earliest Jewish Christianity under James. Ibn al-'Arabi writes of Christ: 'The seal of universal sancity above which there is no other saint is Jesus.'[132]

The Qur'an's general portrayal of 'Isa is undeniably profound. Frithjof Schuon remarks, after mentioning Islam's teaching on Christ's virginal conception and Mary's immaculate conception, that 'it is impossible, even from the Muslim point of view, that all these incomparable privileges should have only a secondary significance.'[133] As Schuon goes on to observe, for the Muslim such exalted views of the Madonna and Child in no way stand in contradiction to or in conflict with devotion to the Prophet Muhammad, perplexing as this compatibility may appear to Christians. As the same author also notes, the Qur'an refers in its own way to Christ's 'divine' aspect: 'Islam seeks to affirm, in its own fashion and according to its own perspective, that Jesus is "true man and true God"... . In admitting the Immaculate Conception and the Virgin Birth, Islam admits in its fashion the Divine Nature of Jesus... .'[134]

Schuon explains that the qualification 'in its fashion' here refers to Islam's care to dialectically 'disassociate the divine from the human'.[135] But even within this limitative framework, the exalted nature of Sufism's veneration of Christ is by no means dampened, as can be seen in Rumi's *Mathnawi*. He tells the story of an idolater who casts a faithful Muslim mother's child into the flames of a pyre for refusing to bow down to an idol. As the mother readied herself to jump into the fire to save her child, the little one speaks in a state of ecstasy, explaining that, 'in this fire I have seen such rest. / In this fire I have seen a world / Wherein every atom possesses the life-giving breath of Jesus.'[136] Furthermore, while definitely by no means denigrating Muhammad, in the Qur'an 'Isa receives quantitatively more honorific titles than the Prophet Muhammad.[137] In order to understand properly the commonalities and providential divergences in the sacred prophetic missions of Jesus and Muhammad, a detailed comparative examination of the Christian and Islamic christologies becomes imperative.

CHAPTER TWO

Islam, Christology
and Divine Filiation

IT IS PROBABLE that early Islamic sources often preserve ancient Jewish and Jewish-Christian traditions which have not survived in Jewish or ecclesiastical writings. It is indisputable that there existed extensive contacts and friendships between Muslims and Christians in the early centuries of Islam.[138] Even with regard to those traditions which developed exclusively within Islam after the polarization between Islam, Judaism and Christianity, many traditions may nevertheless be viewed as legitimate developments along parallel lines of thought which originated independently within either Judaism and/or Christianity. As far as the wider rapprochement between Islam, Judaism and Christianity is concerned, the process can be strengthened by recognizing that the three bodies do not constitute entirely separate religions *per se*, though they certainly do on the outward plane. Historically viewed, Islam represents a formal manifestation emergent from the same transcendent archetype from which Christianity and Judaism emerged, namely, the Abrahamic archetype; and this explains why Islam, even after its historical self-distancing from Judaism and Christianity, continued to develop along several parallel lines found in the other Abrahamic variants. The parallels shared between these three religions can best be understood when we view them each as a formal manifestation of an *Urreligion* in Abrahamic mode.

Many early Christian theologians argued that Islam began as a Christian heresy. Though a fundamentally flawed assessment, this assertion does contain at least a grain of truth in that it recognizes that Islam is not *per se* a separate religion opposed essentially to Christianity; that is, the assertion does recognize a genetic relationship between Islam and Christianity, though it does not consciously realize that the genetic relationship exists at the archetypal or transcendent level. Exoteric Islam formulates its objection to the 'Christian' concept of Christ's divine filiation by banning the terminology of 'God's son', since, in part, in Muhammad's concrete historical context the term was inseparable from associations with pre-Islamic Arabian polytheism, according to which God had given birth in a quasi-physical mode to a multitude of sons and daughters.[139] In banning the term 'God's son', Islamic theologians therefore differ merely at the level of a symbolic verbal articulation which had been inherited by the church from Judaism, whose Hebrew scriptures employed the phrase abundantly, usually to express the metaphorically filial relationship between YHWH and Israel.

A way beyond the impasse between Christian and Islamic terminology regarding the question of divine filiation, in a metaphysical sense at least, is found in those branches of Islamic mysticism which teach, along with Jewish mysticism, an *unio mystica*.[140] It would also be difficult not to concede that the Shiʻi doctrine of the Eternal Imam is ontologically compatible, at least analogically understood, with the Christian doctrine of Christ's association (although not in the former case exhaustive identity) with the divine Logos.[141]

The exalted Islamic concept of Muhammad as Perfect Man could be viewed from a Catholic perspective as at least analogically parallel to the doctrine of the Son of God as the Cosmic, Pleromatic Christ. Frithjof Schuon interprets the phrase Perfect, or Universal Man thusly: '[I]t is "Universal Man" (*al-Insan al-Kamil*) of which the human manifestation is the Prophet, the Logos, the Avatara.'[142] The analogue in Judaism would be the kabbalistic concept of the *Adam Kadmon*.

As many a theologian has recognized, every heresy contains a certain degree of truth, and sometimes quite a lot indeed. Heresies are not uncommonly overreactions against an overemphasis of a valid truth within a generally otherwise orthodox community. Church authorities have at times prematurely labelled a particular articulation of faith as heretical by not realizing that the belief was intended to be understood primarily in an analogical, or even merely metaphorical sense. The Ebionite distinction, discussed in more depth below, between the human 'Jesus' and the supernatural 'Christ' as a symbolic designation of the two natures of Jesus Christ, human and divine, would be a fitting example in this context. The standard Islamic objection to the common representation of Christ's deity in part constitutes a valid rejection of the various Christian heresies which denied the created human nature of Christ, and thus in turn constitutes a justifiable reaction against the otherwise orthodox believers' at times distorting overemphasis on the divine nature of Christ. The problem of the underemphasis of the humanity of Christ was not addressed within modern Catholicism until the early 19th century. On a popular level, one sees this in the early 1800s in the visions of the Augustinian nun Anne Catherine Emmerich, and later, under her influence, in the writings of the great German Catholic theologian Matthias Scheeben.[143] To adore the created human nature of Christ as uncreated, to deny a created status to the human soul of Christ,[144] which is done out of ignorance in certain sectors of fundamentalist Protestant Christianity today, and among many uninformed lay Catholics who should have been taught to know better, would naturally be unorthodox and would need to be corrected. It is possible that certain Christian heretics encountered by the Prophet of Islam denied the created human soul of Christ, and some of the orthodox behaved as if an identification of Christ's human nature with his divine nature were valid, perhaps as an overreaction against certain heresies at the opposite end of the theological spectrum.

By the church addressing the problem of underemphasizing the reality of the created status of Christ's humanity, the rapprochement between Christianity and Islam on the subject of christology could doubtless be deepened. And from the Islamic side, the concept (though without the explicit language) of the Messiah as 'God's Son' could perhaps be more widely understood by way of the teachings within Sufi mysticism on the concepts of *unio mystica* and the Eternal Imam. In this manner both Islamic and Christian thought might be enriched in mutually appropriate and validly traditional ways.

Seyyed Hossein Nasr writes as follows on Islam's classical posture towards Jesus: 'Islam does not accept the idea of incarnation or filial relationship ... . Jesus ... was a major prophet, ... but not a God-man or the son of God.'[145] He then observes that the doctrines of Christ's divine nature and the trinity 'can be understood metaphysically in such a way as to harmonize the two perspectives' of Islam and Christianity.[146] Regarding the Islamic metaphysical understanding of Christ as God, Henry Corbin comments on Ibn al-'Arabi's interpretation: ' ... Christ "is God," that is, he is a theophany, but not as if God could say: "I am Christ (*Masih*), son of Maryam."'[147] From an orthodox Catholic view, Ibn al-'Arabi's statement can be accepted if we interpret 'God' as either the Logos *as such* or the trinitarian 'Father', for according to Catholicism the Logos is not to be identified with the created soul and humanity of Jesus, son of Mary, and neither can the Father be confused with the Son. Although some church fathers in the first and second centuries did simplistically identify Jesus with the pre-existent Logos, according to classical Catholic theology the created nature of Jesus was hypostatically united with the eternal Logos in the unity of one person, and thus consequently, Jesus cannot be identified simplistically with the eternal Logos, given the distinction of the two natures.

Regarding the devotional metaphor of filiation in the sense of a father-son relationship existing between God and humanity, it does appear at times as an acceptable way of speaking in Islamic texts, as in the writings of the Egyptian Sufi Dhu'l-nun: 'Grant me, O God, to seek Thy Satisfaction with my satisfaction, and the Delight of a Father in His child... .'[148] Sufi Shaykh Ahmad al-'Alawi writes that '*Ab*', that is, 'Father', actually 'is one of the Divine Names. By it would Jesus speak unto His Lord, and he used it when he said: "Verily I go unto my Father and your Father", that is, unto my Lord and your

Lord.'[149] As Nasr observes, al-Ghazzali claimed that Jesus was granted divine leave to call God his 'Father', and that 'he never attributed divinity to himself as is commonly understood by Christians'.[150]

The 'common' understanding of the divinity of Jesus among many Christians, especially among uninformed Protestant fundamentalists, agreeing in certain respects with some of the early ante-Nicene church fathers, does not sufficiently appreciate the fact of Jesus's created humanity in contrast with the uncreated Logos, and this simplistic identification is rightly criticized by traditional Catholic theologians. In fact, the christology of the Ebionite Jewish Christians, if understood analogically as it was intended to be, given the Ebionites' Semitic frame of reference and manner of theological articulation, is far from being heretical, and accords better in some respects with traditional Catholic christology than does that of various ante-Nicene apologists, such as 2 Clement, Irenaeus et al. The latter usually based their thought on a sincere but overly identitative interpretation of the Logos statements found in John 1:1ff.

In the Johannine Prologue the Logos is not identified with Jesus, but with God. According to John, the Logos is therefore not a hypostasis in the sense of a pre-incarnational, pre-existent Jesus. Even though later theology saw in John 1:14 a teaching of the incarnation in the sense of hypostatic union, John himself was not addressing in this verse such a question; even less did John identify Jesus simplistically with the Logos. Rather, for John, Jesus is the 'temple' of manifestation of the Logos, as Bruce Chilton observes. As Chilton further notes, to speak of the 'Word' becoming flesh and 'dwelling' in the world alludes to purely Jewish targumic concepts: the Word become flesh is the proclamation of God's Logos by the physical Jesus; the Word's 'dwelling' among us refers to the Shekhinah in the Temple. 'For the law was given through Moses; grace and truth came through Jesus Christ.' Here we have a parallel to the multiple manifestations of the divine pre-existent Logos from the creation in the prophets, and lastly 'in a Son', that we find taught in the Letter to the Hebrews 1:1-3. Both texts refer to a gradual revelation of the Logos, not to a contradictory set of manifestations.[151] Thus, contrary to the generally accepted view of theologians, in John's gospel we have what can be designated a 'low', Semitic and functional christology, not a 'high', Greek and ontological christology. Of course, the functional and ontological overlap to some extent, so that we should speak here of a question of emphasis, but nevertheless, it cannot be denied that it is not Jesus, but the Logos which is presented as pre-existent in John's gospel. And the 'incarnation' of the Logos is also conceptually Jewish and primarily functional; just as God's presence (Shekhinah) dwelt in the temple, so the Logos 'dwelt in us'.[152]

Nestorius, though he erred in certain of his ontological premises, was nevertheless correct in interpreting, in good Jewish-Christian fashion, the Logos's dwelling as a 'tabernacling' in a human 'temple', for this is precisely John's understanding at the 'literal' or textual level.[153] The later ontological understanding (hypostatic union and the like) may be said to be 'implicit' in the biblical texts in the sense of being 'congruent' with them, either metaphorically, analogically or dialectically, but the conciliar concepts are not present at the textual level in the sacred scriptures. Incarnation and trinity in the New Testament are not doctrines; they are present there only at the level of described lived 'experiences'. That is to say, they are of concern to the scriptural authors in so far as they are 'economic' (i.e., manifestations within the economy of salvation history), not primarily 'immanent' (ontologically considered), even though we cannot speak of any absolute distinction between the two modes or categories in this context.

John's 'low' and chiefly functional christology is paralleled by Muhammad's 'low' christology, which itself is eminently 'Johannine'. There is no reason to presuppose an influence of the *Gospel of John* upon Muhammad, but the general tenor and themes of the Qur'anic statements on Jesus agree more with John's gospel than with that of the synoptic gospels. In the Qur'an, Jesus is the 'Word' of God (see *John* 1:1ff.); the Qur'anic Jesus speaks of 'my Lord and your Lord' (see 5:117), a phrase paralleled in *John* 20:17; in Johannine style, the Qur'an stresses the glorification, not the death of Jesus. The list could be expanded, but the point is sufficiently established that the Qur'an shares with John a Semitic and mainly functional Logos christology, freely admitting all legitimate theological divergences despite certain commonalities of language. In other words, it is precisely the Qur'an's parallels to Johannine-like thought and diction that allow us to speak of the Qur'an's 'low', or 'Prophet' christology, which of course is 'exalted' in its own manner.

We should observe at this point that, just as John associates his Logos doctrine with the primordial Light, so does Sufism speak of the Logos as the *Muhammadan Light*. There is no question here of the Sufis borrowing from St. John's gospel. The parallel is but one of countless points of convergence between Christianity and Islam best explained by a mutual descent of the two religions from a single transcendent Abrahamic religious archetype. In the end, we may say that Christianity speaks of the *incarnation* of the Logos, whereas Judaism, Jewish Christianity and Islam would instead speak of the *revelation* or *manifestation* of the Logos.[154]

Here we should inquire further whether or not John's prologue goes beyond pre-Christian theology and philosophy. As regards the creative pre-existent Logos, we have equivalent parallels in the Hebrew scriptures in the figure of the celestial Lady Wisdom (*Proverbs* 8, *Sirach* 24, *Wisdom* 7). A vitally important question is whether according to the Hebrew scriptures the pre-existent Wisdom is eternal or created. The Wisdom literature might seem generally at first glance to assert that heavenly Wisdom is created. The same seems to be maintained by Philo, who teaches that the Logos is the chief angelic being;

a belief also encountered in ancient Jewish Christianity. But it is entirely possible that, given the predominantly functional nature of Hebrew thought, such 'derivative' Catholic concepts as 'begetting' and 'procession' could be encompassed within the semantic field of the Hebrew concept of 'created'; and in fact the Wisdom literature does employ 'begot' and 'proceeded' as synonyms for 'created', as the following texts seem to suggest (emphases added):

Proverbs 8:22-25: The Lord *possessed* (LXX, εκτισεν) me in the beginning of his ways, before he made any thing from the beginning. I was *set up* from eternity, and of old, before the earth was made. The depths were not as yet, and *I was already conceived*, neither had the fountains of waters as yet sprung out. The mountains, with their huge bulk, had not as yet been established: before the hills, *I was brought forth*.

Sirach 1:3-4: Who hath searched out the wisdom of God that *goeth before all things*? Wisdom hath been *created* before all things, and the understanding of prudence from everlasting.

Sirach 24:5, 14: I *came out* of the mouth of the most High, the *firstborn* before all creatures. From the beginning, and before the world, *was I created*, and unto the world to come I shall not cease to be, and in the holy dwelling place I have ministered before him.

Wisdom 7:24: For she is a *breath* of the power of God, and a certain pure *emanation* of the glory of the Almighty God: and therefore no defiled thing cometh into her.

Eastern Christian theology, stressing as it does the transcendence of God and the 'priority' of the Father, is in certain ways formally closer to Judaism's expression of monotheism than is Roman Catholicism, even though the latter also teaches that the Father is neither begotten nor proceeds; but the West's emphasis and theological nuance are in this regard incontestably articulated differently than in Eastern Christianity.

When we shift our focus to Islam, there is a definite tradition of the Logos as eternal and uncreated, imaged as the Heavenly Book, though occasionally some modern theological trends oppose this view. A classical teaching on the eternal nature of the Qur'an is found in the treatise, *Ar-Risalah*, by 'Abd Allah ibn Abi Zaid al-Quairuwani (AH 312-389). Speaking of the divine attributes, this work declares: 'He is too exalted for these attributes to have been created.... . Surely the Qur'an ... was not created.'[155] In the *Wasiya* of Abu Hanifa we read of the relationship of the Qur'an to God: 'It is not He, but neither is it other than He, but in a real sense it is one of His attributes.... . [T]he speech of Allah—exalted be He—is uncreate... .'[156] The *Fiqh al-Akbar* of Abu Hanifa similarly defines: '[N]either [divine] attribute nor name was created... . His attributes existed in pre-eternity... . Our uttering of the Qur'an is created ... , but ... God's word is uncreated.'[157] One final excerpt from a classical Islamic credal statement should be included here, from An-Nasafi: ' ... He has attributes eternally subsisting in His essence. They are not He nor are they other than Him... . [S]peech ... is one of His eternal attributes... . The Qur'an is the speech of Allah – exalted be He – uncreate... .'[158]

Gershom Scholem surveys the history of the Jewish debate on whether the divine Wisdom, *Hokhmah*, is created or uncreated, and whether this Wisdom is a divine hypostasis or a mere literary personification. Beginning with the observation that *Hokhmah* corresponds to *Shekhinah*, Scholem notes that in the Talmudic, midrashic and targumic literature 'the *Shekhinah* is always God Himself,' and 'is not perceived as a distinct hypostasis of God Himself'.[159] With the late midrash on *Proverbs* 22:29 we first encounter the idea of a distinction between *Shekhinah* and God, so that the former has 'been hypostatized as a quality of God'.[160] In general, medieval Jewish philosophers hold that *Shekhinah* is created, having 'no part in the divine essence or unity'.[161] Scholem explains that the proponents of a created *Shekhinah* could not bring themselves to 'endanger the purity of monotheistic belief by recognizing an uncreated hypostasis'.[162]

As for the Johannine prologue, the second aspect to be addressed is that of incarnation. In Judaism there is the tradition of the *Shekhinah* dwelling in the temple, and this is the background of *John* 1:14's phrase, 'and the Logos became flesh and dwelt [literally, "tabernacled"] among [literally, "within"] us.'[163] This *Shekhinah* concept is also the basic background of Philo's statement on the Logos as dwelling in the world, according to *De Fuga et Inventione* xx 110, as Alexander Broadie comments: ' ... Philo speaks of it as clothed in the world, as the soul is clothed in the body... . [T]he Christian concept of the word of God made incarnate is close at hand... .'[164] Here we present *De Fuga et Inventione* xx 110 in the fuller context of the preceding and following passages, the importance of which will become apparent below, when we investigate *Sirach* 50's assimilation to the high priest Simon of the creative personified Wisdom described earlier in *Sirach* 24. Note that the following Philonic passage links together both themes of the high priest and that of the primordial creative Wisdom:

For we say that the high priest is not a man, but is the word of God, who has not only no participation in intentional errors, but none even in those which are involuntary.[165] [109] For Moses says that he cannot be defiled, neither in respect of his father, that is, the mind, nor his mother, that is, the external sense; because, I imagine, he has received imperishable and wholly pure parents, God being his father, who is also the father of all things, and wisdom being his mother, by means of whom the universe arrived at creation; [110] and also because he is anointed with oil, by which I mean that the principal part of him is illuminated with a light like the beams of the sun, so as to be thought worthy to be clothed with garments. And the most ancient word of the living God is clothed with the world as with a garment, for it has put on earth, and water, and air, and fire, and the things which proceed from those elements. But the particular soul is clothed with the body, and the mind of the wise man is clothed with the virtues. [111] And it is said that he will never take the mitre off from his head, he will never lay aside the kingly diadem, the symbol of an authority which is not indeed absolute, but only that of a viceroy, but which is nevertheless an object of admiration. Nor will he 'rend his clothes'; [112] for the word of the living God being the bond of every thing, as has been said before, holds all things together, and binds all the parts, and prevents them from being loosened or separated. And the particular soul, as far as it has received power, does not permit any of the parts of the body to be separated or cut off contrary to their nature; but as far as it depends upon itself, it preserves every thing entire, and conducts the different parts to a harmony and indissoluble union with one another.[166]

Ancient Jewish traditions assimilate the Logos to a particular human being, but most often to one of the past (Moses, Enoch, etc.). But is it not true that the church also explicitly associated the Logos with Jesus only after his earthly departure, that is, after a sufficient time had elapsed allowing for theological reflection upon the person of Jesus? However, it is not correct to say that ancient Judaism never associated a living person with the Logos. As Crispin H. T. Fletcher-Louis has shown, ancient Jews 'worshipped' the living high priest as an embodiment of the Logos-Wisdom.[167] There is also the startling statement in 1 *Chronicles* 29:20, where both God and the king, the latter being by no means dead, are worshipped together: 'And David commanded all the assembly: Bless ye the Lord our God. And all the assembly blessed the Lord the God of their fathers: and they bowed themselves and worshipped God and the king.'

Fletcher-Louis also demonstrates that *Sirach* 50:7 identifies the high priest Simon with the divine hypostatic Glory (the very *kabod* of *Ezekiel* 1:26-28 and *John* 1), and in fact the sacred author Sirach assimilates the Wisdom-Logos of chapter 24 to Simon in chapter 50.[168] Furthermore, the ancient Jewish work known as the *Prayer of Joseph* says that the leading angel of heaven, known as the 'first-born of all creation', 'dwelt among us' in the world as the patriarch Jacob. 1 *Enoch* 42:1-2 also relates that 'Wisdom went out [from heaven] to dwell with

35

the children of the people, but she found no dwelling place,'[169] constituting a striking parallel to John's Logos that descends from heaven, dwells in the world, but is rejected by the people to whom he is sent. Based on these sources, we may conclude that John's prologue does not go beyond any purely Jewish conceptions in its ideas of the pre-existent Logos and the Word being manifest in flesh. It would seem that only the later conciliar formulations concerning hypostatic union, which are in any event not explicitly present in John's gospel, go beyond ancient Judaism's boundaries.

To turn to the theme of apotheosis in ancient Jewish literature and theology, certainly we can say that to call a human person 'God', whether that man be identified as Moses, Enoch, or the heavenly Son of Man, is to make a statement not totally unrelated to ontology. But again we must keep in mind both aspects of the ontologically functional and the functionally ontological when encountering the statement that such-and-such a figure 'is' God. What this means is that a divine status (an ontological statement) is bestowed (a functional statement) by the eternal and uncreated God. In a recent study, Richard Bauckham stresses that at the time the New Testament originated, Judaism had integrated Greek thought sufficiently that a functional description of a certain entity implies an ontological statement.[170] But Bauckham overlooks the point that such an ontological statement in ancient Judaism is to be understood primarily along functional lines, so that if a sacred figure is described as 'God', that figure 'is' God because of the activity of God the Creator. Yet it would be fully correct to state that if an ancient Jewish text calls a human an 'angel' or 'God', then such would not be a purely functional statement, for it also presupposes an ontological implication of some sort.[171] But the bestowal of 'angelic' or 'divine' status upon a human being remains just that: a *bestowal* from the divine favour.[172] We might also consider al-Hallaj's proclamation, *Ana'l-Haqq*, 'I am the Truth,' that is, 'I am God.' The later traditional Sufi interpretation of these words is that they mean not that al-Hallaj claimed to be God, but that the Sufi had 'passed away' in mystic extinction to the point that God spoke through the mouth of al-Hallaj.[173]

In a recent study Darrell D. Hannah argues against a purely functional interpretation of Paul's christology in *1 Corinthians* 15. Hannah concludes that Paul's christology is inconsistent, simultaneously 'high' (in *Philippians* 2 and *1 Corinthians* 8:6) and 'subordinationist' (in *1 Corinthians* 3, 11, and 15).[174] But to divide various Pauline texts into 'high' and 'subordinationist' categories is the result of Hannah failing to synthesize ontology and functionalism in Paul's thought. There are no 'high' and 'low' divisions in the apostle's christology; rather all the texts cited by Hannah can be understood properly once we see them as functionally ontological. His christology is not at one time 'high' and at another time 'low', but functionally ontological in all the texts under consideration: Christ's divine status (an ontological statement) is always the result of the divine activity of God (a functional statement) upon Christ's humanity.[175] One flaw in Hannah's essay is his interpretation of *Apocalypse* 3:21 as implying two divine thrones, one belonging to the Father and another belonging to Christ:[176] 'To him that shall overcome, I will give to sit with me in my throne: as I also have overcome and am set down with my Father in his throne.' But this text is actually emphasizing that Christ's throne is none other than his Father's throne. This makes better sense than an idea of two divine thrones, for as even Hannah argues, everywhere else in the *Apocalypse* only one divine throne is envisaged. But the greatest flaw in Hannah's essay is his failure to appreciate the central significance of *Apocalypse* 3:21's post mortem (not strictly 'eschatological' as Hannah assumes[177]) promise to martyrs to share in the throne of the Father. This undermines the argument that Christ, specifically because he shares the Father's throne, must therefore be divine in the fullest sense and therefore also worthy of unrestricted divine worship, as if God 'the Father' were the Messiah. *Apocalypse* 3:21 indicates that Christ's sharing in the Father's throne means an exaltation of his *created* human nature, an exaltation also bestowed upon all believers, for they also have a share in the divine throne (or at least all martyrs, if we want to confine ourselves strictly to the text of the *Apocalypse*). Again, what we have here is an example of a functionally ontological christology.[178]

Hannah also calls into question the standard apotheosis interpretation of Moses' dream in the *ca.* 2nd century BCE *Exagoge* by Ezekiel the Tragedian. Hannah's first objection to the standard interpretation of Moses as undergoing apotheosis is the text speaking of Moses as 'mortal' in contrast to God's 'own divine nature'.[179] But this argument has little weight, for it is self-understood that the Moses who undergoes apotheosis must indeed be a mortal. And the fact that it is a mortal who is subsequently 'divinized' demonstrates that we are speaking of a *bestowal* by God, that is, a functional reality, admittedly with secondary ontological implications.

To deal with Hannah's second objection to the standard interpretation, we give here the *Exagoge*'s account of Moses' dream:

I thought upon Mount Sinai's summit I saw
A mighty throne that reached to heaven's high vault,
Whereon there sat a man of noblest mien
Wearing a royal crown; whose left hand held
A mighty sceptre; and his right to me
Made sign, and I stood forth before the throne.
He gave me then the sceptre and the crown,
And bade me sit upon the royal throne,
From which himself removed. Thence I looked forth
Upon the earth's wide circle, and beneath

The earth itself, and high above the heaven.
Then at my feet, behold! a thousand stars
Began to fall, and I their number told,

As they passed by me like an armed host:
And I in terror started up from sleep.
Then his father-in-law thus interprets the dream:
This sign from God bodes good to thee, my friend.
Would I might live to see thy lot fulfilled!
A mighty throne shalt thou set up, and be
Thyself the leader and the judge of men!
And as over all the peopled earth thine eye
Looked forth, and underneath the earth, and high
Above God's heaven; so shall thy mind survey
All things in time, past, present, and to come.[180]

Hannah retorts, in line with Richard Bauckham's interpretation, that this says nothing 'about Moses' heavenly status'. The matter, he argues, is 'more mundane' than that. Moses is simply described as 'God's earthly counterpart: "What God is in relation to the cosmos, Moses will be in relation to Israel."'[181] Lastly, Hannah asserts that the stars bowing to Moses does not refer to angelic worship but mere 'homage' from humans. These are not unreasonable arguments; yet when we return to the text itself, we are struck afresh by the startling imagery of God being described as a man on the divine throne (in agreement with *Ezekiel* 1:26-28) and then by Moses, a mortal, assuming that very same throne which is clearly divine. Furthermore, no authority has ever argued that the process of apotheosis implies that the mortal under consideration assumes any share in God's rule in other than a derivative sense, that is, of having the share of rule bestowed upon the individual human *qua* human.

Neither does Hannah's interpretation seem to do full justice to the passage's comments on Moses' universally comprehensive gaze, both spatially and temporally, in that it is said that he viewed all three worlds (heaven, earth and *sheol*), implying his sight would reach into past, present and future. It does appear that the rule of Moses in the *Exagoge* is limited to Israel, but that does not cancel out the fact that to rule God's chosen people one must still share in the divine rule, and that that rule is by implication a participation to whatever degree in God's throne.[182] Furthermore, Moses' ability to gaze over heaven, earth and *sheol* would seem to indicate that he is being described in terms of the *Adam Kadmon*, i.e., as the 'universal Man', whose 'body' is coextensive with the very cosmos, like the Hindu Purusha.[183] Even if in this passage of the *Exagoge* Moses is not equated with the *Adam Kadmon*, the very fact that Ezekiel the Tragedian apparently dares to apply its cosmic imagery to the mortal Moses is in itself quite revealing. Despite any possible limitation in the text regarding

Moses ruling only Israel, it is thus understandable that other ancient Jewish literary works do seem to associate Moses and the *Adam Kadmon* in a more plenary manner.

In the *Testament of Moses* 11:16, Moses is 'the master of the world' and 'the divine prophet for the whole earth', 'the perfect teacher in the world', and in terms reminiscent of personified Wisdom in *Wisdom* 7:22 ('For in her is the spirit ... sacred, ... manifold, subtle'), Moses' 'sacred spirit' is 'manifold and incomprehensible'.[184] Because the *Testament of Moses* 1:14 also teaches the pre-existence of Moses, we may firmly conclude that this ancient work assimilates the Logos to Moses. The question of whether the *Exagoge*'s stars that bow to Moses represent angels or mere humans (we feel the latter is the more likely), as in the dream of Joseph in *Genesis* 37:9-10, is a secondary question, for angelic worship is not a necessary consequence of apotheosis. What we have in any event in the *Exagoge*, is an example that parallels *Apocalypse* 3:21's promise of a human or 'created' share in God's throne.

Before leaving Hannah's essay, we should examine his interpretation of *Philippians* 2. He argues against a common interpretation that the Son did not possess the Divine Name until after his exaltation, for the Son was in the 'form of God' even before the incarnation. But if by 'Son' Hannah understands simply (or simplistically) 'Jesus', then his position cannot be accepted as standard Christian theology. According to the latter we would have to say that not 'Jesus of Nazareth', but the Logos pre-existed in the 'form of God'. According to Catholic theology, the pre-existent Logos was hypostatically united with the created nature of the man Jesus in the incarnation. The man Jesus's created human nature was hypostatically united with the pre-existent Logos, and Jesus received the Divine Name at his exaltation. Jesus did not possess the Divine Name before the incarnation, for not 'Jesus' but the 'Logos' pre-existed. It is impossible that as a Jew, Paul could have confused the created human nature of the Messiah with God, even after his acceptance of Jesus as Messiah. The human nature of Christ is, on the contrary, functionally associated with God, who bestows apotheosis upon this created nature. Thus Bauckham's rejection of the 'developmental model, according to which the New Testament sets a christological direction only completed in the fourth century' as 'seriously flawed',[185] would be unacceptable to Catholic theology if left unqualified. Paul and John had no conception of the later christological dogmas as articulated with the Greek philosophical distinctions of human and divine natures, hypostatic union, etc., and the apostles had no need for such articulations. To arrive at its full 'immanent' understanding of christology, the church needed centuries of theological reflection. The christology of the New Testament speaks of the events of the economy of salvation history, with 'immanent' implications, to be sure. The later councils developed these secondary ontological implications and made them primary, whereas in the New Testament they were mostly of an implicate or principial order.[186] Hannah is labouring under the common theologically simplistic misperception of Jesus as Logos in an exhaustive or 'identitative' sense that is rightly, from even a Christian perspective, the object of 'prophetic' criticism and denunciation in the Qur'an.

As we quoted above from *De Fuga et Inventione* III, Philo says that the high priest, whom he in some sense identifies with the Logos, possesses 'an authority which is not indeed absolute, but only that of a viceroy, but which is nevertheless an object of admiration'. Based on this we can conclude that for Philo an 'incarnation', or better, theophanic 'embodiment', or manifestation of the Logos would be worthy of a relative worship. The same applies to all other ancient Jewish texts that speak of salvation figures who undergo apotheosis and angelic worship. This also holds for several New Testament texts. In *Philippians* 2 and throughout the Johannine *Apocalypse*, it is the humanity of Jesus of Nazareth, or the 'lamb of God', not the Logos *as such* that is glorified through resurrection and exaltation to God's throne; the Logos as such needs no such glorification, for the Logos is the divine Glory (*kabod*) itself. Therefore, even according to Catholic theology, it is the exaltation of the created humanity of Jesus of Nazareth that is under consideration, and by definition we are speaking of a reality that cannot be worshipped specifically *as uncreated*.

It should be noted that the worship of the exalted Jesus by the prostration of all creation such as described in *Philippians* 2, could not be *per se* unacceptable to Islam, for the same type of worship was demanded by God to be given to the earthly 'caliph' Adam by the angels, as recorded in Qur'an 2:34, in agreement with previous Christian tradition:[187] 'And when We said unto the angels: Prostrate yourselves before Adam, they fell prostrate, all save Iblis. He demurred through pride, and so became a disbeliever.' And Qur'an 3:59 declares: 'Lo! the likeness of Jesus with Allah is as the likeness of Adam.' Thus the Catholic dogma that justifies veneration of the humanity of Jesus (e.g., devotion to the Sacred Heart) in a certain sense possesses Semitic monotheistic archetypal parallels.

And as it is specifically the glorified humanity of Christ that is worshipped in *Philippians* 2, so it is the exalted human Jesus as the Lamb of God that receives cosmic veneration in the *Apocalypse*. Therefore, texts like *Apocalypse* 5:13 are not proof-texts of the divine nature of Christ: 'And every creature which is in heaven and on the earth and under the earth, and such as are in the sea, and all that are in them, I heard all saying: To him that sitteth on the throne and to the Lamb, benediction and honour and glory and power, for ever and ever.' The glorified humanity of Christ is worthy of worship because its apotheosis is effected and bestowed by God who as Creator is worthy of worship. Indeed, all the *Apocalypse* passages on the 'divine' Lamb refer to the humanity, not divinity, of Christ. This is why the same *Apocalypse* that ascribes to Christ such divine titles as Alpha and Omega (see 1:8; 22:13), also speaks of Christ in terms of an angel in 14:15-16 (emphases added): 'And I saw: and behold a white cloud and upon the cloud one sitting like to *the Son of man*, having on his head a crown of gold and in his hand a sharp sickle. *And another angel* came out from the temple, crying with a loud voice to him that sat upon the cloud: Thrust in thy sickle and reap, because the hour is come to reap. For the harvest of the earth is ripe.' Here the one like the Son of Man who reaps the harvest of the earth is Christ, for in 19:11-21 the vintaging of the earth is clearly assigned to him; yet 14:15's phrase '*another* angel' suggests the Son of Man 'is' an 'angelic' entity himself.[188]

Therefore, not only do the themes of pre-existence and 'incarnation' in the Johannine prologue not go beyond ancient Jewish theology, the theme of Jesus's apotheosis and universal worship in the *Philippians* 2 hymn also remains within the parameters of ancient Jewish monotheistic thought. In *1 Enoch* 48:1-5 and 62:4-7, 9, the Son of Man receives cosmic adoration: 48:5: 'All who dwell on earth shall fall down and worship before him [the Son of Man], And will praise and bless and celebrate with song the Lord of Spirits [the Ancient of Days].' 62:5-7, 9:

5. [T]hey [shall] see that Son of Man sitting on the throne of his glory.
6. And the kings and the mighty and all who possess the earth shall bless and glorify and extol him who rules over all, who was hidden.
7. For from the beginning the Son of Man was hidden, and the Most High preserved him in the presence of His might, and revealed him to the elect.
9. And all the kings and the mighty and the exalted and those who rule the earth
Shall fall down before him on their faces,
And worship and set their hope upon that Son of Man,
And petition him and supplicate for mercy at his hands.

In *1 Enoch* 71 we learn that the Son of Man who receives worship is none other than the patriarch Enoch himself.

Similarly, in *3 Enoch* chapters 9-15, Enoch is transfigured in heaven into the angel Metatron, sits on his predestined throne next to God, is crowned with the very Name of God, is given the title of the Lesser YHWH, rules over heaven and earth, and receives angelic worship. Despite some differences, we could not ask for a more structurally equivalent parallel to the *Philippians* 2 hymn. In *3 Enoch* 48C:10, Enoch is explicitly identified with the Word of God mentioned in *Isaiah* 55:11: 'So shall my word be, which shall go forth from my mouth: it shall not return to me void, but it shall do whatsoever I please, and shall prosper in the things for which I sent it.'

We should also make reference to an ancient Jewish *Orphica* poem, which is given here according to the longer recension known from Eusebius. Third person pronouns referring to God are capitalized, while those referring to Moses are placed in lower case in order to distinguish between the two, although the final 'He' in upper case may possibly refer simultaneously to both God and to Moses after the latter's apotheosis:

> I sing to those who lawfully may hear:
> Depart, and close the doors, all ye uninitiated,
> Under sentence by the ordinances of the just,
> The law divine announced to all mankind.
> But thou, Musaeus, child of the bright Moon,
> Lend me thine ear; for I declare the truth to you.
> Let not the former fancies of thy mind
> Rob thee of the dear and blessed eternal life.
> Look to the word divine, scrutinize it closely,
> And guide thereby the deep thoughts of thine heart.
> Walk wisely in the way, and look to none,
> Save to the immortal Framer of the cosmos:
> For thus of Him an ancient story speaks:
> He is One, complete in Himself, all else by Him
> Made complete: ever coursing within His works,
> By mortal eyes unseen, seen by mind alone.
> It is not He that out of good
> Makes evil to spring up for mortal men.
> Both love and hatred wait upon His steps,
> And war and pestilence, and sorrow and tears:
> For there is none but He. All other things
> Would be easy to behold, could'st thou but first
> Behold Himself here present upon earth.
> The footsteps and the mighty hand of God
> Whenever I see, I'll show them thee, my son:
> But Him I cannot see, so dense a cloud
> In tenfold darkness wraps our feeble sight.
> Him in His power no mortal could behold,
> Save one, a scion of Chaldaean race:
> For he was skilled to mark the sun's bright path,
> And how in even circle round the earth
> The starry sphere on its own axis turns,
> And winds their chariot guide over sea and sky;
> A bright comet heralding his great birth.
> And then he, high above heaven stationed,

Sits on a golden throne, and plants his feet
On the broad earth; his right hand he extends
Over Ocean's farthest bound; the eternal hills
Tremble in their deep heart, nor can endure
his mighty power. And still above the heavens
Alone he sits celestial, and completes all on earth,
He himself as beginning, middle, and end.
So men of old, so tells the Nile-born sage,
Taught by the twofold tablet of God's law;
Nor otherwise dare I of him to speak:
In heart and limbs I tremble at the thought,
How He from heaven all things in order rules.
Draw near in thought, my son; but guard thy tongue
With care, and store this doctrine in thine heart.[189]

This piece of *Orphica* reflects traditional Jewish monotheism, for it presents God as One and as Creator of all. After the affirmation of the divine Unity, the hymn alludes to the heavenly God's earthly theophany to Moses the Chaldaean. His birth is heralded by a flaming comet, congruent with Moses' later education in the Egyptian astronomical sciences, according to standard Jewish tradition. Reminiscent of Ezekiel the Tragedian's description of the all-encompassing scope of Moses' post-apotheosis gaze upon the universe of heaven, earth and *sheol*, our Orpheus hymn narrates Moses' ascent to the heavenly throne, from where the prophet also stands upon earth and extends his right hand over the ocean, a frequently encountered symbol of *sheol* as a watery abyss or netherworld. Moses is the 'beginning, middle, and end', once again reminiscent of Ezekiel the Tragedian's declaration concerning Moses' universal knowledge of all time, past, present and future. The phrase, 'beginning, middle, and end', as M. Lafargue remarks, is a traditional divine title, not only in Greek philosophy (see Plato, *Laws*, 715e),[190] but also found in varying forms in Jewish and Christian sacred scriptures (see *Isaiah* 41:4, 44:6, 48:12; *Apocalypse* 1:8, 17, 21:6, 22:13). The final line enjoins the initiate to guard in secrecy 'this doctrine', that is, the teaching of the hymn in general, which would seem to mean the doctrine of apotheosis, whereby a human is made to share, by the bestowal of the grace of participation, in the nature and rule of God. This process involves, as in New Testament texts on the glorification of Jesus's created humanity, the attribution to a human being – but not qua human – of divine titles and functions of world creation, cosmic rule, and the reception of adoration and reverential fear from the world of humanity.[191]

We would argue, based on the cumulative evidence examined above from ancient Judaism, that the New Testament accounts of the worship of Jesus refer not to a worship of the divine nature, but to the worship, in a qualified sense of homage or honour, of the glorified, exalted, *created* humanity of Christ, and that this mode of worship is paralleled in the Jewish and Islamic accounts of the worship of Adam, Enoch, Moses, the Jewish high priest, etc. The ancient Jewish practice of assigning the appellation of 'God' to human beings (Moses, the high priest, Melchizedek, etc.) likewise constitutes a parallel to the New Testament's designation of Christ as 'God'. It is a functional appellation with ontological implications. To fail to distinguish between the created humanity of Christ and the eternal Logos – despite the unity of the two natures in the one person of Jesus Christ according to Christian belief – leads to conclusions that are deservedly assailed in the Qur'an, even from a traditional Christian perspective.

To address further the question of the created or uncreated status of the Logos, we observe that in the Johannine prologue, the light of *Genesis* 1:3 ('And God said: Light be made! And light was made') is clearly identified as the Logos. Since such 'light' was 'made', John would seem, according to a purely historical view, to assume a created status for the Logos. But for John there may not be a simple or complete identification of the Logos as the primordial Light; the Logos for him may be uncreated, while the created Light may be derived from the Logos. Paul also seems to somehow identify the light of creation with the Logos in *2 Corinthians* 4:6, though Paul is more ambiguous, because more symbolical, in his articulation: 'For God, who commanded the light to shine out of darkness, hath shined in our hearts, to give the light of the knowledge of the glory of God, in the face of Christ Jesus.' Here it appears that Paul allegorizes 'light' as 'knowledge of God's glory' (probably meant as a divine hypostasis), which is somehow associated with the 'face' of Christ. Here the 'face' probably is a metaphor for 'eyes' as the receptacle of light. Is Paul then implying that the knowledge of God (the light of *Genesis* 1:3) emerges from the Logos? It is well known that in classical Greek poetry 'light' is a poetic synonym of 'man', enabling ancient Jews to interpret *Genesis* 1:3's 'light' as 'the Man', that is, the Messiah or Logos. *Genesis* 1:3 recounts the 'making' of the primordial light; yet this alludes not to a creation of the primordial Light, but describes its entrance onto the plane of creation.

As Boyarin observes, R. Schnackenburg's contention that the Johannine prologue's notion of the pre-existent Logos goes beyond the doctrine of the pre-existent Wisdom or Logos of ancient Judaism cannot be supported.[192] Schnackenburg claims that *John* contains 'New Testament' revelation beyond that of Judaism regarding an uncreated, eternal Logos who pre-existed creation, in contrast with the 'Old Testament' Wisdom, who was supposedly merely 'God's companion and partner in creation'. But as Boyarin clarifies, John's statement that the Logos was 'with God in the beginning' says no more and no less than *Proverbs* 8 says of Wisdom, who also declares of herself that she 'was with Him in the beginning'. According to the Qur'anic Light Verse, 'God is the Light of the heavens and the earth'; and such identitative language would seem to suggest an uncreated light. Yet the light can be spoken of as created insofar as it enters into the created plane. Similarly, in Islamic thought it is sometimes maintained that the Holy Spirit is both uncreated and created.[193] Judaism stresses the created status of the Holy Spirit, who is identified with the divine Light. The kabbalist Judah ben Barzillai al-Bargeloni writes concerning the creation of the world: '[God] first created the Holy Spirit, to be a sign of His divinity, which was seen by the prophets and the angels.'[194]

Regarding Philo's Logos concept, Daniel Boyarin writes that the famous allegorical interpreter did not borrow his ideas from any Greek or Roman philosophy, for there is no fitting parallel to Philo's version of the Logos in Platonism, Aristotelianism or Stoicism, a fact referred to in the work of Darrell Hannah.[195] Philo's Logos concept is a native Jewish idea derived from theological reflection upon the Hebrew scriptures. Boyarin cites *Quis rerum divinarum heres sit* 205-06, in which Philo teaches that the Logos is the 'highest in age' (which would seem to imply a created status), and who is given 'to stand on the border and separate the creature from the Creator'. Philo describes the Logos as 'neither uncreated by God, nor created as you, but midway between the two extremes... .'[196] Boyarin comments: 'Philo oscillates on the point of the ambiguity between separate existence of the Logos, God's Son (e.g., in *De agricultura* 51), and its total incorporation within the godhead.'[197]

Because Nicaea, however, involves a primacy of ontology over biblical functionalism, it would not be out of place to explore Philo's attitude toward speculation on the divine Essence in order to test Boyarin's claim. Philo fundamentally agrees with Aristotle that, although we could never fully comprehend God, nevertheless, as Alexander Broadie explains, 'even if our image of god fails to correspond with the facts, it might still be considered a necessary aid to thought about god.'[198] In *De Specialibus Legibus* I vi. 32, Philo separates the question of the existence of God from the question of precisely what the divine Essence is in itself. The latter is 'difficult' if not 'impossible to solve'. For Philo, in *De Posteritate Caini* xlvii 167-9, to 'enquire about essence or quality in God, is a folly... .'[199] But as Broadie explains, the unknowability of God's essence should not prevent the human mind 'from approximating as nearly as possible to an intellectual grasp of it'. Broadie refers to *De Specialibus Legibus* I vii 36, 40: 'For nothing is better than to search for the true God, even if the discovery of Him eludes human capacity... . For the very seeking, even without finding, is felicity in itself.'[200] As Broadie claims, what is most important is whether the search into the divine Essence is carried out in humility or arrogance.[201]

As for the origin of the Logos, Philo holds in *De Cherubim* ix 28 that 'it was conceived before' all things.[202] Additionally, this 'conception' would have occurred outside of time, so that we would have a 'logical or an ontological priority rather than a temporal precedence'.[203] Yet Philo also writes in *Legum Allegoriae* III lxi 175 that the Logos is the 'eldest of created things'.[204] This should be interpreted in the light of the Philonic statement already quoted above, that the Logos is 'neither uncreated by God, nor created as' humans are, 'but midway between the two extremes'. Therefore the Logos is 'created', but not as humans are. Could this be reconciled dialectically with the Catholic formula concerning the Logos, that he is 'begotten, not made'? Broadie cogently suggests that for Philo, the Logos is the first divine emanation.[205] In the end we may conclude that Philo speaks in functionally ontological modes, and that his musings on the divine Essence in relation to the Logos are intended to be understood as imperfect hints at an essentially unknowable mystery. It is a mystery, however, that must be searched into in a spirit of humility, and within this search lies the present beatitude of the human mind. Aquinas in his *Summa contra gentiles* LI writes decisively: 'Hence, if God's essence is to be seen, the intellect must see it through the divine essence itself, so that in such vision the divine essence shall be at once the object which is seen and that whereby it is seen.'

To revisit the theme of the Ebionites, they believed the divine 'Christ' descended upon the human 'Jesus' at his baptism and then forsook him just before his ascent to God. Taken as literal statements, this may seem rather bizarre to modern Christian sensibilities, but assimilated analogically in an ancient 'Semitic' manner, it simply means that the divine nature cannot be subject to death. What for the precise Greek philosophical language of later Catholic theology would be unacceptable, becomes acceptable once we understand it metaphorically, that is, the names 'Jesus' and 'Christ' were the Ebionites' way of speaking of the human and divine natures of Christ; and the Jewish-Christian articulation cannot be considered heretical, since it merely repeats, in admittedly more concrete metaphorical mode, the Hebrew scriptures' general teaching on the descent of the Spirit upon YHWH's prophets.

Indeed, Michael Goulder points out that the so-called 'adoptionist' christology is nothing other than the Old Testament theology of prophetic possession by the Spirit. Adoptionist christology, understood metaphorically, as it was originally intended to be, is by no means heretical in its essence, and as Goulder points out, the term 'adoptionist christology' should probably be abandoned by theologians and replaced with a more accurate description of this primitive Jewish-Christian belief, namely, 'possessionist christology'.[206] Goulder, generally inclined to see too great a distance between Ebionite and New Testament christologies, would perhaps be surprised to find his description of the 'possessionist' model, as well as the Ebionite True Prophet concept, eminently matched in almost all essentials in Edward Schillebeeckx's Roman Catholic description of the New Testament 'Prophet' and 'Pneuma possession' christologies.[207]

Some of the church fathers' representations of Ebionite christology as merely 'adoptionist' is misleading. In the *Clementine Homilies* 16 we have an instructive account of Ebionite christology. In 16:11, the Gnostic Simon appeals to *Genesis* 1:26 to argue that there are two gods: 'Let *us* make man... .' Peter counters Simon in 16:12 by arguing that the 'us' implies the generated Wisdom of God, and not any second god. But if Christ is associated with Wisdom, which is the Logos in an equivalent sense, then the Ebionite doctrine is not strictly 'adoptionist':

> And Peter answered: 'One is He who said to His Wisdom, "Let us make man." But His Wisdom was that with which He Himself always rejoiced as with His own spirit. It is united as soul to God, but it is extended by Him, as hand, fashioning the universe. On this account, also, one man was made, and from him went forth also the female. And being a unity generically, it is yet a duality, for by expansion and contraction the unity is thought to be a duality. So that I act rightly in offering up all the honour to one God as to parents.'[208]

In 16:15, Peter explains that Christ never claimed to be a second god alongside the true God.

> And Peter answered: 'Our Lord neither asserted that there were gods except the Creator of all, nor did he proclaim himself to be God,[209] but he with reason pronounced blessed him who called him the Son of that God who has arranged the universe.' And Simon answered: 'Does it not seem to you, then, that he who comes from God is God?'[210]

In 16:16, Peter explains that the Father alone is unbegotten. If we keep in mind that in Jewish Christianity, as in Judaism, the word 'God' is reserved solely for the Father, then there would be nothing unorthodox in the text that follows:

> 'In addition to this, it is the peculiarity of the Father not to have been begotten, but of the Son to have been begotten; but what is begotten cannot be compared with that which is unbegotten or self-begotten.' ... And Peter said: 'Why do you not see that if the one happens to be self-begotten or unbegotten, they cannot be called the same; nor can it be asserted of him who has been begotten that he is of the same substance as he is who has begotten him?'[211]

The Gnostic Simon counters that Christ claimed to be a second god, based on *Matthew* 11:27: 'No one knows the Father but the Son, nor does any one know the Son but the Father, and they to whom the Son may wish to reveal Him.' Peter offers his interpretation of this verse in *Clementine Homilies* 17:13:

> ' ... He, being the Son from the beginning, was alone appointed to give the revelation to those to whom he wishes to give it. And thus the first man Adam must have heard of him; and Enoch, who pleased God, must have known him; and Noah, the righteous one, must have become acquainted with him; and Abraham his friend must have understood him; and Isaac must have perceived him; and Jacob, who wrestled with him, must have believed in him; and the revelation must have been given to all among the people who were worthy.'[212]

The ending of this passage is simply an alternate formulation of the Ebionite True Prophet christology, according to which the prophets beginning with Adam knew the Logos specifically, since they themselves were manifestations of the Logos, yet naturally in different modes and to various degrees.[213]

To revisit Islamic christology at this point, it is significant that, whereas the Qur'an declares, 'Say not God is the son of Mary,' it does not command, 'Say not the son of Mary is God.' Consider this passage from the Qur'an:

> They indeed have disbelieved who say: Lo! Allah is the Messiah, son of Mary. Say: Who then can do aught against Allah, if He had willed to destroy the Messiah son of Mary, and his mother and everyone on earth? Allah's is the Sovereignty of the heavens and the earth and all that is between them. He createth what He will. And Allah is Able to do all things (5:17).

The point is the same as Ibn al-'Arabi's, referred to above.[214] Given the Qur'an's thoroughgoing emphasis on the infinite gulf between the creator and the created, or Absolute Being as opposed to relative (created, contingent) being, it is understandable that Islamic theology de-emphasizes the created human nature and soul of Jesus. As Frithjof Schuon explains, this de-emphasis is not done 'with an intrinsically pejorative intention, but merely to stress the littleness of the creature before its Creator... .'[215] As we will have occasion to note below, the Dominican theologian Fr. Thomas F. O'Meara reminds us that even from Aquinas's Christian viewpoint, Christ's humanity 'remains distant and minute compared to the Word of God', and as the angelic doctor expresses himself on the matter: 'The power of a divine person is infinite and cannot be limited to anything created' (*Summa Theologiae* 3 q. 7, a. 3).

According to Ibn al-'Arabi, relative, i.e., contingent being, by stark contrast to Absolute Being, may be called in a certain sense non-being. To clarify this idea, we will here combine al-'Arabi's Semitic and oriental approach with that of the 'Greco-Roman' articulation of Western Christianity. What al-'Arabi is proposing is simply that only God is the *Ipsum Esse*, whereas the being of created entities is derived *absolutely and entirely* from the Creator, and moreover, without God's sustaining power a created entity would simply cease to exist. Therefore, contingent being does not have its own existence; being is derived from, that is, created by, the *Ipsum Esse*. Created entities have no existence in or from themselves, but only in and from the *Ipsum Esse*. As William Chittick and Peter Lamborn Wilson remark on al-'Arabi's ideas: 'So all entities considered in themselves are nonexistent, whereas considered in relation to Being they are the possibilities of Self-Manifestation inherent within It.'[216] Entified being is not identical to *Ipsum Esse*, which is simply to say the creature is not the Creator.[217]

Catholic dogma holds that in view of the aspect of union implied in the *unio secundum hypostasim*, and because Jesus Christ is one person and not two, what is predicated or said of Christ's divine nature is also applicable to his humanity. Accordingly, Mary is called the Mother of *God*. But this manner of speaking must not be divorced from the historical context in which it arose, a context which reveals that it is fundamentally a *negative* proposition, that is, it was formulated in order to combat certain heretical notions. Additionally, the shared attributive language, applied in Catholic theology to the one person of Jesus Christ possessing two natures, obviously operates within a conceptual model that is *relative* and *limitative*. Indeed, if the definite boundaries implied in the dogma were lost sight of, one would end up by identifying the human nature of Christ with the divine Logos, which would be irrational and heretical. And in view of the infinite distance between the created humanity of Christ and the Creator, which is the distance between creature and Creator, the conciliar dogma under discussion here could be said to be, according to a certain dialectical manner of speaking, *infinitely* relative. In fact, in speaking of Mary as the Mother of *God*, we have an interesting example of Greek philosophical theology operating in a mode that, although it utilizes ontology, is primarily *functional*. If one were to interpret it as primarily ontological, the result would be sheer blasphemy from both a Catholic and an Islamic perspective.

Some of the ante-Nicene fathers' simplistic identification of Jesus with the eternal Logos, rightly criticized mutually by both Islamic and post-Nicene Catholic theology, nevertheless can be somewhat justified from a Catholic viewpoint, in that the identification was an attempt to emphasize the unity of the person of Jesus Christ in virtue of the hypostatic union. And in fact the Qur'an also justifies the underlying concern in a metaphysical sense, in that it also in a certain way establishes an integral (though not identitative) relationship between Jesus and the Logos by employing the formal articulation announcing that 'Jesus was ... God's Word and a Spirit from Him' (see 4:171).

Of course, other Qur'anic passages clarify the statement so that a simplistic identification is in the end excluded. For instance, consider Qur'an 3:45: '(And remember) when the angels said: O Mary! Lo! Allah giveth thee glad tidings of a Word from him, whose name is the Messiah, Jesus, son of Mary, illustrious in the world and the Hereafter, and one of those brought near (unto Allah).' Note the indefinite form, 'a Word'; similarly, the *Letter to the Hebrews* 1:1 refers to Christ as 'a Son', without the definite article. The burden of Qur'an 4:171 is to emphasize the created status of Jesus, who is 'only' *God's* Word and Spirit. The emphasis is therefore God, not His Word and Spirit Jesus. However, the usage of the indefinite article should not be understood in a derogatory sense, especially given Islam's respect for all of God's messengers. Moreover, as each prophet possesses a certain uniqueness, so does Jesus in that his human origins are paralleled in a pre-eminent sense only by one other prophet, namely Adam, who was created by direct divine activity. As Qur'an 3:59 establishes: 'Lo! the likeness of Jesus with Allah is as the likeness of Adam. He created him of dust, then He said unto him: Be! and he is.' Doubtless this unique origin of Jesus among the prophets is one of the main reasons why in post-Qur'anic Islamic texts, 'Spirit and Word of God', without the sense of the indefinite article, became the dominant formal christological title for Jesus. Nevertheless, it should be remarked that 'Spirit of God' is also an Islamic title for the angel Gabriel, and John the Baptist's birth is described in Qur'an 3:39 as 'a confirmation of a word from Allah'. So it should be understood that 'word' and 'spirit' are not associated exclusively with Jesus in Islam, and this is to be expected, given the varying meanings and nuances of the two terms occurring in different contexts.

To recapitulate, we may say that the Qur'anic statements criticizing christological doctrines are not directed against orthodox, but against heterodox Christian articulations, namely, against the identification of the Father with the Son and the denial of the created status of Jesus's human nature and soul. There is nothing in the essence of the Qur'an's christological attacks that should trouble an insightful Christian theologian. Muhammad by necessity naturally censured the term 'son of God' because of the danger represented by Arabian polytheism, which spoke of several divinities as God's 'sons' and 'daughters' in a quasi-physical sense. But the same reality to which informed Christians refer by using the phrase 'son of God' is alluded to in the Qur'an, according to an esoteric perspective and in a metaphysical sense, under other titles such as 'Word of God' and 'Spirit of God'.

CHAPTER THREE

Logos as Book and Person: the Qur'an and Christ

T HE PARALLEL HAS often been drawn between the Islamic doctrine of the 'inliteration' of God's Word in the written Qur'an and the Christian doctrine of the incarnation. Seyyed Hossein Nasr offers the following insightful observation by comparing the Qur'an and the eucharist: 'Arabic is the sacred language of Islam and Qur'anic Arabic plays a role in Islam analogous to the role of the body of Christ in Christianity.'[218]

Since it was so already in John Damascene's time, we may assume that from the very beginning of Islam it was considered blasphemy to deny the eternal and uncreated nature and status of the Qur'an. To assume that Islam borrowed the concept of the eternally pre-existent heavenly Word from Christians is the conclusion of an intellectually shallow historicist methodology, based on a preoccupation with establishing and then explaining thematic parallels as the sole result of intellectual genealogical descent. The possibility that a single idea could arise simultaneously within two different groups, and that the origin of such an idea may be explained by a common descent from a transcendent archetypal pattern, does not even occur to a scholar operating from a strict historicist *Weltanschauung*. Although the eternity of the Qur'an is denied by Shi'i Muslim authorities today, perhaps for philosophical reasons and for fear of the idea's polemical misuse or exploitation by Christians, it is beyond dispute that the uncreated status of the Qur'an is an historically orthodox Sunni tenet of faith. As F. Buhl explains: 'The Mu'tazilis and the more free-thinking theologians raised a protest, it is true, but after Ash'ari himself, in the last version of his dogmatics, had championed the view that the written or recited Qur'an is identical in being and reality with the uncreated and eternal word of God, the victory was won by the orthodox school.'[219] Speaking of the pre-existent *Muhammadan Light*, Louis Massignon explains that 'orthodoxy has always carefully placed the doctrine of the uncreated Qur'an above this cult.'[220]

Frithjof Schuon reflects the traditional Sunni understanding of the uncreated Qur'an in the following statement: 'For Muslim orthodoxy the Qur'an is … the uncreated Word of God – uncreated though expressing itself through created elements such as words, sounds and letters … .'[221] The pre-existent heavenly book 'inliterated' as the 'historical' Qur'an finds essentially identical homologues in Jewish apocalyptic, wisdom and rabbinic literature. Already in the canonical scriptures the Hebrew sacred writers identify the Torah as an historical manifestation of the eternal, pre-existent Wisdom. The identification is explicit in *Sirach* 24 and *Baruch* 3 and 4. That we are approaching a sacred mystery in the speculative doctrine of the pre-existent heavenly book that parallels the Christian dogma of the incarnation is borne out by the fact that the church has traditionally adapted both passages from *Sirach* and *Baruch* in its liturgy and theology as prophecies of the incarnation and as protological descriptions of the pre-existent Logos.

From the perspective of the teaching on the uncreated heavenly book, it can be said that rabbinical Judaism and Sunni Islam do not deny the uncreated, eternal nature of God's 'Logos'; the central difference between these two and Christianity is that whereas according to Judaism and Islam the Logos dwells among humans in the 'body' of a book, or 'as' a book, according to Christianity the Logos manifested itself by being united with the nature of a man. But in view of the created human nature of Christ, there can be no simplistic, undifferentiated identity established between Jesus's creaturely status and the Logos. It was always this simplistic identification that disturbed Judaism, Jewish Christianity and Islam, and rightly so from a truly orthodox Christian view. Moving from the supraformal to the formal level must always imply and necessitate an element of contingency on the plane of manifestation, whether this be applied to the supraformal heavenly book in its formal written manifestation in history, or to the Logos in relation to any of its 'human' revelations in the world.

At the opening of John's gospel we read of the pre-existent creative Logos. At one level the 'Word' that creates is an allusion to *Genesis* chapter 1, where God's spoken word effects creation. God's word of 'let there be' occurs in the *Genesis* creation account ten times; this certainly contributed to the later doctrine of the ten *sefirot*, or 'numbers', encountered in the Kabbalah, which also connects the ten creative utterances of *Genesis* 1 with the ten commandments. The ten divine creative utterances were then personified as the tenfold, yet unitive Word of God, or Logos. This Logos as literary personification of the *Genesis* ten creative words, or declarations, appears as personified Wisdom (חכמה or σοφια) in *Proverbs* 8, *Sirach* 24, *Wisdom* 7, and *Baruch* 3 and 4. This personified Wisdom is then explicitly identified as the pre-existent, creative Law, or Torah in the Jewish Wisdom literature.

At the most fundamental level, the Logos of John's opening chapter is not derived from Hellenistic philosophy, but rather from the creation account in

Genesis and other Hebrew scriptural Wisdom literature passages. Since *Sirach* 24:32 and *Baruch* 3:38-4:1 already identified the pre-existent Logos with the Torah, *John* 1:17 must be understood not as implying an opposition, but as explicating a unitive pattern of progressive manifestational fulfillment: 'For the law was given by Moses; grace and truth came by Jesus Christ.' That is, the pre-existent Logos was first manifested in Judaic history through Moses in the form of the Torah; later the Logos is manifested again, but in a different mode, namely, as Jesus Christ, an embodiment of grace and truth, two attributes of Wisdom found in the Vulgate version of *Sirach* 24:25: 'In me is all grace of the way and of the truth, in me is all hope of life and of virtue' (*In me gratia omnis viae et veritatis; in me omnis spes vitae et virtutis*).[222] According to Islamic logic, one could expand John's statement by asserting that Moses gave the Torah, then Jesus came and established grace and truth in the Gospel, and finally, Muhammad came and revealed the Qur'an as a synthesis of law and grace in truth:

> And We caused Jesus, son of Mary, to follow in their footsteps, confirming that which was (revealed) before him, and We bestowed on him the Gospel wherein is guidance and a light, confirming that which was (revealed) before it in the Torah – a guidance and an admonition unto those who ward off (evil) … . And unto thee [Muhammad] have We revealed the Scripture with the truth, confirming whatever Scripture was before it … . For each We have appointed a divine law and a traced-out way. Had Allah willed He could have made you one community. But that He may try you by that which He hath given you (He hath made you as ye are). So vie one with another in good works. Unto Allah ye will all return, and He will then inform you of that wherein ye differ (5:46, 48).[223]

These two ayat contain a sublime explanation of religious diversity as providential, in a striking parallel with Nicholas of Cusa's teaching in his treatise, *De pace fidei*. The various religions, according to this perspective, are varying formal manifestations of the one supraformal 'substantial' Truth, and the concrete praxis that is to result, again providentially, from the confrontation of such diversity is not mean-spirited polemics, but mutual competition in good works. Consider also Qur'an 4:149: 'Allah loveth not the utterance of harsh speech save by one who hath been wronged.' Similarly we read in Qur'an 29:46: 'And argue not with the People of the Scripture [Christians and Jews] unless it be in (a way) that is courteous, save with such of them as do wrong (against you); and say: We believe in that which hath been revealed unto us and revealed unto you (aforetime); our God and your God is One, and unto Him we (all) surrender.' Moderation of vocal articulation is demanded not only in religious disputation, but also in worship; Qur'an 17:110: 'And thou [Muhammad], be not loud voiced in thy worship nor yet silent therein, but follow a way between.'

The same points are made by Nicholas of Cusa in his *De pace fidei* ch. XIX, where he argues that the diversity of religions is providential, for each believing one's own religion to be 'the best' inspires the followers of the various religions to outdo each other in good works: 'Where conformity of mode cannot be had [between the world religions], nations are entitled to their own devotions and ceremonies, provided faith and peace be maintained. Perhaps as a result of a certain diversity devotion will even be increased, since each nation will endeavour with zeal and diligence to make its own rite [religion] more splendid, in order that in this respect it may excel some other (nation) and thereby obtain greater merit with God and (greater) praise in the world.'[224]

Disputes arising from differences of expression and theological articulation between the various religions, necessary because of the divine sanction of cultural plurality, will be resolved by God at the Last Judgment. And perhaps everyone, as the Sufis have perennially taught, will then be surprised at the nature of the Divine clarification. As Rabbi Jacob Neusner writes: ' ... God is known to spring surprises on us. The one thing that will not surprise me is that, in the future as in the past, Islam, Judaism, Buddhism, Zoroastrianism, and Christianity, in most of their various subsystems, will go on in accord with their own eternal rhythms.'[225]

If it be countered that because of the differences existing between Islam and Christianity, they therefore cannot descend from the same transcendent archetype, the answer is that every manifestation of a supraformal archetype on the formal plane will necessarily exhibit variation on account of the formal differences inherent in the diverse mental and linguistic cultures of humanity. The situation between Christianity and Islam is similar paradigmatically to the formal modifications that the supraformal archetype of Judaism underwent within Christianity. The formal differences between Judaism, Christianity and Islam are to be traced back to the plurality which characterizes all phenomenal manifestation or entification; the 'discontinuities' in the three Abrahamic religious traditions are actually more extrinsic than intrinsic, for the variations are like separate lines which at some point intersect at the center or level of the primordial Abrahamic religious archetype. Thus the supraformal and formal realities give rise to what may be called continuities and discontinuities, some coinciding or overlapping at either the transcendent or the phenomenal categories of being and manifestation. That formal differences of even a quite profound nature can issue from the same transcendent archetype is demonstrated by Jewish monotheism in contrast to the church's trinitarianism. Since, as St. Thomas observes, the doctrine of the trinity is a mystery of faith not directly accessible to human reason unaided by divine revelation, we can conclude that, although the trinity is an exoteric belief of Christianity, in relation to Judaism and Islam any analogous form of the belief could exist – to be sure in a quite attenuated form – only at the esoteric level. Therefore, in relation to the three Abrahamic religions, any polymorphous articulation of the divine unity outside Christianity is to be found only in mystical or speculative theology, as in Sufism's integration, in a metaphysical sense, of *unio mystica* and the *Nur Muhammadi*, the Shi'i doctrine of the eternal, pre-existent Imam, and the Kabbalah's ten sefirotic eternal creational emanations. That these ideas do indeed exist in the Sufic, Shi'i and kabbalistic systems indicates that the formal differences regarding these doctrines between the three religions are more 'accidental' or 'relative' than 'substantial' or 'essential'.

Contemplating the progressive triune paradigm of Moses, Jesus and Muhammad, we once again are reminded of the early Jewish-Christian doctrine of the True Prophet as Logos manifestation and its polymorphous appearance(s) throughout history. If we ask whether there is evidence in any sense in the records of the early Great Church in support of a multiplicity of Logos manifestations, we will find it interestingly[226] in the opening verses of the *Epistle to the Hebrews*:

(1) God, who, at sundry times and in divers manners, spoke in times past to the fathers in the prophets, (2) In these last days, hath spoken to us in a Son, whom he hath appointed heir of all things, by whom he also made the worlds. (3) Who being the brightness of his glory and the figure of his substance and upholding all things by the word of his power, making purgation of sins, sitteth on the right hand of the majesty on high.

(1) Multifariam et multis modis olim Deus loquens patribus in prophetis (2) novissime diebus istis locutus est nobis in Filio quem constituit heredem universorum per quem fecit et saecula (3) qui cum sit splendor gloriae et figura substantiae eius portansque omnia verbo virtutis suae purgationem peccatorum faciens sedit ad dexteram Maiestatis in excelsis.[227]

Jerome's Latin version here is quite faithful to the original Greek, especially with regard to the phrases, 'in prophetis', 'novissime diebus' and 'in Filio'. Before we explore some of the theological implications of these terms, we will note that verse 1's proclamation regarding God's speaking refers to the divine pre-existent Logos. This can be inferred from verse 2's declaration concerning God's speaking 'in Filio' in the eschatological days of the Messiah, who according to Christian theology was hypostatically united with the pre-existent Logos, 'by whom he also made the worlds'. The last phrase undeniably alludes to those

Jewish texts on personified Wisdom through whom God creates the world (see *Proverbs* 8, *Sirach* 24, *Wisdom* 7), and it is not coincidental that verse 3's ideas and vocabulary are mirrored in the Greek text of *Wisdom* 7.

Regarding the phrase 'in prophetis' (εν τοις προφηταις), we should keep in mind that one of the most notoriously difficult elements of any language's grammar is presented by prepositions. Though most would translate 'εν' in verse 1 with 'by', if we remain strictly literal, the closest translation would be 'in'. Thus we are told that God has spoken, or manifested his divine pre-existent and primordial creative Logos, 'in the prophets', that is, the Jewish prophets. In a different mode, that is, in a plenary mode, the Logos was manifested 'in Filio' (εν υιω); the absence of the definite article suggests the strict translation 'in *a* Son', not 'in *the* Son'. The theological significance of the absence of the definite article in the Greek text implies that the manifestation of the Logos throughout salvation history cannot be absolutely restricted to Jesus Christ. The Logos manifested 'in a Son' occurred in 'novissime diebus', in the 'most recent days', or 'επ εσχατου των ημερων τουτων' (*these last days*). It must be admitted that the term 'novissime diebus' in the present context does not explicitly necessitate a sense of a *definitive*, that is, a final, Logos manifestation; it merely functions as a temporal contrast to the earlier times (*olim*) when God manifested his Logos 'in the prophets'. 'Novissime diebus' does not by any means necessitate that there could be no further manifestations of the Logos after Christ.

Hebrews 1:1-3 implies that the divine Logos has been manifested in a variety of modes, 'multis modis' (πολυτροπως): in the past, 'in the prophets',[228] at a later point, 'in a Son'. That the Logos manifestations of former times (*olim*) are described as 'multifariam' (πολυμερως), 'fragmentary' or 'in part', admittedly suggests that the later revelation 'in a Son' is a plenary manifestation, though not necessarily definitive or final in an exclusive sense, but in an inclusive sense open to the future. The theoretical question could therefore rightly be raised as to whether a *plenary* manifestation could not reoccur. The verses can be held as teaching a multiplicity of Logos manifestations in varying modes and degrees culminating 'in a Son' in the 'last days', but not as excluding the possibility of a further Logos manifestation.

As Daniel Boyarin argues, *John* 1:9-13 refers to the pre-incarnate Logos, who was received by men before the birth of Jesus of Nazareth.[229] The interpretation that sees these Johannine verses as referring to the incarnate Logos became dominant only with Maldonatus in the 16th century.[230] The fathers held to the same interpretation, namely, that the Logos visited Abraham and other Hebrew worthies, usually in the form of an angel or an angel disguised as a man. But could *John* 1 not be referring to the same concept found in *Hebrews* 1:1-3 of multiple Logos manifestations as embodied in the prophets, who are sent to the people and either accepted or rejected by them? Indeed, according to Schillebeeckx, the Johannine prologue, at the pre-canonical level at least, did teach that the Logos was incarnated (embodied) in Moses, John the Baptist, and then finally in Jesus. But in light of *Hebrews* 1:1-3, there should be no reason for a Catholic theologian such as Schillebeeckx to consign, as he does for fear of heterodoxy, an idea of multiple Logos manifestations to a reputed pre-canonical stage of theology.[231] Boyarin interprets the Johannine prologue as teaching that the Torah was 'an earlier attempt of the Logos to enter the world.... . The Torah simply needed a better exegete, the *Logos Ensarkos...* .'[232] Indeed, 'Christ is the Logos who personifies the Torah.'[233]

Can we find any further support in traditional Christian theology for the possibility of a multiplicity of Logos incarnations? As Dominican theologian Thomas F. O'Meara concludes, we do indeed find such evidence in Thomas Aquinas, for whom the idea of the created status of Jesus 'as identical with the Word of God' is both 'heretical and absurd' because it contradicts the doctrine of the hypostatic union.[234] Aquinas maintains, in O'Meara's formulation, that Christ's humanity 'remains distant and minute compared to the Word of God', and in the angelic doctor's own words, 'The power of a divine person is infinite and cannot be limited to anything created [3 q. 7, a. 3].'[235]

As Peter C. Phan similarly formulates this situation: 'The Logos ... is not exhaustively embodied in Jesus of Nazareth who was spatially and temporally limited.... . There is a "distinction-in-identity" or "identity-in-distinction"... . Hence, the activities of the Logos, though inseparable from those of Jesus, are also distinct from and go beyond Jesus' activities, both before and after the Incarnation.'[236] As Phan notes, this has nothing to do with the proposition condemned in the Vatican document *Dominus Iesus*, namely, the theory of an imperfect or defective revelation of Jesus Christ.[237]

Karl Rahner reflects as follows upon the same truth concerning Christ's humanity: ' ... Christ in reality and in all truth is a man with all this involves: a human consciousness which is aware in adoration of its own infinite distance in relation to God.'[238] On the question of the possibility of other Logos incarnations besides that of Jesus of Nazareth, O'Meara writes that, 'the life of Jesus on earth does not curtail the divine Word's being and life.... . Aquinas asked if the Word of God (or the two other divine persons) could be incarnate in a further creature. He answered affirmatively.'[239] O'Meara then quotes from 3, q. 3, a. 7: 'If a divine person could not assume another [created nature], then the personal mode of the divine nature would be enclosed by one human nature. But it is impossible for the Uncreated to be circumscribed by the created. Whether we look at the divine power itself or its personhood (the term of the union [with Jesus]), one must say that the divine person can assume more than one human being.'[240] Compare the following observation by Frithjof Schuon: 'The Logos is one, but its modes of human manifestation may differ without in any way detracting from its quality as Logos.'[241]

We garner the above arguments not in order to assert that Muhammad was an incarnation of the Logos – for Islamic theology speaks of divine theophany rather than incarnation – but in order to indicate that the Christian idea of the absolute and unique appearance of the Logos in hypostatic union with Jesus of Nazareth must be understood in a relative sense. As Peter C. Phan remarks, 'Christ's uniqueness is not exclusive or absolute but *constitutive* and *relational*.'[242] Our author reminds us that Jesus did not teach all truth to the apostles, but explained that the Holy Spirit would unfold such to them only after his ascension (see *John* 16:12-13).[243]

Neither do we argue for a total identity between the Christian concept of incarnation and the Islamic concept of theophanic manifestation. We wish only to maintain that they are not mutually exclusive, or totally contradictory. They stand in a similar relationship to each other as does *John* 1:14's Jewish concept of the manifestation of the *Shekhinah* in a human being and the church's later dogma of the incarnation, as expressed in Greek philosophical terminology. In any event, the relationship between the Christian and Islamic systems is suggested by the Sufi Logos doctrine of the Muhammadan Light, which certainly justifies Frithjof Schuon's assertion that the Islamic mystics have assimilated Muhammad to the Logos, even though Islam is not one of the avataric, or incarnational religions. We could therefore say that Islam assimilates Muhammad to the Logos through the mode of theophanic manifestation rather than through the mode of incarnation. But since both are varying modes of Logos manifestation, the Islamic and Christian perspectives meet at a certain metaphysical point.

Frithjof Schuon describes the approach to this subject taken by Islam, which insists that God 'does not descend into manifestation, He projects Himself therein, as the sun projects itself through its light; and it is this projection that permits humanity to participate in Him.'[244] The same author explains that, even though Islam rejects the idea of incarnation for Muhammad, nevertheless, 'we would reply that a certain Divine Aspect took on under particular cyclic circumstances a particular earthly form', in accord with various sayings of the Prophet of Islam such as: '"He who has seen me has seen God" (*El Haqq*, "The Truth"); "I am He and He is I, save that I am he who I am and He is He who He is."'[245] Schuon reminds us of 'an Arabic saying that "Muhammad is a mortal, but not as other mortals; (in comparison with them) he is like a jewel among pebbles,"'[246] before asserting that 'each traditional form [religion] identifies its founder with the divine Logos.'[247] Schuon also remarks that 'in his inner reality, Muhammad, like Christ, is identified with the Word....'[248] The same author records elsewhere the two following *ahadith*: 'I am Ahmad without *mim*' (that is, the Prophet is *Ahad*, which is God's Name, '[the] One') and 'I am an Arab (*'Arabi*) without *'ayn*' (that is *Rabbi*, 'my Lord').[249]

In the *Gospel of the Hebrews*, as quoted later in this paragraph, we read of the Spirit coming to rest in its fullness within the Prophet Jesus. Interestingly, when we turn to *Sirach* 24:11-12, 15, we also find pre-existent Wisdom speaking of seeking rest: 'And by my power I have trodden under my feet the hearts of all the high and low: and in all these I sought rest, and I shall abide in the inheritance of the Lord. Then the creator of all things commanded, and said to me: and he that made me, rested in my tabernacle.... . And so I was established in Zion, and in the holy city I likewise rested, and my power was in Jerusalem.' The concomitant themes of rest and rule ('power') contained in this verse are interestingly paralleled in an ancient work related to the *Gospel of the Hebrews*, namely, the Greek *Gospel of Thomas*, fragment 2, 'and when he reigns, he will rest'.[250] According to Jerome's commentary on *Isaiah* 11:2, the *Gospel of the Hebrews* stated: 'And it came to pass when the Lord was come up out of the water, the whole fount of the Holy Spirit descended and rested upon him, and said unto him: My son, in all prophets was I waiting for thee that thou shouldst come, and I might rest in thee. For thou art my rest, thou art my first begotten son, that reignest for ever.'[251]

In the same commentary, Jerome records a similar statement from the *Gospel of the Hebrews*: 'The full fount of the Holy Spirit descended upon him. For the Lord is the Spirit and where the Spirit is, there is liberty.' The second sentence might be an explanatory gloss by St. Jerome, or it may have been found already in the *Gospel of the Hebrews* and thus may have been quoted by St. Paul in *2 Corinthians* 3:17. We may also note that the *Gospel of the Hebrews'* teaching on the definitive manifestation of the Logos as the divine 'rest' finds some intriguing thematic parallels in the *Letter to the Hebrews*, namely, in the multiplicity of Logos manifestations taught in the opening verses, and the theme of the divine 'rest' developed later in the same epistle. Could it be that the Jewish Christians who used the *Gospel of the Hebrews* were from the same or a related community to whom the *Letter to the Hebrews* was addressed? If so, then the Letter's opening verses could be a sort of conciliatory concession to the readers' beliefs regarding the multiplicity of Logos manifestations in the prophets culminating in the True Prophet Jesus, in whom the Logos permanently 'rests'. That the *Letter to the Hebrews* 1:1-3 juxtaposes the 'former' prophets with the later 'Son', reminds us again of the *Gospel of the Hebrews'* designation of Christ as 'Son' at his baptism, as recorded by Jerome. Finally, the *Letter to the Hebrews* 1:3 and 10:12 agrees with the *Gospel of the Hebrews* in identifying the crucifixion with Jesus's ascension to God, a position eminently reminiscent of the *Gospel of John's* presentation of the crucifixion as Jesus's glorification.

In the Jerome passages we see the same combination of resting and reigning encountered in *Sirach* 24 and in the *Gospel of Thomas*. And as Islamic theology teaches that God's revelation has been sent to all peoples and nations, so that the prophets number 124,000, Wisdom accordingly proclaims of herself in *Sirach* 24:9-10: '[I] have stood in all the earth: and in every people, and in every nation I have had the chief rule.' Similarly, according to *Acts* 14:15-17, throughout the ages, God did not leave himself without a witness in any nation, though the witnesses in this particular context are specified as the blessings of nature.

In view of the analogue, if not homologue, of the pre-existent heavenly book described in the Jewish scriptures with the early Christian concept of Christ as Logos manifestation, we should ask ourselves if there are any traces in the literary remains of primitive Jewish Christianity which would seem to indicate that the original followers of Jesus developed their christology based on the idea of the eternal heavenly book. In fact, Jean Daniélou, in a classic, even if dated, study of Jewish Christianity, has documented just such a tradition. After noting that 'Book' (*biblion*) is a name for the pre-existent Logos in Philo's *Legum Allegoriae* I, 8:19, Daniélou cites from the Syriac *Odes of Solomon* 23, a Jewish-Christian hymn from *c.*100 CE, which states that the 'thought' of God 'was like a Letter'. God's 'thought' is of course his eternal Logos, here identified with a Letter. Toward the end of *Ode* 23, in verse 19, we read: 'And the Letter was a great Tablet [Gr. *pinakidion*], which was wholly written by the Finger of God.' Daniélou comments: '[T]he tablet written by the finger of God plainly refers to the tablets given to Moses on Sinai, and thus identifies the latter with the heavenly tablets of Jewish apocalyptic speculation.'[252] This sheds light on the correct interpretation of *Colossians* 2:14: 'Blotting out the handwriting of the decree that was against us, which was contrary to us. And he hath taken the same out of the way, fastening it to the cross.' Here it is clearly implied that Christ is a book fastened to the cross, a book written by the finger of God, that is, the pre-existent Torah manifested in history first under Moses, and then in the person of Jesus. Thus in *Colossians* 2:14, the book is not an indirect, but rather a direct image of Christ, the symbol being clearly identified with him.[253]

That *Ode* 23 portrays the Logos as a Letter that becomes a great Tablet is an extraordinary statement when we recall that in Islam, the pre-existent Qur'an is described as a cosmic tablet written upon by the pen of God. Before examining the metaphysical import of the symbolism, we will reproduce an account mirroring the traditional Islamic mythic narration of creation:

> Know that the very first thing which Allah created was the marvelous Tablet of Destiny upon which is written not only all that happened in the Past, or that will happen in the Present or the Future, but also every human being's lot for ever.... . The Tablet of Destiny was made out of an immense white pearl, and it has two leaves like those of a door.... . Allah next created a great pen formed out of a single gem. The pen is so long that it would take one five hundred years to travel from end to

end of it. It is split at one end like an ordinary pen, and pointed, and from the point light flowed forth in the same way that ink flows from common pens, or water gushes from a fountain. Then the voice of Allah thundered forth the one word 'Write,' and the sound caused the pen, which was full of life and intelligence, to tremble, and immediately the point began to race across the tablet from right to left, and to inscribe the things that had been, and that then were, and that would happen until the Day of Resurrection. When the tablet was filled with writing, the pen dried up, and it and the tablet were removed, and are preserved in the Treasury of Allah, who alone knows all that is written.[254]

Seyyed Hossein Nasr explicates the theological verities implicit in such metaphoric images in the following manner: '[T]he Qur'an leads naturally to the symbolism of the Pen and the Tablet... . The Pen symbolizes the Word, the Logos, the Intellect and the Tablet Universal substance.'[255] We may confidently conclude that the main reason a heavenly book christology would seem odd to modern Christians is that early on the church lost touch, for various reasons, with its Jewish matrix and Semitic thought world, moving away from the 'functional' language of Semitic mythic metaphor to the 'substantial' philosophical discourse of the Greco-Roman world.[256] But that the heavenly book is a legitimate theological concept for christology in the church is demonstrated by the fact of its presence in several Jewish biblical books; texts which the church holds as sacred scripture.

The Qur'an repeatedly stresses, in response to the crowds' demand for a miraculous sign from Muhammad to prove his divine apostleship, that no sign would be given except that of the Qur'an itself. Similarly, we read in *Matthew* 12:38-39: 'Then some of the scribes and Pharisees answered him, saying: Master, we would see a sign from thee. Who answering said to them: An evil and adulterous generation seeketh a sign: and a sign shall not be given it, but the sign of Jonas the prophet.' The same sentiment is recorded in *John* 4:48: 'Jesus therefore said to him: Unless you see signs and wonders, you believe not.' Interestingly, in Arabic, a verse of the Qur'an is called an *aya*, or literally, a 'sign' (plural, *ayat*). The 'sign of Jonas' mentioned by Jesus refers to the preaching of repentance, the Last Judgment, and Christ's resurrection, or exaltation to God. Central teachings of the 'signs' (verses) of the Qur'an are similarly the preaching of repentance as preparation for the resurrection and the Last Judgment. Muhammad's challenge to his miraculous sign-demanding opponents, to write a sura matching the majesty of the Qur'an, does not primarily imply that a poet could not conceivably compose a literary work at least remotely *similar* in style to the Qur'an's poetic beauty. But even if such were to be achieved in a tenuous sense, the Qur'anic claim would retain force, for the significance of the Qur'an in this context is above all the fact that, regardless of the question of its literary qualities, its spiritual potency is demonstrated by its having served for over a millennium as the sacred text of a world religion, indeed, the latest and final world religion.[257]

CHAPTER FOUR

Dialectical Synthesis of Qur'anic and Gospel Narratives: Crucifixion as Ascension

RITHJOF SCHUON, INTRODUCING a discussion on the varying ecclesiastical and Qur'anic interpretations of Christ's crucifixion, begins by stating: 'In the sacred Texts there may be symbolical or dialectical antinomies, but not contradictions. It is always a difference of point of view … even in cases like that of divergent Gospel narratives.'[258] To account for the gospels 'contradicting' the Qur'an's crucifixion narrative by claiming that the Christian scriptures have been 'changed' and 'corrupted' is all too easy an assertion made by some authors, and is self-defeating, especially in its crasser forms, for the very method of higher criticism that sees a history of redactional changes in the Jewish and Christian scriptures also imputes the same to the Qur'anic text. Certain changes have occurred in scriptures, but illegitimate 'corruptions' would seem to be ultimately irreconcilable with the metaphysical truth that the great religions' writings are sacred and from Heaven. To claim that God gave a written revelation to humanity and that it was then subsequently corrupted *as such*, would seem to imply that God was imperfect in power, being unable to preserve from corruption that which had been formerly revealed. The Qur'an does not clearly teach that the Christian scriptures *as such* or in their essence were corrupted. Qur'an 2:59: 'But the evil doers changed that word into another than that spoken to them, and we sent down upon those evil doers wrath from heaven, for that they had done amiss.' Islamic tradition allows the opinion that this statement refers to oral misinterpretation of the scriptures, rather than to a real corruption of heavenly inspired scriptures. As Frithjof Schuon writes, the Hanbalite Ibn Taymiyyah accused the Jews and Christians of falsifying the interpretations of the scriptures, not the scriptures themselves.[259] In the same passage, Schuon alludes to the freedom with which the Old Testament is sometimes quoted in the New Testament, as well as the different textual readings existing between the Greek Septuagint and Hebrew versions of the Jewish scriptures; these constitute examples of what may appear to some as 'falsification', yet in fact the situation is rather that 'the same idea is divinely "rethought" in relation to a new human receptacle.'[260]

The Prophet of Islam never proclaimed that one should reject the Torah and Gospel as it existed concretely in written form in his time, neither is there any such claim in the Qur'an, although *ahadith* warn against scriptural misinterpretation made by the interpreters of the bible. If the Prophet believed that the Jewish and Christian scriptures had been fundamentally falsified at the written level, he no doubt would have stated so in unambiguous terms. In any event, it cannot be denied from an historical perspective that, already centuries before the rise of Islam, the bible was substantially the same as it is in its present-day form; the evidence of the Dead Sea Scrolls and pre-Islamic papyri and codices substantiates this claim.

If we concede that both the Christian and Qur'anic scriptures have been integrally preserved, we must then face the issues raised by one of their most striking apparent contradictions, namely, the accounts of Christ's crucifixion. The central Qur'anic teaching on the crucifixion is contained in sura 4:

> 4:157: And because of their saying: We slew the Messiah, Jesus son of Mary, Allah's messenger – they slew him not nor crucified him, but it appeared so unto them; and lo! those who disagree concerning it are in doubt thereof; they have no knowledge thereof save pursuit of a conjecture; they slew him not for certain [or: they did not really slay him].
>
> 4:158: But Allah took him up unto Himself. Allah was ever Mighty, Wise.

What immediately strikes us is that the exaltation of Jesus to God described in 4:158 is reminiscent of certain New Testament theologies, especially those embedded in the *Gospel of John* and in the *Philippians* 2 christological hymn, which interpret the death of Christ as his exaltation to God. Moreover, Qur'an 3:169 allows us to speak dialectically of a simultaneous relative denial and affirmation of death for martyrs in general: 'Think not of those, who are slain in the way of Allah, as dead. Nay, they are living. With their Lord they have provision.' Qur'an 3:169 is in perfect accord with the teaching of Christ directed against the Sadducees, namely, that God is God of the living, not of the dead, so that Abraham, Isaac and Jacob are not dead in an absolute sense, but alive (see *Luke* 20:37-38). Moreover, the Qur'an's particular nuance agrees in spirit with the emphasis of St. John's gospel, which interprets the very death of Christ on the cross precisely as his exaltation to God in heaven. In this context we would do well to remember that the Islamic view of the crucifixion pre-existed in the earliest age of Christianity; as Frithjof Schuon remarks: 'It should be noted that the idea that Christ was not crucified but was taken directly to Heaven existed already at the time of the apostles,' so that the idea could not have arisen first in Islam.[261]

Immediately after Qur'an 4:158's allusion to Christ's exaltation to God at the time of the perceived crucifixion, we read in 4:159: 'There is not one of the People of the Scripture but will believe in him before his death, and on the Day of Resurrection he will be a witness against them.' This is a particularly enigmatic aya, and it has been subjected to widely differing exegetical treatments through the centuries. For our purposes, we will first examine one of the more standard views, according to which Jesus will die after his second coming.

Abu Huraira is cited in Abu Salih Shu'aib b. Muhammad al-Baihaqi, where the former speaks 'concerning the descent of Jesus a second time in the Last Days'. Jesus will return to 'destroy the Antichrist, the lying ad-Dajjal'. Then will come a time of peace for the world, and 'Jesus will remain on earth for forty years, will get married and have children.[262] Then he will die, and the Muslims pray over him and bury him in Madina beside [the grave of] 'Umar.'[263] Muhammad b. al-Qasim, the Persian, cites the same tradition from Abu Huraira.[264]

The Jewish apocalyptic work *4 Ezra* (= *2 Esdras*), accepted by the semi-canonical *Epistle of Barnabas*, St. Ambrose and other fathers as authoritative, teaches, in accordance with Islamic tradition, that the Messiah will die at the end of the world, after a 400 year messianic reign, in contrast to the Islamic tradition of a 40 year reign. The Syriac text refers to a 30 year messianic reign, but this is no doubt a secondary reading referring to Jesus's approximate age at his ascension, interpreting the Christian era as the beginning of the *eschaton*, in agreement with the New Testament in general.

4 Ezra 7:26-35:
26. Behold the time shall come, and it shall be when the signs shall come which I have foretold thee, and the bride shall appear, and appearing she shall be revealed that now is hid with the earth:
27. And every one that is delivered from the foresaid evils, he shall see my marvelous things.
28. For my son shall be revealed with them that are with him, and they shall rejoice that are left in the four hundred years.
29. And it shall be after these years, that my son the Messiah shall die: and all men that have breath,
30. And the world shall be turned into the primordial silence seven days, as in the former judgments, so that none shall be left.
31. And it shall be after seven days, and the world shall be raised up that yet waketh not, and that which is corruptible shall perish:

32. And the earth shall render the things that sleep in it, and the dust them that dwell in it with silence, and the chambers shall render the souls that are commended to them.

33. And the Highest shall be revealed upon the seat of judgment, and miseries shall pass, and long sufferance shall be gathered together.

34. And judgment only shall remain, truth shall stand, and faith shall wax strong,

35. And the work shall follow, and the reward shall be revealed, and justice shall awake, and injustice shall not have dominion.

The Islamic tradition which places the death of the Messiah at the end of the world thus has a background in Jewish tradition, namely, in *4 Ezra*, a work accepted by several church fathers as authoritative if not canonical, and a book that also profoundly and extensively influenced the medieval liturgy of the Catholic Church. However it may have been interpreted, the imagery and text were at least acceptable to the church fathers.

Another Islamic *hadith* speaks of Jesus's reign as 4,000 years instead of 40. The implication for our present purposes would seem to be that the 40 years tradition is a later historicization of an originally suprahistorical, eschatological event or reign:

> It is related that one day the rain and thunder and lightning were fierce about Jesus (Peace be upon him!), so he began to seek something under which he might shelter. His eye fell on a tent far off, so he came to it; but behold there was a woman in it, so he turned away from it. Then he saw a cave in a hill and came to it, but behold there was a lion in it. Then he put his hand on it and said, 'My God, Thou hast given everything an abode, and Thou hast not given me an abode.' Then God (Exalted is He!) revealed to him, 'Your abode is in the dwelling of My mercy. Verily I will give to you in marriage on the Day of Resurrection a hundred houris whom I have created with My hand, and I will give a feast at your wedding for four thousand years, each day of which is like the duration of the present world, and I will command one to proclaim, "Where are those who were ascetics in the world? Visit the marriage of the ascetic in the world, Jesus, son of Mary."'[265]

Yet another Islamic traditional narrative implies the death of at least Christ's human nature, and the removal or ascension of his 'divine nature'. In this account, Christ's great commission to the apostles is given before the crucifixion as opposed to after the resurrection, where it is situated chronologically in the canonical gospels:

Then when God (Exalted is He!) wished to take him and raise him to Himself, his disciples gathered with him in Jerusalem in a room belonging to one of his (female) companions, and he said, 'Verily I am going to my Father and your Father, and I am giving you an injunction before *the departure of my divine nature* and am making with you a covenant and a pledge. So he who receives my injunction and fulfils my covenant will be with me to-morrow; but he who does not receive my injunction, I have nothing to do with him, and he has nothing to do with me.' Then they said to him, 'What is it?' He replied, 'Go to the kings of the ends of the earth and convey to them what I have charged you with, and summon them to that to which I have summoned you, and do not deceive them, and do not fear them, *for when I leave my humanity I shall be standing in heaven at the right hand of the throne of my Father and your Father, and shall be with you wherever you go* and shall strengthen you with help and strength by the permission of my Father. Go to them and summon them with gentleness and cure them and command them to be kind and forbid them what is unlawful, until you are killed, or crucified, or rejected from the earth.' Then they asked, 'What is the verification of what you command us?' He replied, 'I am the first who does that.' And he went out the next day and appeared to the people and began to summon them and admonish them and warn them until he was taken and carried to the king of the Children of Israel. Then he ordered him to be crucified, *and his humanity was crucified* and his hands were nailed to the two pieces of wood of the cross, and he remained on the cross from dawn to afternoon. And he asked for water, and was given vinegar to drink, and he was pierced with a lance. *Then he was buried where the cross was* and forty people were put in charge of the grave; and all this happened in the presence of his companions and his disciples. Then when they saw that happen to him, they were sure and knew that he had commanded them nothing in which he was different from them. *Three days afterwards they gathered in the place where he promised them to appear to them* and they saw those signs which (had been arranged) between him and them; *and the news spread among the Children of Israel that the Messiah had not been killed.* Then the grave was dug up, and *the humanity was not found.* The parties among them disagreed, and there was a great amount of talk which is too long to be recounted. Then verily those disciples who had accepted his injunction separated in the country and each of them went his own way. One went to the west, one to Abyssinia, two to Rome, two to the king of Antioch, one to Persia, one to India, and two remained in the dwellings of the Children of Israel summoning them to the opinion of the Messiah until most of them were killed, and the Messiah's claim was spread in east and west by the deeds of the disciples.[266]

Phrases such as 'the departure of my divine nature' and 'his humanity was crucified' admittedly reflect an Ebionite-Nestorian theological trajectory. If a traditional Christian theologian understands the terms in an analogical sense and applies a *pia interpretatio* to them, then they can be accepted as metaphysically accentuating the orthodox distinction existing between the two natures of Christ, rather than as necessarily denying the unity of person with regard to the Messiah (in his incarnation or his crucifixion), a unity of person which, as Aquinas maintains in *Summa contra gentiles* IV:39, must be maintained by Christian faith. Yet Aquinas simultaneously insists in the same passage that in addition to the belief in the unity of Jesus Christ's person, nevertheless the two natures in question, the human and divine, exist not in a relationship of strict identity, but rather of unity (in hypostatic mode), so that the human nature of Jesus Christ is not to be strictly identified with the uncreated eternal Logos, and therefore this created human nature cannot fully circumscribe the uncreated Logos.[267] Furthermore, according to Aquinas, strictly speaking the union of the two natures occurs not in the *natures* themselves, but in the *person* of Jesus Christ, for combining two dissimilar natures would result in a change in both, and this is excluded because the divine nature is immutable.[268]

Because of the distinction of natures, while acknowledging the unity of person, Aquinas nevertheless correctly denies that 'Christ's Passion is attributed to him in respect of his Godhead,' for as he explains, 'the union of the human nature with the Divine was effected in the Person, in the hypostasis, in the suppositum, yet observing the distinction of natures; so that it is the same Person and hypostasis of the Divine and human natures, while each nature retains that which is proper to it.' The angelic doctor continues as follows: '[T]he Passion is to be attributed to the suppositum of the Divine Nature, not because of the Divine Nature, which is impassible, but by reason of the human nature... . Therefore Christ's Passion belongs to the "suppositum" of the Divine Nature by reason of the passible nature assumed, but not on account of the impassible Divine Nature.'[269] Thomas continues by observing the following: 'Athanasius says (Ep. ad Epict.): "The Word is impassible whose Nature is Divine." But what is impassible cannot suffer; consequently, Christ's Passion did not concern his Godhead.' Furthermore, our authority goes on to state: 'The Lord of glory is said to be crucified, not as the Lord of glory, but as a man capable of suffering.' To summarize, although, in view of the unity of the Messiah's person, Aquinas writes in *Summa contra gentiles* IV:39, 'For since Holy Scripture without any distinction assigns the things of God to the Man Christ, and the things of the Man Christ to God, he must be one and the same person, of whom both varieties of attributes are predicable,' nevertheless, in view of the distinction of natures, in *Summa theologiae* 3, q16, a5 he denies the dual proposition that 'what belongs to the Son of Man can be predicated of the divine nature and what belongs to the Son of God predicated of the human nature... .' If we therefore interpret the phrase 'his humanity was crucified' in the Thomistic sense that 'Christ's Passion is not to be attributed to him in respect of his Godhead' and that 'Christ's Passion did not concern his Godhead,' and if we then interpret the phrase 'the departure of my divine nature' as a metaphorical or analogical reference to the impassibility of the divine nature, then such Ebionite-Nestorian phraseology can be seen as relaying an element of truth which is in accord with traditional Orthodox, Catholic and Protestant theology. Similarly, if understood appropriately, Schuon's teaching can be acceptable to Christian theology when he writes that the Qur'anic assertion that 'Christ was not killed in reality' is true 'not only as regards the Divine nature of the God-man', but also in view of his human nature which was resurrected.[270]

Ibn Ishaq teaches that Jesus was both earthly and celestial, that is, human and angelic.[271] Al-Razi in his *tafsir* on sura 4:157 explains that the philosophers maintain that Jesus possessed an earthly (physical) and a celestial (spiritual) nature, and that it is an allowable opinion for a Muslim to hold that the death of Christ applies to his earthly rather than to his celestial nature,[272] a view which is essentially in accord with the Nestorian formulation. The latter articulation, we repeat, if taken literally is rejected by traditional Christian theology; but if understood in the abstract sense, it can be brought analogically into accord with the Thomistic metaphysical statement that 'Christ's Passion did not concern his Godhead.'

While recognizing the validity and applicability of the above Scholastic precisions, we can nevertheless also give due weight to the following comments of Schuon, who when speaking of christological controversies, observes that in contrast to much of exoteric dogma as formulated by councils, it would often be better simply to let biblical language remain as it is, 'in a holy indetermination that excludes no aspect of truth and does not crystallize one aspect to the detriment of the others.'[273] In accord with this insight, Schuon elsewhere mentions groups such as the 'Dyophysites, Monophysites, Aphthartodocetae, Phartolatrae, Agnoetae, Aktistetae, and Kristolatrae,' who apparently wanted 'to pin down' christological 'questions which are not of crucial importance' relating to 'things which the Revelation did not deem it indispensable to be altogether precise about... .'[274]

To return to Islamic belief concerning the crucifixion, further divergence of opinion is witnessed to in the following tradition: 'Ibn al Athir said in the *Kamil*: The learned have differed concerning his death before his being raised up. Some say, "He was raised up and did not die." Others say, "No, God made him die for three hours." Others say, "For seven hours, then He brought him back to life." And those who say this are expounding His saying (Exalted is He!), "Verily I will cause you to die and will raise you to Myself" (Qur'an 3:55).'[275] As Edward Schillebeeckx notes, 'In the Targums we find an Aramaic word which means both "die" and "be lifted up" (*anabasis*), the double meaning of which we also find in the *Gospel of John* in connection with the death of Jesus: "elevation" (of the cross) and "exaltation" to God. The Targum on *Ps.* 68:18 speaks of the death of Moses as an exaltation or an ascent to heaven... .'[276]

In the end, it would seem that the Qur'anic viewpoint could overlap with the Jewish-Christian conception of the crucifixion as ascension, for according to the latter the crucifixion does not primarily or even essentially mean the death of Jesus, but his exaltation to God. That is, Jesus was indeed crucified, in the sense that he was nailed to the cross; he even 'suffered for us' (*1 Peter* 2:21) on the cross; but he did not die there in a definitive sense, but was raised to God even while nailed to the cross. Or as John teaches, Jesus's crucifixion is not death, but life. Peter expresses this same dialectic in *1 Peter* 3:18: 'Because Christ also died once for our sins, the just for the unjust: that he might offer us to God, being put to death indeed in the flesh, but enlivened in the spirit.' He was put to death 'in the flesh', that is, according to the human viewpoint, but was raised 'in the spirit', that is, according to the divine viewpoint. In general, the synoptic gospels reflect the 'human' perspective of the events of Good Friday, while John, the Jewish-Christian gospels and the Qur'an reflect the 'divine' perspective.

Seyyed Hossein Nasr has approached the theme of the crucifixion both practically and theoretically: 'It could be said that this event was greater than any single description of it... . [T]he crucifixion and the idea of redemption it signifies are perhaps the most difficult of all aspects of Christianity for an ordinary Muslim to grasp.'[277] Nasr is of course correct in stating that the average Muslim will find the standard Christian interpretation of the crucifixion somewhat bizarre. But on the other hand, as Nasr himself observes, the idea of a vicarious martyrdom and redemption plays a fundamental role in Shi'i theology. It should be emphasized here that a dialectical approach is needed to reconcile the various divergent interpretations of the crucifixion, resurrection and ascension of Christ in the New Testament itself. The approach of New Testament theology is one of unity of spirit embodied in simultaneously diverse theological articulations. That there exist so many different interpretations of the crucifixion already within the New Testament supports Nasr's assertion that 'this event was greater than any single description of it.'

In an essay exploring the wide-ranging docetic conceptions of both the crucifixion and of the Shi'i Imamate, Henri Corbin cites the following line from the *Acts of Peter*, in which Peter states concerning his perception of Christ's transfiguration, *Talem eum vidi qualem capere potui*,[278] that is, 'I saw him according to my capacity.' In the *Acts of John* we read concerning the crucifixion: 'Thou hearest that I suffered, yet I did not suffer; that I suffered not, yet did I suffer; ... And in a word, what they say of me, that befell me not. But that which they say not, that did I suffer.'[279] Here it would seem that both the Pauline 'affirmation' and the Jacobean 'denial' of the crucifixion are simultaneously affirmed and denied; the logic behind this posture is the realization that what took place at the end of Christ's sojourn on earth is ultimately beyond exact or exhaustive description. Every statement concerning such a transcendent event must contain both truth – insofar as the formulation exists as a pointer towards the supraformal Truth – and 'falsity' – insofar as no doctrinal expression can fully encompass the supraformal Truth to which its words point. The Hesychasts teach that the light of the transfiguration of Jesus would not have been visible to the physical eye.[280] The same could be said of the 'crucified' or 'resurrected' Jesus. This is not to deny the reality of the transfiguration, crucifixion or ascension of Jesus Christ; on the contrary, as St. Paul writes in the context of a discussion concerning the resurrected body: 'For the things that are seen pass away, but the things that are unseen are eternal' (2 *Corinthians* 4:18). The transfigured or transcendent status of Christ's ascended body is clearly specified for us when St. Paul in 1 *Corinthians* 15 places his vision of the ascended heavenly Christ in the very same category as the appearances of the resurrected Christ to the twelve apostles before the ascension. This is not to deny a 'formal substance' to the person of the ascended Christ, but it is to insist upon its transfigured state and its non-earthly materiality. The resurrected or ascended Christ was by no means a figment of the apostles' imaginations; and to say these appearances were of the order of 'visions' in no way implies any correspondence between unreal 'figments of imagination' and true 'visions', for the latter are supernatural modes of perception of transcendent realities which exist in a more 'real' mode than does the densest physical materiality.

In yet another work, Seyyed Hossein Nasr returns to the theme of the crucifixion, and argues that the problem of the different approaches taken by Islam and Christianity may in fact be resolved, at least to a certain extent, only by calling into question modern epistemological biases: 'One could say that a major cosmic event as the end of the earthly life of Christ could in fact be "seen" and "known" in more than one way, and that it is God's will that Christianity should be given to "see" that end in one way and Islam in another.'[281]

As for the diversity of New Testament approaches, Luke's account of Christ's ascension placed forty days after the resurrection, as described in his *Book of Acts* 1:3, is an historicization of the event of Christ's exaltation to God on Good Friday, as we will explicate below. According to the main accounts of all the gospels, *Matthew* 28:1, 20, *Mark* 16:9, 19, *John* 20:1, 17, and even Luke's own gospel at 24:1, 51, Christ's ascension is recorded not as taking place forty days after the resurrection, but on Easter Sunday itself. Other New Testament passages associate the resurrection with a simultaneous ascension, such as *Ephesians* 1:19-22 and similar texts. The canonical gospel tradition of the ascension on Easter Sunday is witnessed to in a number of early extracanonical Christian documents.

The *Epistle of Barnabas* 15:26 reflects this position: 'Wherefore also we keep the eighth day for rejoicing, in the which Jesus rose from the dead and also having been manifested ascended into the heavens.' Similarly, the *Apology* of Aristedes 15: 'After three days he came to life again and ascended into heaven.'[282] The *Gospel of Peter*, by describing the cross on Easter Sunday as reaching into the heavens, implies that the ascension was inseparable from the resurrection, as does verse 56 of the same gospel: 'He is not there for he is risen and has departed to the place from which he had been sent.'

The ending of the *Epistle of the Apostles* (chapter 51), redacted within a few decades of the *Gospel of John*, in agreement with the four gospels, places the ascension three days after the crucifixion:

> And when he had said this, and had finished his discourse with us, he said unto us again: Behold, on the third day and at the third hour shall he come which hath sent me, that I may depart with him. And as he so spake, there was thunder and lightning and an earthquake, and the heavens parted asunder, and there appeared a bright cloud which bore him up. And *there came* voices of many angels, rejoicing and singing praises and saying: Gather us, O Priest, unto the light of the majesty. And when they drew nigh unto the firmament, we heard his voice *saying unto us*: Depart hence in peace.[283]

Neither does the *Testament of Levi* 9:5 separate the resurrection from the ascension: 'And he shall ascend from Hades and shall pass from earth to heaven.'[284] The *Sybilline Oracles* 9:16 has Christ and the saints of *Matthew* 27:53 rise and ascend on Easter Sunday.[285]

The number 40 used by Luke is, as Catholic and Protestant scholarship now generally recognizes, a non-chronological symbolic number;[286] accordingly, other symbolic numbers were employed in the early church to designate the length of time between the resurrection and ascension. The archaic late first-century Jewish-Christian *Ascension of Isaiah*, one of the earliest witnesses to the dogma of the immaculate conception of Mary, extends the 40 days to 545 days. The *Apocryphon of James*, incorporating Jewish-Christian tradition, places the ascension 550 days after the resurrection. Similar Jewish-Christian traditions were adopted by Ptolemy and the Ophites, who extended the 40 days to eighteen months, which closely approximates the variants of 545 and 550 days.[287] Perhaps the symbolism and assumption operative here is that Christ's post-resurrection ministry should fittingly be of comparable length to his pre-resurrection ministry. Finally, the *Pistis Sophia* 1:1 lengthens the period to eleven years,[288] possibly reflecting the tradition that a number of years passed before the apostles left Jerusalem to fulfill the preaching mission to the nations, after being scattered by persecution.

The *Gospel of John* and the *Philippians* 2 christological hymn both preserve an early interpretation that viewed the exaltation of Christ as inseparable from the crucifixion itself. *Colossians* 2:15 declares the triumph over the principalities and powers took place on the cross, whereas this triumph is usually assigned elsewhere in the New Testament to the resurrection. *Hebrews* 10:12 startlingly associates the crucifixion with the ascension to God's right hand, speaking of Christ who, 'when he had offered one sacrifice for sins for ever, sat down on the right hand of God.'[289]

Raymond Brown explains in his commentary on the *Gospel of John* that in specifying 40 days, 'Luke is not giving us a date for the glorification of Jesus'; it is 'incidental' for the purpose of introducing Pentecost, as can be shown by the fact that elsewhere he places the ascension on Easter Sunday.[290] Brown also clarifies concerning the post-resurrection appearances, that we cannot take the idea of 'ascension' in a sense of mythological topography. Christ ascends, meaning that he enters heaven, or the divine sphere of being, not the skies 'above' the earth. Therefore, Christ after his resurrection appears from heaven, not from any chronological point of an earthly sojourn of 40 days. After the resurrection, Christ exists in an eschatological mode: 'The time and place that characterize earthly existence no longer apply to him ... ; and so we cannot imagine his dwelling some place on earth for forty days while he is making appearances and before he departs for heaven. From the moment that God raises Jesus up, he is in heaven or with God.'[291] Brown then reminds us that exegetes, including Pierre Benoit, have demonstrated that some New Testament texts 'acknowledge the identity of the resurrection and the ascension', including *Acts* 2:32-33, 5:30-31, *Romans* 8:34, *Ephesians* 1:20, *Philippians* 2:8-9, *1 Peter* 3:21-22, and *Luke* 24:26.[292] Moreover, 'the Jesus of *Matt* xxviii 16-20 who appears after the resurrection is a Jesus to whom all power in heaven and on earth has been given.'[293] Brown interjects that in view of John's presentation of crucifixion as glorification, '[p]erhaps it would have been more logical if John had joined the author of the *Epistle to the Hebrews* [10:12] in having Jesus go directly to the Father from the cross, for the resurrection does not fit easily into John's theology of the crucifixion.'[294] For John, the crucifixion, resurrection and ascension are all 'part of one action and one "hour."'[295] John is forced, Brown points out, to adapt into a 'sequential narrative' an event that transcends space and time; the 'temporal' narration of events *sub specie aeternitatis* cannot be taken literally in a chronological sense.[296]

A number of ancient extracanonical texts also present the crucifixion as Christ's ascension to God. According to Coptic Cyril, the *Gospel of the Hebrews* taught: 'After they had raised him up on the cross, the Father took him up into heaven unto himself.'[297] The *Gospel of Peter* likewise records: 'And the Lord cried out aloud saying: My power, my power, thou hast forsaken me. And when he had so said, he was taken up.'[298] In the *Acts of John*, one of the titles of the cross is 'Resurrection'; in the *Odes of Solomon* 22, the triumph over the principalities occurs simultaneously on the cross, in hell, and in heaven.[299] Perhaps the most theologically intriguing interpretation is that of the *Apocalypse of Peter*, which situates the ascension at the time of Christ's earthly transfiguration upon Mount Tabor.[300] Whatever may be said of this solution, given the immense popularity and semi-canonical status the work enjoyed over a period of several centuries, we can safely say that the ascension's symbolic representation as the transfiguration was not in the least disturbing to the early Christians. In fact, in placing the ascension at the transfiguration, Peter, in typical Jewish-Christian fashion, simply bypasses the crucifixion by 'replacing' it with the exaltation. In other words, the canonical account of the transfiguration is in Peter not a 'misplaced' resurrection narrative in the traditional sense, but rather a typically Jewish-Christian 'crucifixion as exaltation' narrative. That is, Peter's transfiguration account indirectly speaks of the cross by describing the ascension.

We should also note that in *2 Peter* 1:16ff., where we would expect Peter to refer to the resurrection as proof that the gospel is not founded on myth, but on eyewitness testimony, he instead refers to the transfiguration. Since general scholarly opinion holds that *2 Peter* and the *Apocalypse of Peter* are genealogically related, it would seem congruent to argue that in both the transfiguration is conceived of as the ascension. Indeed, there is no specific or formal mention of either the death or resurrection of Christ in all of *2 Peter*. Our thesis is that both are referred to indirectly by means of Peter's reference to the transfiguration. *John* 1:14's, 'and we beheld his glory' is equivalent to *2 Peter* 1:16b-17a: 'but we were eyewitnesses of his greatness. For he received from God the Father honour and glory.' *John* 1:14 also refers to the transfiguration, but we would argue that it is the transfiguration as ascension that John refers to, for otherwise there would be no reference in the Johannine prologue to Christ's most glorious achievement of the cross as exaltation; the very goal, according to Christian theology, of Christ's mission. This incidentally solves the riddle of why there is no transfiguration account in John, for it is indeed there in the form of the crucifixion-ascension narrative. Again, John's gospel overlaps with the Jewish-Christian theology that always stresses the exaltation in the first category, and never the crucifixion in isolation from the exaltation.

Daniélou consistently holds that in the original version of *Matthew* 27:53, the saints rose on Good Friday 'at the moment of the Passion', and not on Easter Sunday.[301] Accordingly, it was later redaction in the *Gospel of Matthew* 27:53 that tried to obscure this early close proximity of crucifixion and exaltation, for various admittedly legitimate theological reasons and concerns of liturgical symbolism, by having the Jewish saints rise from their graves *after* Christ's resurrection on Easter Sunday. That the saints' resurrection occurred on Good Friday is supported by some versions of the *Gospel of Nicodemus*, Shem-Tob's

Hebrew version of the *Gospel of Matthew*, and the *Pepys Harmony*, which M. E. Boismard argues contains readings more primitive than Tatian's *Diatessaron*.[302] Here we cite *Matthew* 27:50-54, with emphasis added in verse 53:

> 50. And Jesus again crying with a loud voice, yielded up the ghost.
> 51. And behold the veil of the temple was rent in two from the top even to the bottom: and the earth quaked and the rocks were rent.
> 52. And the graves were opened: and many bodies of the saints that had slept arose,
> 53. And coming out of the tombs *after his resurrection*, came into the holy city and appeared to many.
> 54. Now the centurion and they that were with him watching Jesus, having seen the earthquake and the things that were done, were sore afraid, saying: Indeed this was the Son of God.

The *Gospel of Nicodemus* relates the same events as follows:

> And it was about the sixth hour, and darkness was upon the face of the whole earth until the ninth hour.

> And while the sun was eclipsed, behold the veil of the temple was rent from the top, to the bottom; and the rocks also were rent, and the graves opened, and many bodies of saints, which slept, arose.

> And about the ninth hour Jesus cried out with a loud voice, *Eli, Eli, lama sabacthani?* Which being interpreted is, My God, My God, why hast thou forsaken me?[303]

Tatian's *Diatessaron* reads, based on the Arabic version, 'the tombs were opened; and the bodies of many saints which slept, arose and came forth; and after his resurrection they entered into the holy city and appeared unto many.'[304] Tatian seems to reflect a compromise text in which the saints rise on Good Friday but do not enter Jerusalem until Easter Sunday. Shem-Tob's Hebrew version of *Matthew* 27:53 reads: 'They came out of their graves and after (this) they entered the holy city and were revealed to many.'[305] Since there is no reason why we should suspect that later Christians would have wanted to reverse the chronology to denigrate the supremacy of Christ as 'firstfruits of the resurrection' (cf. *1 Corinthians* 15:20), we seem to be led to the conclusion that canonical *Matthew*'s chronology is in all likelihood a secondary development. According to St. Paul, Christ is the 'first fruits' of the resurrection; from a Christian theological perspective, he therefore must have risen *before* the Jewish saints, who according to the earliest traditions, as we have concluded, rose on Good Friday: *Ergo* Christ must have risen before the Jewish saints, on Good Friday at the very 'instant' of his 'death'.

Daniélou notes that the teaching of Christ assigned to the pre-passion period in *John* 14-17, is presented as post-resurrection discourses in the *Epistle of the Apostles*, written just a few decades after John.[306] Even though chronology in the gospels is rarely intended to be taken in a literal historical sense, the difference between John and the *Epistle of the Apostles* is really simply that the latter, at least indirectly, is influenced by the original conception of the crucifixion as the exaltation to God; therefore, what John places immediately before the crucifixion, the *Epistle of the Apostles* logically places immediately before the ascension. The latter carried through John's own emphasis on the crucifixion as glorification more thoroughly than the gospel writer himself has. In this way, the later work actually recovers the church's earliest theological 'chronology' as formulated at the pre-canonical level, according to the reconstruction posited in this monograph.

That the resurrection happened on Good Friday was the early belief preserved in the Johannine communities, and this is why they celebrated Easter on the Western church's Good Friday. The theological implications are astounding, and it is understandable that a Western pope once threatened to excommunicate the entire Eastern church over the matter. Anton Baumstark argued that the Johannine communities celebrated Easter on Good Friday because their founder John felt the crucifixion to be emotionally more important for him, because he was the only apostle who stayed at the foot of the cross, and that the West held Easter Sunday in higher esteem because it was more important for Peter, who had fled in disgrace from Christ on Good Friday.[307] This is doubtless a valid theological insight into the personalities of the apostles, but it fails to get to the bottom of the matter historically or theologically, in that it does not integrate the fact that the Johannine spirituality was heir to a dialectical tension between a simultaneous belief in the exaltation on Good Friday and on the 'third day'. In praxis, the former position proved victorious, which makes sense, given that such is the dominant theme of John's gospel, with the 'third day' tradition somewhat secondarily grafted onto the end of the narrative, reflecting a subsequent periodization of the 'suprahistorical' event of Christ's exaltation to God's right hand. But as Baumstark also notes, even in Rome the crucifixion and resurrection were celebrated together on Easter; this again reflects the enduring influence of the original conception that did not separate the crucifixion from the exaltation to God, that is, that Christ 'ascended' to God on Good Friday.

Like Luke's historicization of the ascension forty days after the resurrection, so the tradition of Christ's resurrection three days after the crucifixion is certainly a profound and providentially sanctioned theological statement, but is not literally an historical statement, at least not in the sense of strict chronology. This is indicated above all by the varying traditions, some referring generally to the resurrection 'on the third day', some to 'after three days', some to 'within three days', yet others to 'after three days and nights'.[308] We may reconstruct the historicization process that developed in the earliest days of the church as follows: The glorification of Jesus was at first situated on Good Friday; later this was historicized by means of the numerically symbolical 'three days' motif; the latter was finally extended to a numerically symbolical 40 day period, and then to yet other symbolically equivalent time lapses of varying lengths. That the exaltation of Christ to God was inseparable metaphysically from the crucifixion, is a statement that has been casually asserted by Catholic theologians for decades when discussing John's theology, but it has not truly been taken seriously, and its theological implications remain unconfronted both for within the church and in relation to the dialogue with Islam.[309] In the final analysis, Nasr's words on the end of Jesus's life on earth should be recalled, namely, 'this event was greater than any single description of it.' Or as St. Gregory of Nyssa remarked, 'It is impossible to expound all the meaning contained in the cross.'[310]

Frithjof Schuon confirms that the Qur'anic and biblical data on the crucifixion can be dialectically reconciled: '[T]he Qur'an, by its apparent denial of Christ's death, is simply affirming that Christ was not killed in reality – which is obvious not only as regards the Divine nature of the God-man, but also as regards His human nature, since it was resurrected... .'[311] The variation between the Islamic and Christian understanding of the crucifixion is one of an 'outward' difference, and such divergences 'may be contested *ad extra*', or at the exoteric level, yet remain 'incontestable *ad intra*', or at the esoteric level.[312] The exoteric dogma of each religion adapts itself 'to the mental predispositions of the human collectivity concerned'.[313] Schuon notes further: 'In an analogous sense it is said in Islam that "the divergence of the exegetists is a blessing."'[314] Exoteric dogma is necessarily relative, for it is a metaphorical, analogical or dialectical formulation of the absolute Truth, which human language can never grasp or express fully; thus dogma is essentially 'simplification'.[315] Elsewhere Schuon dialectically reconciles the two perspectives on the crucifixion by explaining that the cross is the central truth of Christianity, whereas the central truth of Islam is the unity of God, and the intense focus upon this latter truth does not allow Islam to see the crucifixion as the supreme Truth; the Muslim 'denial' of the cross is on one level 'Platonic or gnostic'.[316]

Claus Schedl suggests that in Qur'an sura 4:157 the emphasis should be put upon the word 'him' rather than upon the word 'not': 'They did not kill *him* and they did not crucify *him*,' rather than the more usual emphasis, 'They did *not* kill him and they did *not* crucify him.'[317] The difference in accentuation here may be subtle grammatically, but it is profound in its theological implications. Regarding the literal reading, 'He was made similar to them,' Schedl observes that sura 4:157 also contains the complete title 'the Messiah, Jesus Son of

Mary, God's Messenger,' whereas all earlier passages maintain Jesus's 'double character': 'On the one side is 'Isa, human like the other figures of salvation history, and therefore not "God's Son"; on the other side, however, he is the great "miraculous sign" of God. Because he was conceived through the "Spirit" (19:17) and was strengthened "with Spirit" (2:253), he is simply named "Spirit from him (God)" (4:171).'[318] Schedl therefore interprets sura 4:157 as follows: '"They did not kill and crucify him (the Spirit-Messiah)." ... Between the crucified one and the Spirit-Messiah there is no identity, rather only an appearance-similarity. However, 'Isa, upon whom the Spirit descended, has the greatest similarity with the Spirit-Messiah.'[319] There is thus no need to speculate on a *Doppelgänger* of Jesus, such as Simon of Cyrene or Judas Iscariot, who may have been crucified in place of Jesus. There is no *Doppelgänger*, only the Messiah's double character, 'on the one side the Spirit-gifted Messiah and God's Messenger, on the other side the human 'Isa, Maryam's son.'[320]

Schedl delineates various parallels between the Qur'anic treatment of the crucifixion and passages from two Nag Hammadi texts, *Second Discourse of Great Seth* and the *Apocalypse of Peter*. Sura 3 ayat 54 and 55 declare that the plan of the enemies of Christ was defeated by God's own plan, which culminated in the ascension of Christ. *Second Discourse of Great Seth* 55.6 similarly speaks of a plan against Christ; a plan to crucify him which was defeated by the ascension of Christ, who speaks thusly: 'And on account of this I assumed their appearance,' or literally, 'On account of this I made myself similar to them,' the exact phraseology found in sura 4:157's Arabic text;[321] so that in the Nag Hammadi and Qur'anic texts, 'the invisible Spirit-Messiah was "made similar" "to them", that is, to humans in general and to Jews in particular, in that he assumed human "form." His actual existence as "Son of the Greatest" remained concealed to them. The Spirit-Messiah was rather (at the crucifixion) "taken up on high."'[322] Schedl neglects to mention at this point yet another rather precise correspondence between sura 4:157 and *Second Discourse of Great Seth*; the Qur'anic phrase 'they did not kill him or crucify him ..., but he/it was made to appear so to them' corresponds to the following line of the Nag Hammadi text: 'They punished me (with death), yet I did not really die, rather only in appearance.'

Schedl insists that this Qur'anic paradigm of the human 'Isa and the Spirit-Messiah corresponds to a Gnosticism which the church can only consider as heretical in orientation and articulation; this, however, overlooks the fact that the paradigm under consideration corresponds precisely with the early Jewish-Christian Ebionite doctrine of Jesus Christ, which designates the human nature as 'Jesus', and the celestial or divine nature as 'Christ'. Frithjof Schuon employs this typical Jewish-Christian distinction when he writes: 'It is important to emphasize that when Christ says, "I am the Way, the Truth, and the Life," this is absolutely true of the Divine Word ("Christ"), and relatively true of its human manifestation ("Jesus").'[323] Furthermore, that the 'Christ', or Holy Spirit, descended upon 'Jesus' at his baptism, and departed from him at the cross implies that the divine nature, 'Christ', could not be subject to death. This is an eminently Jewish theological posture from the Second Temple era; for throughout the Parables in *1 Enoch*, the Messiah is conceived of as a celestial pre-existent entity, not as an earthly or human being who pre-exists as such in heaven. For the earliest Jewish Christians, therefore, Jesus 'was' the Christ in the sense that the divine nature called 'the Christ' or 'the Spirit' descended upon the human Jesus, not that Jesus was simplistically and exhaustively identified with 'the Christ'. The word 'Christ' in this context obviously possesses a quite different meaning than it bears in Pauline Christianity. Once we understand the Jewish-Christian usage of 'Christ' as a synonym for 'Holy Spirit', 'divine nature', 'Logos', or 'eternal Son', then the Ebionite christology intriguingly assumes an orthodox character, for the paradigm then basically coincides with Aquinas's doctrine that the eternal Logos cannot be simplistically and exhaustively identified with Jesus's created humanity. Jesus can be called the Christ insofar as the two natures are united, yet there can be no confusion of the two natures. In Schedl's language, as quoted above, 'Between the crucified one and the Spirit-Messiah there is no identity.... . However, 'Isa, upon whom the Spirit descended, has the greatest similarity with the Spirit-Messiah.'

CHAPTER FIVE

Positive Christian Responses
to Islam

C HRISTIAN THEOLOGIANS' ASSERTION that Muhammad was a false
prophet, or perhaps even a remote precursor to the eschatological
Anti-Christ, has by no means been the only ecclesiastical response to
the phenomenon of Islam. As early a figure as Assyrian Nestorian patriarch
Timothy, who died in 823, wrote to the 'Abbasid caliph al-Mahdi: 'Muhammad
is "worthy of all praise" and "walked in the path of the prophets" because he
taught the unity of God; ... he taught about God, his word and his spirit.'[324]
It would be disrespectful to charge the Christian patriarch in this context with
fear or especially with having uttered anything contrary to the Faith for mere
expediency. In his statement to the caliph, Timothy denies neither Christ nor
his unique role in the economy of salvation for Christians; indeed he praises
Muhammad in part for teaching about God's 'word and his spirit', which are
two of the standard Islamic titles for Jesus Christ derived from the Qur'an.

The Franciscan Louis Massignon called for a 'spiritual Copernican
revolution' in the Catholic Church in relation to the question of the
authenticity of Muhammad's prophetic call.[325] Patriarch Timothy's and
Massignon's examples show us that a positive evaluation within Christianity
of Muhammad's Prophethood is by no means unprecedented historically
in earlier or later centuries. Neither has the 12th-13th-century Christian
abjuration, 'I anathematize the god of Muhammad,'[326] been the only response
to the question of Islamic belief. John Paul II, in his April 3, 1991 Ramadan
message to Muslims wrote: 'I close my greeting to you with the words of one
of my predecessors, Pope Gregory VII who in 1076 wrote to Al-Nasir, the
Muslim Ruler of Bijaya, present day Algeria: "Almighty God, who wishes that
all should be saved and none lost, approves nothing in so much as that after
loving Him one should love his fellow man, and that one should not do to
others, what one does not want done to oneself. You and we owe this charity
to ourselves especially because we believe in and confess one God, admittedly,

in a different way, and daily praise and venerate him, the creator of the world and ruler of this world.'"[327] If Muslims worship the same God as Christians, then the church cannot in good logic legitimately call Muslims 'infidels' or 'pagans'. The same of course applies to Jews who likewise believe in the one God of Abraham.

The great confidant of Pope Pius II, Cardinal Nicholas of Cusa, in his treatise, *De pace fidei* (1453), shows us that neither was the common writing off of Islam as a 'false religion' the only response of Catholic authorities to the phenomenon of Islam. Nicholas of Cusa frames his treatise in the form of a heavenly council at which the Christ as the Word appears together with representatives of the various world religions. To the Muslim representative, Christ replies: 'Therefore, all men declare together with you that there is one Absolute Wisdom, which they presuppose and which is the one God.' Muslim: 'So it is. And no one who has understanding can affirm anything different.' Christ: 'Therefore, for all those who are of sound understanding there is one religion and worship, which is presupposed in all the diversity of rites [= religions].'[328] Ernst Cassirer explains that Nicholas of Cusa's early cosmological principle of equal distance and nearness of creatures to God was applied to the religious universe in *De pace fidei*: '[N]o body is closer or farther from the divine ...; rather, each is "immediate to God." ... [F]or Cusanus the cosmos of religions is equally near and far from God... .'[329] Yet this 'truly grand "tolerance" ... is anything but indifference,' for 'whereas the signs are subject to change and to modification, what they signify is not.'[330] If the heavenly religions, like all beings and entities, have an immediate relationship to the Divine, then 'none of [their] points of view has any priority,' for each view participates in 'accidentality' and 'necessity.'[331] Thus the universal and the particular 'interpenetrate each other.'[332]

According to the Qur'an, all revealed religions are of divine origin and are varying forms of a common transcendent archetype, and in actuality the forms constitute in essence a single supra-formal religion. As Frithjof Schuon declares: '[F]undamentally, there is only one religion with various forms, for humanity is one and the spirit is one... .'[333] To break or divide the one primordial religion into various sects is to claim that only one of the religions, to the exclusion of all others in an absolute sense, is the source of revelation and salvation. Ultimately only God is Absolute, and such absoluteness cannot be ascribed to any religion that originates from Him; to absolutize a religion in this manner would constitute an act of idolatry, of *shirk*. The primordial unity of religion is the message proclaimed in sura 23:52-53: 'And lo! this your religion is one religion and I am your Lord, so keep your duty unto Me. But they (mankind) have broken their religion among them into sects, each sect rejoicing in its tenets.' Thus aya 58, by referring to revelations in the plural, as does the Qur'an generally, requires not only recognition of Muhammad's revelation, but also of all previous revelations or religions, for they are all expressions of the primordial religion: 'And those who believe in the *revelations* of their Lord.' And as the Qur'an repeatedly stresses, it is up to God on judgment day to shed light upon that in which the various sects and religions differ (cf. 5:48).

Later in his *De pace fidei*, Nicholas of Cusa has Christ explain concerning the trinity: 'Now, in the manner in which Arabs and Jews deny the Trinity, assuredly it ought to be denied by all.'[334] On the question of the divinity of Christ, Nicholas of Cusa has St. Peter at the heavenly council proclaim to a Persian Muslim: 'Together with you, I steadfastly deny that the Eternal is temporal.' Peter explains the doctrine of the two natures of Christ and states concerning the human nature: '... He was not the Word of God in accordance with that nature.'[335] Furthermore, 'the human [nature] does not pass over into the divine [nature].'[336] In short, Nicholas of Cusa has the Logos in heaven state that the manner in which Muslims deny the trinity and divinity of Christ ought to be denied by all.[337]

In agreement with Nicholas of Cusa, Frithjof Schuon observes that 'the negation of the Christian Trinity in the Qur'an' is merely 'extrinsic and conditional,'[338] therefore, neither intrinsic nor unconditional. As Nicholas of Cusa's *De pace fidei* has Christ explain in heavenly council: 'As Creator, God is trine and one; as Infinite, He is neither trine nor one nor any of those things that can be spoken of.'[339] Schuon agrees substantially with this view when he writes: 'It is expressly said in that Islamic credo, the *Fiqh al-Akbar* of Abu Hanifah, that Allah is unique, not in the sense of number, but in the sense that He is without associate.'[340]

Regarding the trinitarian dogma, Frithjof Schuon remarks that although Islam 'had ... to limit its expansion, ... this in no way prejudices the existence, within Islam, of the universal truth that is expressed by the dogma in question.'[341] Schuon furthermore states that within the church the idea of the 'trinitarian relationships' was 'providentially and necessarily adopted.'[342] Again we read that 'a Christianity that denies the Divinity of Christ denies the reason for its own existence.'[343] If it be objected that Jewish Christianity denied the divinity of Christ, we answer that the Ebionites contested this truth in merely an extrinsic manner, that is, they objected only to the Hellenistic philosophical articulation of the Great Church. In view of the Ebionite doctrine of the True Prophet, it cannot be doubted that they saw in Christ a plenary Logos manifestation. The following Islamic *hadith* of Jesus witnesses to a shared Jewish-Christian and Islamic conception of the theophanic nature of the Messiah. In this saying, Christ denies having said that he was God in the absolute sense, but simultaneously maintains the truth of his theophanic reality: 'Jesus (Peace be upon him!) said, "If I had said it, Thou wouldest have known it (see Qur'an 5:116), because Thou art He who speaks in my form, and Thou art the tongue with which I speak, making it sure that Thou alone art in my desire and in my person."'[344]

Qur'an 5:73's criticism of the trinity condemns those who refer to Christ as the 'third of three': 'They surely disbelieve who say: Lo! Allah is the third of three; when there is no God save the One God. If they desist not from so saying a painful doom will fall on those of them who disbelieve.' That the 'third of three' refers to Christ is plain from the opening of the preceding aya, 5:72: 'They surely disbelieve who say: Lo! Allah is the Messiah, son of Mary.' In the Great Church's trinitarian formula, however, the Son is the second hypostasis enumerated, not the third (the formula being 'Father, *Son*, and Holy Spirit'). The Qur'an is condemning the polytheistic trinity of the heretical Gnostics, whose trinitarian formula of 'Father, Mother, and Son'[345] quite literally places Christ as 'the third of three.' Further confirmation for our interpretation is found in 5:75, which emphasizes that Christ and his mother were both subject to mortality and that 'they both used to eat (earthly) food.' This implies that the position attacked here held that Christ and Mary were immortal in their physical humanity and thus did not have to eat. In short, the position here attacked was that of unqualified Gnostic docetism which denied the physical reality of Christ's body.

As a final piece of evidence, 5:116 shows that this aberrant trinitarian belief incorporated Mary into the Godhead: 'And when Allah saith: O Jesus, son of Mary! Didst thou say unto mankind: Take me and my mother for two gods beside Allah? he saith: Be glorified! It was not mine to utter that to which I had no right.' We know that the Collydrians of Arabia worshipped the Virgin Mary as God, since they offered a Eucharistic sacrifice to her.[346] It would appear that they, in a Gnosticizing fashion, assimilated the Virgin Mary to the Holy Spirit in a simplistic and exhaustive sense, since the 'Spirit', being grammatically feminine in Hebrew, Syriac and other Semitic languages, was the divine person referred to as Mother in the classical Gnostic trinitarian formula, 'Father, Mother, and Son.'

The traditional Christian slur against Muhammad, that he did not understand the church's trnitarian belief, is therefore unfounded. The Qur'an quite correctly understands and condemns aberrant Gnostic trinitarianism. This, incidentally, argues against any intrinsically heretical docetic conception in the Qur'anic account of the crucifixion where it uses the word 'appear' (see Qur'an 4:157).

Louis Gardet concludes that the Qur'anic passages that have been identified by some Muslim theologians as attacking the church's doctrines of trinity and incarnation do not in fact fit the church's own position: 'What they are refuting is not orthodox Christian belief at all but heretical views which the Church herself repudiates.'[347] While we agree with Gardet's assertion, he does not seem to have given sufficient attention to the question of whether the Islamic criticisms could in fact at times function as a legitimate 'prophetic' corrective to the church, when she may manifest certain disequilibria in her exposition of various aspects of christological and trinitarian dogmas. That she does experience such imbalances, especially at the level of popular piety, but not confined to that area alone, is self-evident from even a cursory reading of ecclesiastical history. Our comments on this point should not end on a negative note; we should observe that the Qur'an's attacks against wayward followers of Christ in sura 5 climax in the final two verses, with a majestic promise of Paradise (119) and an exalted affirmation of Allah's omnipotence (120): 'Allah saith: This is a day in which their truthfulness profiteth the truthful, for theirs are Gardens underneath which rivers flow, wherein they are secure for ever, Allah taking pleasure in them and they in Him. That is the great triumph. Unto Allah belongeth the Sovereignty of the heavens and the earth and whatsoever is therein, and He is Able to do all things.'

In an important essay, David A. Kerr surveys recent Christian theological reflection upon the Prophethood of Muhammad. He first summarizes Louis Massignon's interpretation. Massignon distinguishes between positive and negative prophecy. Positive prophecy announces a 'reversal of human values', whereas negative prophecy preaches the eschatological judgment.[348] Muhammad was primarily a 'negative' prophet announcing the day of judgment. According to Massignon, Muhammad announces the eschatological sign of Mary's virginity, which is a truth that finds final fulfillment in the second coming of her son Jesus Christ. In this sense, the Arabian Prophet is a 'Marian sign'.[349] As Kerr explains, Massignon seems to imply that just as Mary's virginity was unique, so Muhammad was the unique, or definitive, 'negative, eschatological' prophet.[350] In this way, 'Massignon gave positive significance to Muhammad's "post-Christian" chronology: if his prophethood occurred after Jesus' first coming, it is his very anticipation of the Second Coming that commends him for Christian acceptance as an authentically eschatological prophet.'[351] Massignon's views on Muhammad's Prophethood were published in the Roman Catholic missionary journal, *Rhythmes du Monde* (Paris), in 1948 (vol. 3, pp. 7-16), and were never condemned by his church.[352]

Kerr then analyzes the research of Canon Charles Ledit, who posited a threefold 'Abrahamic community embracing Jews, Christians, and Muslims.'[353] Ledit identified two Thomistic categories of prophecy, 'theological prophecy' which culminated in Christ, and 'directive prophecy' which existed before Christ and outside Israel (e.g., Adam, Noah, Melchizedek, Job, Ahikar, Daniel), and which continues to operate after Christ as a means of offering guidance and direction for the 'spiritual welfare of the elect'.[354] Thus for Ledit, Muhammad is a 'directive prophet', and indeed, 'the culminating point of "extra-biblical" prophecy' in that he, as 'a son of Abraham', prepares Israel for the day of judgment.[355]

The Maronite Catholic priest Michael Hayek argues that even though according to the Jewish perspective Ishmael was rejected, 'he yet remains the child of Abram/Abraham, for which reason he cannot be deemed theologically extraneous to the purpose of God in "the Abrahamic cycle" of faith.'[356] Ishmael constitutes an 'Old Testament in the Old Testament', in the sense that he represents a type of 'natural' monotheistic religion or faith, since Abraham did pray in *Genesis* 17:18: 'O that Ishmael might live before Thee,' in contrast to the Isaac typology of 'miraculous' faith. Thus we arrive at a typology of the 'rejected' and the 'accepted', and Ishmael's natural faith constitutes the 'preparation' for the 'supernatural', revealed faith of Isaac.[357] Indeed, Ishmael's very name means 'God has heard', making it difficult to maintain his rejection as permanent or intrinsic.[358] Though Kerr does not mention Christ's sayings on the first being last and the last first (cf. *Matthew* 20:16), and the accepted being rejected and vice versa (cf. *Matthew* 21:43), these sayings of Jesus certainly could be applied fruitfully to the typology involved with the 'rejected' Ishmael whose 'descendant religion' confirms, as Hayek phrases it, the 'biblical truth' of God's acceptance of 'all who believe', even outside of Israel (and the church by extension); thus Islam confirms this truth of God's infinite love of the 'outsider' in an unparalleled, 'impressive, massive and continuous manner'.[359] Father Hayek concludes that Muhammad is the 'prophet of the "excluded" faithful', who preaches the eschatological return of Christ, 'which alone can bring into being the "universal Messianic reconciliation" of Jews, Christians, and Muslims.'[360]

Other notable views surveyed by Kerr include that of Eastern Orthodox Bishop George Khodr, who asserts that there is a reciprocal '"hidden bond" between Christ and Muhammad, the mystery of which will only be revealed with Christ's Second Advent.'[361] For Hans Küng, Islam and the church share a dialectical 'continuum in discontinuity'.[362] Küng points out that Vatican II, while praising the monotheistic faith of millions of Muslims around the world, through 'embarrassment' neglected to praise the precise historical source of that Islamic monotheism, namely, the Prophet Muhammad.[363] For Montgomery Watt, the genuineness of Muhammad's Prophethood is demonstrated by Christ's dictum, 'by their fruits you shall know them,' which fits Islam, given Muslims' 'general moral well-being'.[364] But as Kerr explains, all the authors surveyed in this context represent Christians speaking to other Christians, who unfortunately mostly fail to integrate understandings of Muhammad's Prophethood as embodied in Islamic theology and piety.[365] Yet it can be graciously conceded that such self-understandings of the 'other' can serve as a useful foundation and beginning for interreligious dialogue. What is necessary in any event in the church's understanding of Islam, is simultaneously an avoidance of a sentimental ecumenism that would deny the vital importance of religious differences on the formal level, and a recognition of an underlying unity between the Abrahamic faiths on the supra-formal and transcendent plane.

CHAPTER SIX

Sufism and Western Historicism

S EYYED HOSSEIN NASR observes that in the 19th century, 'the Persian Sufi poet Hatif Isfahani praised Christianity as being an affirmation of Divine Unity provided its doctrine of trinity is understood in its metaphysical significance.'[366] The Algerian Sufi Shaykh al-'Alawi Ahmad agrees. Al-Jili and a whole host of other Sufis adopted the same attitude toward the Hindu Vedas, resembling 'those Sufis who tried to interpret the Christian Trinity as an assertion rather than a negation of Divine Unity.'[367] Ibn al-'Arabi taught that Christ was a 'theophany' of God and the 'seal of sanctity', and that he was quite justifiably called the 'son' of God, in a non-physical and non-polytheistic sense of course. There was naturally no acceptance of the doctrine of the trinity at the exoteric level, but the Sufis recognized that Christian terminology regarding divine filiation and trinity is acceptable from a mystical, speculative or metaphysical viewpoint. The great Sufi poet Rumi had several Christian disciples, and this great Persian poet had no qualms about teaching that both traditions, Islam and Christianity, upheld the same message of Divine Unity and *unio mystica*. As Frithjof Schuon comments, the mufti's area of competence is that of the 'commonplaces of practical life', and regarding the 'formula of *At-Tawhid*, or monotheism', the mufti may not interfere, for the 'import that a man gives to this formula is his personal affair, since it depends upon his Sufism'.[368]

The *Religionsgeschichte* school of interpretation that attributes Sufism *per se* or its origin to Neoplatonism or to related movements has been exposed as untenable in an unqualified form since the work of Louis Massignon, who demonstrated that Sufism is derived principally from the Qur'an, not from extraneous sources. To be sure, technical terms were at times borrowed from other traditions, but they were used to express native concepts or to unfold trajectories already inherent within the Islamic archetype. As Seyyed Hossein Nasr writes, historical borrowings are in any event, 'secondary in comparison with the living body of an authentic religion that must of necessity originate from Heaven.'[369] Furthermore, one cannot summarily 'explain away major elements of a religion by simple recourse to historical borrowing as we see in the treatment of Islamic esoterism in the form of Sufism by so many Western orientalists.... '[370]

Fortunately, much of Western critical scholarship on Sufism is beginning to move away from the historicism of the last few centuries. In a major new critical sourcebook of Sufi texts, Carl W. Ernst, Professor and Chair of the Department of Religious Studies at the University of North Carolina at Chapel Hill, speaks of Sufism's 'origins in the Prophet Muhammad and the Qur'anic revelation.... '[371] Ernst rightly deplores the previous state of scholarship on the phenomenon of Sufism by explaining that western scholars admired Sufism to the extent that they believed that it originated in non-Islamic sources such as 'Christianity, yoga, or Buddhism.'[372] As Michael Sells documents, the origins of Islamic mysticism are to be located in the Qur'an, early Islamic rites, and in the visionary narrations of Muhammad's ascent (*Mi'raj*) through the seven heavens culminating in a vision of the throne of Allah. Additionally, pre-Islamic Arabic love poetry, and not Neoplatonism, provided to an extent previously overlooked by most orientalists many of the key literary symbols of later Sufi mystical poetry and theology of the Beloved.[373] Later Islamic mysticism was merely augmented, not created, by contact with Neoplatonism. Consider, for instance, the Islamic concept of the universal Return or cosmic recapitulation, which we might call *al-Ruj'ah* in a parallel sense with the Christian concept of *apokatastasis*, again paralleled by Neoplatonism's concept of the cyclical return of the cosmic cumulative Omega to the divine originative Alpha. It can be said that it was more the case that the Sufis read Neoplatonic texts in light of the 'Return' verses in the Qur'an, rather than that they read the Qur'an in light of Neoplatonic texts.[374] The *Religionsgeschichte* school has actually reversed the historical facts. The Sufi doctrine of the Return existed already in Muhammad's teaching, as witnessed to in several *ahadith* and in the Qur'an, and thus well before Islam's encounter with Neoplatonic philosophy.

In any event, it is simply inconsistent and self-defeating for a Christian scholar to invoke the *Religionsgeschichte* school's interpretation of Sufism's origins, since the very same school of thought is loathed by traditional Christians, because it argues, based on the very same methodological principles, that Christianity's sacraments were borrowed from Greek mystery religions, and that the ancient Jewish feasts were derived genetically from antecedent pagan Near Eastern models. The explanation of these similarities is that there was a transcendent 'overlap' situated in the archetypal realm between the Greek mystery religions and ancient Christianity, a parallelism fully and rightly exploited by the patristic writers.

In the same sense, a thoughtful Christian should have no objection to Nasr when he states that Sufism, and even Islam *as such*, are not derived from historical Judaism or Christianity, and that the parallels between the three

Abrahamic religions exist because of 'the common transcendent archetype of Judaism, Christianity and Islam.'[375] Similarly, in his *Ideals and Realities of Islam*, Nasr comments on the early church fathers' profound integration of Greek and Roman philosophy, noting that such absorption of extraneous elements, 'is true in fact of every living spiritual tradition which like a live organism accepts material from its surroundings and transforms it into what conforms to its own organic needs.'[376] Frithjof Schuon similarly explains the dynamic discussed by Nasr in the following manner: '[T]he intellectual originality of the Muslims can only proceed from a Revelation.'[377]

Nasr has written a very penetrating tribute to Louis Massignon, who was a Third Order Franciscan, in which he recalls an Islamic–Catholic dialogue conference held in 1958 at the Dominican monastery of Tioumliline in the Atlas Mountains. Nasr remarks in his tribute that Massignon was a close friend of the Servant of God Charles de Foucald, who, 'rather than try to convert the Muslims, he tried to become a kind of witness to Christianity to them and to befriend them as people following another version of his religion and the message that comes from God.'[378] As we will seek to demonstrate in our chapter on the 'ternary nature of monotheism', de Foucald's position in no way violates Christ's injunction to the church to preach his commandments to all the world.

CHAPTER SEVEN

The Transcendent Unity of Religions

WHEN WE COMPARE the various gospel accounts of what is commonly called the great commission to the apostles, we are struck by the similarity of themes shared by all the accounts, but also by the simultaneous variation in individual wording:

Matthew 28:18-20:
All power is given to me in heaven and in earth.
Going therefore, teach ye all nations; baptizing them in the name of the Father, and of the Son, and of the Holy Ghost.[379] Teaching them to observe all things whatsoever I have commanded you: and behold I am with you all days, even to the consummation of the world.
Mark 16:15-16:
Go ye into the whole world, and preach the gospel to every creature. He that believeth and is baptized, shall be saved: but he that believeth not shall be condemned.

Luke 24:47-49:
And that penance and remission of sins should be preached in his name, unto all nations, beginning at Jerusalem.
And you are witnesses of these things.
And I send you the promise of my Father upon you: but stay in the city, till you be endued with power from on high.

Acts 1:8
But you shall receive the power of the Holy Ghost coming upon you, and you shall be witnesses unto me in Jerusalem, and in all Judea, and Samaria, and even unto the uttermost part of the earth.

John 20:21-23:
As the Father hath sent me, I also send you.
Receive ye the Holy Ghost.
Whose sins you shall forgive, they are forgiven them; and whose sins you shall retain, they are retained.

Mark: The Freer Logion:
The time of Satan's years of power has reached fulfillment, but soon other abominations will come. Yet for the sake of sinners I was given over to death, that they might return to the truth, cease sinning, and inherit the spiritual and unending majesty of righteousness in heaven.

It would strain credibility to insist that the above six accounts, five canonical and one extra-canonical, of the great commission represent separate sayings of Christ, as if he delivered the great commission on five or six different occasions, and that each gospel writer then simply independently recorded a distinct saying. If we accept that the post-resurrection sayings were not spoken or communicated by Christ in physically audible words to the apostles, we could surmise that he interiorly imparted to them only the general sense or themes of his message, leaving each of the apostles free to formulate the mystical impressions in concrete words of his own choosing.

These variations, in which general themes are the same whereas the individual words are different, may be compared to the repetition of a piece of music; as long as the main melody stays at least generally the same, the accompanying counterpoint or harmony notes may vary greatly, even ad lib, without affecting the integrity and overall identity of the song. Analogously, myths are like musical pieces. There may be dozens of Greek myths about any one particular deity. Yet each myth, despite often significant variations in plot line, purpose, characters and chronology, is tied together by an overarching and uniting element or theme. The general structure remains the same, while individual aspects such as characters or plot chronology may vary.

The universal mythological element may be understood 'literally', whereas the varying 'particulars' cannot be taken 'literally' without turning them into contradictions of each other. The mythic mentality does not view the variations as literal and therefore as contradictions. They are like counterpoint or harmony notes that may be freely changed without detriment to the main melody, or to the universal mythological theme at hand. Inner content differs, outer or overall structure remains more or less the same.

This model also helps explain the variations in the Jewish targums and in the gospels, in which chronology is not always intended to be taken literally. Once the chronology of the gospel narrative events is in every case taken literally, that is, solely as historical rather than metaphysical in mode, then they become irreconcilable contradictions; and in any event the metaphysical is more 'true' than the historical, because the former is more abiding. The solution is that the variations we are considering are not contradictions, because the gospels' chronologies were never meant to be taken in a historical sense in every instance. The interpretative domains and functions of the universal order are not to be applied to or identified with those of a particular order. Similarly, Christ's words recorded in the gospels are often characterized by a targumic fluidity.[380] Consider the following two verses: *Matthew* 12:28: 'But, if I by the Spirit of God cast out devils, then is the kingdom of God come upon you.' *Luke* 11:20: 'But, if I by the finger of God cast out devils, doubtless the kingdom of God is come upon you.' The theme remains the same, whereas the author-translator is free to change the particular verbal formulation into equivalent concepts. The *Gospel of John*, in which Christ's teaching is formulated at the verbal particular level in a hieratic tone almost entirely absent from the synoptic gospels, is a prime example of the retention of a common, general semantic and thematic content accompanied by an extensive verbal particular variation and freedom.

The failure of some previous Christian writers to distinguish rabbinic particular fluidity resulted in many unfortunate anti-Jewish remarks. The following prejudiced statement from a Jesuit is typical of the era; Fernand Prat, S.J., after labelling the talmud and midrash a 'confused, incoherent, and contradictory mass of trash', makes the comment: 'In the slough of the Apocrypha and the rabbinical writings a few particles of gold can be sometimes met with, but with how much dross are they combined!'[381] Abdullah Yusuf Ali similarly writes of Jewish sacred legends as 'Jewish stuff',' 'some' of which was 'absurd', and which for Ali unfortunately were incorporated in certain older Qur'an commentaries.[382]

Our modified mytheme concept can also be compared in an analogous sense with the distinction between the exoteric and the esoteric dimensions of faith and practice in the various world religions. To mention Islamic devotion, one speaks of 99 divine names; yet there is only one divine essence or being. The 99 names are therefore divine modes of manifestation in the created cosmos. The diversity of religions reflects in a certain sense the diversity of divine names,[383] and according to Islamic thought, as Schuon remarks, 'every religion is founded upon a Revelation emanating from one and the same infinite Consciousness, or from the same celestial Will... .'[384] The diverse religions are, however, connected in differing degrees at the level of esoteric, that is, mystical or metaphysical truth, although being simultaneously divergent at the exoteric level, which is the domain of dogmatic theology.

Because of the reality of exoteric divergences, only a false ecumenism could ignore the 'contradictions' in the various beliefs of the world religions; but on the other hand, only a rigorist would deny that there are many parallels existing between the world religions at the inward level, and to a lesser extent at the dogmatic level. Of course a parallel does not imply or necessitate an identity, but it does indicate some degree of relatedness or compatibility, which would constitute material commonality sufficient for the foundations of ecumenical inter-religious dialogue and mutual understanding. Naturally, mysticism and dogmatic theology cannot be diametrically opposed in any sound religious system; rather must they mutually support, modify and inform each other.

Speaking in analogous terms, Schuon calls the archetypal parallels between religions, 'universalities', and the various religions' dogmas 'particulars'.[385] The 'universal' Truth experienced immediately in mystical enlightenment is then translated into 'particular' truths, or formulations of truths, by the representatives of the various religions, with varying degrees of accuracy or completeness.[386] Thus the terms esoteric and exoteric are comparable to universal and particular, or even to substance and form.[387] Schuon also calls these pairs the unitive and separative modes.[388]

We may summarize our argumentation by repeating that a modified mytheme concept employing the support of analogical amplitude may help us not only to understand the similarities and differences in such texts as the targums, midrash, talmud, the canonical gospels, world myths and apocalyptic visions, but may also assist in the analysis and evaluation of the continuities and discontinuities existing between the world religions.

In that for Christian theology the dogmas of incarnation and trinity are not directly accessible to human reason, but must be, as St. Thomas and Catholic theology in general maintain, revealed directly by God, they reflect supraformal realities. Being supraformal, they cannot be fully and exactly explicated or articulated discursively and logically. When transcendent realities enter the formal level, such as the event of 'incarnation' within human history, they are by virtue of their suprarational-revelational status accessible and sense-able to human perception only as if through a prism. This point can be illustrated by Catholic theologian Hans Urs von Balthasar's description of the post-resurrection narratives which involve 'Legitimate refractions of the single inexpressible reality into the multiple colors of the spectrum,' and it is, moreover, 'not good policy to wish to reconcile, at any price, particular images at the level of the earthly, phenomenal order... .'[389]

The resurrection, post-resurrection discourses, and ascension of Christ can each be described as an 'incomprehensible event',[390] a 'primordial phenomenon'.[391] Moreover, 'Luke himself can have experienced no contradiction between an "Ascension" identical with the Resurrection, and a manifestation of that Ascension at the end of the time of the appearances.'[392] Von Balthasar approves of Gerhard Lohfink's assertion that 'a *glorificatio in fierei* and *in facto* are scarcely distinguishable for an event which takes place outside the time and space of the old aeon,' and as Pierre Benoit concludes, there is no need to apply a 'chronological element' to the post-resurrection appearances.[393] The gospels' 'periodisation' of such events must not be taken literally, for as Lohfink declares, 'the same transcendent event can manifest itself in any number of appearances.... Moreover, the infinite richness of the transcendent event can never be perfectly shown forth in the finite.'[394] In addition, 'Words, like (scenic) images remain of necessity "limit expressions" for a reality which ... overflows ... the latter's receptive capacities.'[395] Von Balthasar also speaks of 'figural language'[396] necessary to describe the resurrection and ascension, which 'are for our temporal and mortal world something eschatological.... [E]schatological affirmations ... remain always "limit-affirmations."'[397]

The suprahistorical dimension of the resurrection, a dimension which necessitates only a limited, indirect and fluid formal description, also applies in varying degrees not only to the crucifixion, *descensus ad inferos*, and ascension, but also to realities such as the virginal birth of Christ, the immaculate conception of Mary, divine filiation, incarnation, hypostatic union and trinity. These doctrines may validly and in a perfectly orthodox manner be subject to a richly diverse variety of theological articulations that 'literally', though not 'absolutely', 'contradict' each other. Like the post-resurrection narratives, the supraformal, or better, transcendent 'event' of divine filiation and 'incarnation' cannot be perceived or comprehended as they are in themselves. Such realities can be expressed only approximatively; the formal dogmatic articulations of these transcendent realities must be taken symbolically, metaphorically or analogically, but not literally.

Accordingly, the situation with the post-resurrection narratives applies also, as we have noted, to the dogmas of incarnation and trinity, truths that cannot be deduced by unaided reason, and which are knowable only through revelation, for they lie beyond reason, not that they are not reasonable or cannot be discussed reasonably. Yet the formally articulated revelation retains the character of fluidity marking the post-resurrection narratives, a situation parallel to all theological discussion and dogmatic formulation of incarnation and trinity. The theological and dogmatic precision of experts is necessary and fully natural, for after all, the supraformal realities have manifested themselves in the concrete world of forms, that is, at the formal level of complexity as opposed to the 'simple' or 'simplex' transcendent realm; but the dogmatic formulations never lose their relativity and can only indirectly point to supraformal realites, even though they do so in a manner adequate to the purpose for which they are given.

Discourse about incarnation and trinity is therefore of a different category than doctrines directly accessible to human reason alone, unaided by revelation, such as the immortality of the soul, or, as Islamic theology and *Romans* 1 agrees, the existence of the One creator God.[398] All metaphysical realities such as hypostases, eternal generation, hypostatic union, remain mysteries and approximative concepts and articulations at the formal level. That dogmas are extrapolated by reflection upon truths revealed by heaven ensures that the dogmas *effectively* point indirectly to the supraformal truths, that is, effectively and sufficiently for the group to which the revelation is directed; the dogmas reveal something of their supraformal counterparts, but never every dimension inherent in them.

Joseph Cardinal Ratzinger, now Pope Benedict XVI, emphasizes the esoteric nature of the doctrine of the trinity by reminding us that it 'is a sort of cipher for the insolubility of the mystery of God.... . We can only speak rightly about him if we ... leave him as the uncomprehended... .'[399] Benedict XVI explains that, given the limited and limitative nature of all theological discourse, especially concerning mysteries of faith non-deducible by reason unaided by revelation, our spiritual gaze 'can always look from one side and so grasp only one particular aspect, which seems to contradict the other... . Only by circling round, by looking and describing from different, apparently contrary angles', are we able to hint at the truth adequately, but always only partially.[400]

Of course, the imperfect nature of the dogmatic statements concerning the trinity does not cancel out the fact that 'contact with the reality does take place'.[401] But certainly, because of the inevitable 'infinite indirectness'[402] of speech about the triune God, Benedict XVI's main burden is to demonstrate the strictly esoteric or 'hidden' nature, in the Dionysian[403] sense of a negative and apophatic-tending theology, of trinitarian dogma, which constitutes 'a realm in which Christian theology must be more aware of its limits than it has often been in the past'.[404] Not only is trinitarian dogma characterized by a limitation of *allusion*, it fundamentally employs the language of *illusion*. As Benedict XVI reminds us, *persona* and *prosopon* 'belong to the language of the theatre', referring as they do to the actor's *mask*.[405] Indeed, the various key theological terms finally approved by the church and adopted for her trinitarian discourse were all at one time or another formerly condemned by the same church. This applies, among others, to *persona*, *prosopon*, and even *homousios*.[406] Benedict XVI comments that what the terms' former condemnations imply is that even after their later adoption, 'it is only through the negation ... implicit in [them], that they are usable.'[407] At the formal level, therefore, trinitarian discourse always remains essentially 'contradictory', for the underlying reality being 'esoteric' or 'hidden', all explication which attempts to make it 'visible' in dogma must necessarily result in a certain 'illusion', as an apophatically-inclined approach would describe it. In other words, as Karl Rahner phrases this situation, 'the Trinity is an absolute mystery (Denziger 1795, 1915) which is not perspicuous to reason even after being revealed (on which see also *Collectio Lacensis*, VII, pp. 507 c.525 BC).'[408] This is not to say that one cannot discuss and explore a theological or metaphysical mystery in a rational manner, but we must bear in mind the human limitations of the exploration, and the humility and reverential awe with which we should respond to all mysteries of faith.

To return to our former topic, just as the post-resurrection discourses *literally*, but not *absolutely*, contradict each other in details, so do various theologies of christology and trinitarianism both within Christianity and without. But that is of the nature of things when the formal articulation of supraformal realities confronts us. As the canonical post-resurrection narratives show, even the *revealed* formal expressions may in a certain sense *literally*, though not *absolutely*, contradict each other. In the past, experts were inclined to mistake literal for absolute contradictions, whence the fruitless and unnecessary attempts at gospel harmonization going all the way back to Origen's Jewish Alexandrian allegorical method, profound as it admittedly might be.

In the light of this discussion, we may posit that there are truths that can be best understood at the esoteric level, that is, by means of a negative theology, as Dionysius maintains. Such esoteric truths are those which cannot be known through reason alone, unaided by divine revelation. If we make the esoteric exoteric, then we confuse categories. By making the esoteric exoteric, we mean taking dogmas in a literal and complete sense rather than in a limitative symbolical, analogical or metaphorical sense, for dogma only partially unveils at the formal level the supraformal realities as they subsist in plenary mode in themselves.

Here Schuon's discussion of different spiritual points of view may be helpful.[409] He uses the example of viewing two points on a circumference from different angles. From one visual perspective there will be a continuity between the two points, from another, discontinuity.[410] In that the two points are 'linked' on the one circumference, they constitute a unity; but in that the two points are placed at different locations on the circumference, they constitute a sort of visual 'contradiction'. Moreover, 'this contradiction will reach its maximum when the two points are situated at the extremities of a diameter of the circle'; at the same time, 'this extreme opposition or contradiction only appears as a result of isolating the points ... from the circle and ignoring the existence of the latter.'[411] The circle represents supraformal Truth,[412] the points are dogmatic articulation of formal truths. Schuon argues that his model of spiritual points of view being similarly limited as are physical points of view is fitting or congruent, based on the principle of similarity or continuity between the physical and spiritual realms, for 'the physical world ... is but a reflection of spiritual realities.'[413] We could here refer to Aristotle's comment on fittingness, admittedly on a different subject, at the end of *Politics* I 1254a: 'And if this is true of the body, how much more just that a similar distinction should exist in the soul?'

We could also speak of viewing a point in the distance from each of the four different cardinal directions. We can never reduce the view from the south angle to the view from the north angle any more than we can say that south is north. Yet though the angles are different, the point in the distance remains the same reality. Analogously, validly differing spiritual or theological points of view cannot be reduced to each other, but neither are they always necessarily absolute contradictions; they may only constitute 'apparent' contradictions. As Schuon explains concerning the providential separation of religions: 'The theological point of view, in fact, can never combine two different perspectives in a single dogma and this accounts for the divergence between Christianity and Islam ... .'[414]

As soon as we associate the resurrection with the crucifixion – and from a Christian perspective one may legitimately do so in light of St. John's identification of the crucifixion with Jesus's glorification – then the contradictions between the gospels and the Qur'an concerning the crucifixion immediately reveal themselves as 'literal', but not as absolute contradictions, just as the gospel post-resurrection narratives contain only literal as opposed to absolute contradictions. The impossibility of a formal articulation completely expressing or conveying a supraformal reality explains why, as Schuon says in reference to Christ, there arose such a 'profusion of divergent doctrines concerning His nature from the very beginning of Christianity'.[415] As Karl Rahner asserts, the incarnation, even after it is revealed by God, remains one of 'the absolute mysteries of faith'.[416] But Rahner teaches that by extension the incarnation 'also includes Jesus' human life, his death and resurrection'.[417] Thus we may speak in a sense of the utter mystery of the crucifixion as analogous to the mysteries of incarnation and trinity, lending support to Schuon's argumentation concerning the underlying reasons for the doctrinal divergences regarding Christ's nature as related specifically to his crucifixion. Speaking of the crucifixion accounts in the gospels and Qur'an 4:157-58, Schuon explains that discerning the distinction between history and symbolism in scripture is at times either 'difficult' or 'even impossible'.[418]

Given the power of a genuine dogma to convey a sufficient degree of illuminative reference to the supraformal Truth, a dogma, although always remaining relative, nevertheless functions in an 'absolute' sense within the community upon which a particular revelation has been bestowed. Such a combination of absoluteness and relativity is expressed by Schuon's dialectical concept of the 'relatively absolute', as expounded in his *The Transcendent Unity of Religions*.[419] To deny the referential power of dogma to illuminate supraformal Truth would represent a fundamental misunderstanding of the nature and function of theological reflection in a faith community, and is rightly condemned as an error in the Vatican document *Dominus Iesus*. When the same document refuses to allow that the sacred scriptures of non-Christian religions are inspired *in the same sense* as the Bible, the denial is more functional and extrinsic than 'substantial' and intrinsic. From a traditional viewpoint, though one may concede that God has spoken in other sacred books, and that such works contain the revelation of the one universal Creator, nevertheless, one must recognize that the divinely revealed religions and their scriptures are providentially intended to remain separate. The divinely revealed forms of religion should not be eroded by any unprincipled process of syncretism. Even within a single religion, namely, Christianity, the Gospels retain a function and value distinct from that of the Torah, although the Torah is equally held as sacred scripture by the church.

In order for a Christian to explain the presence of genuine miracles outside the church, one might invoke Karl Rahner's distinction between 'miracles of confirmation' and 'miracles of mercy'.[420] Rahner applied the distinction to certain cases within the church, but may not Christian theologians at the very least also apply the category of 'miracles of confirmation' to the church and that of 'miracles of mercy' to non-Christian religions? Since scriptural inspiration is a sort of 'miracle', one might posit, from a Catholic viewpoint, an *'inspiration of confirmation'* for the bible in contrast to an *'inspiration* of mercy' for the sacred scriptures of other religions. This 'Rahnerian' approach of 'inspiration of mercy' to non-Christian religious texts would make eminent sense in this paradigm when applied to the Qur'an, for in the latter both the Prophet of Islam and the scripture revealed through him are designated as 'a mercy' sent from God. Though the Qur'anic 'mercy' in this context and Rahner's idea of 'mercy' involved in miracles are not identical, nevertheless, they would appear to overlap to a sufficient degree to justify the comparison. In any event, in this context one must be wary of slipping into the invalid theory of a purely 'natural mysticism' in order to explain away the truly divine origin and reality of miracles in all the various heavenly inspired religions. As Frithjof Schuon incisively writes: '[T]he similarities and the number of miracles in all the different religions are too great not to have significance... .'[421]

CHAPTER EIGHT

The Ternary Nature of Abrahamic Monotheism

A CCORDING TO FRITHJOF SCHUON, Abrahamic monotheism was transmitted through the lines of his sons Isaac and Ishmael. The monotheistic faith of the Israelite line of Isaac was later renewed and codified by Moses, and that at a time when monotheism was in decline among the descendents of Ishmael.[422] But whereas in the Israelite line Moses assumes a certain superiority over Abraham, in the Ishmaelite line Abraham retains spiritual centrality. Christ 'closes the Mosaic line and concludes the Bible, gloriously and irrevocably'.[423] But 'the Ishmaelite, and still Abrahamic, line was situated outside this cycle ... ; it called in its turn for a glorious completion, not Sinaitic and Christly in character, but Abrahamic and Muhammadan... .'[424]

Qur'an 3:67 succinctly encapsulates the Islamic self-identity based on a primordial association that in a sense 'circumvents' Judaism and Christianity without by any means excluding Moses or Christ: 'Abraham was not a Jew, nor yet a Christian; but he was an upright man who had surrendered (to Allah), and he was not of the idolaters.' The same line of reasoning is more fully present in Qur'an 2:135-40, which we cite here in its entirety:

135. And they say: Be Jews or Christians, then ye will be rightly guided. Say (unto them, O Muhammad): Nay, but (we follow) the religion of Abraham, the upright, and he was not of the idolaters.

136. Say (O Muslims): We believe in Allah and that which is revealed unto us and that which was revealed unto Abraham, and Ishmael, and Isaac, and Jacob, and the tribes, and that which Moses and Jesus received, and that which the prophets received from their Lord. We make no distinction between any of them, and unto Him we have surrendered.

137. And if they believe in the like of that which ye believe, then are they rightly guided. But if they turn away, then are they in schism, and

Allah will suffice thee (for defence) against them. He is the Hearer, the Knower.

138. (We take our) colour from Allah, and who is better than Allah at colouring? We are His worshippers.[425]

139. Say (unto the People of the Scripture): Dispute ye with us concerning Allah when He is our Lord and your Lord? Ours are our works and yours your works. We look to Him alone.

140. Or say ye that Abraham, and Ishmael, and Isaac, and Jacob, and the tribes were Jews or Christians? Say: Do ye know best, or doth Allah? And who is more unjust than he who hideth a testimony which he hath received from Allah? Allah is not unaware of what ye do.[426]

That aya 135 does not advocate an intrinsic rejection of Christianity and Judaism in their essence is demonstrated by aya 136's inclusion of Christ and Moses in the list of prophets to whom Muslims give credence. The words in aya 137, 'if they believe in the like of that which ye believe', refer to an acceptance of all God's messengers, and implies a censure of 'picking and choosing' from among them; the latter is defined by aya 137 as 'schism'. We can infer from aya 138 that choosing to believe in all of God's messengers is equivalent to following divinely sanctioned religion in a principial, unconditional sense. In aya 139, the Qur'an, in accord with the logic of the passage under discussion, asks the Christians and Jews why they would dispute with the Prophet, since he follows the message of both of their religions' founders: 'Ours are our works and yours your works. We look to Him alone'; that is, God has given to each group their own particular revelation, and 'we', that is, all three groups, depend upon God. As a conclusion to the argumentation, aya 140 points forward to Qur'an 3:67, with which we began our interpretation above: 'Abraham was not a Jew, nor yet a Christian; but he was an upright man who had surrendered (to Allah).' To argue that God could not give different revelations to different peoples would be tantamount to questioning the divine power and wisdom; therefore aya 140's rhetorical question: 'Do ye know best, or doth Allah?'

Like the patriarch Abraham, the religion of Islam is desert-nomadic in far more essential ways than Moses and Judaism: 'Islam and Abrahamism are basically religions of nomads without history, scorched by the ever present and ever eternal Divine Sun. In the face of this Sun, man is nothing ...'[427] Titus Burckhardt adds that Mecca, where Abraham and Ishmael constructed the Kaaba, 'is the forgotten Sacred City – forgotten both by Judaism, which is ignorant of the prophetic role of Ishmael, and by Christianity, which inherited the same point of view.'[428] Such 'ignorance' is, from Schuon's perspective, providential, given the validly divergent formal trajectories of Ishmael and Isaac, both of whose religions were of necessity distinct manifestations emanating from the singular Abrahamic religious archetype.

According to the paradigm under discussion, it could be said that the Abrahamic covenant was first renewed by Moses, secondly by Jesus, and lastly by Muhammad. That the Prophet of Islam should not be excluded from the ranks of the first two renewers, Moses and Jesus, is established by the fact that the Qur'an recognizes Moses and Jesus as prophets, and by the fact of Muhammad's descent from Abraham's son Ishmael. Of course, though essential continuities with the original Abrahamic archetype remained, the mode and character of each renewal possessed particular and extrinsic or relative discontinuities with the same primordial Abrahamic covenant, which bestowed upon each faith community its own unique spiritual character and genius, that is, their very raison d'etre. But before exploring how each of the three Abrahamic monotheistic variants both differ and agree in certain aspects with each other, we must first digress and deal with certain secondary apologetic matters which may not be agreeable to all, but are nevertheless necessary, given the historical rejection of Islam by the majority of ecclesiastical authorities. These points are presented here not in order to convince opponents that the arguments are true, but merely to show that the propositions are not inherently without reason.

Regarding the cardinal question of the genuineness of the Prophethood of Muhammad, Schuon posits that if he had been a false prophet, Christ would surely have foretold the fact, 'for it is inconceivable that Christ, when speaking of the future, should have passed over in silence a manifestation of such magnitude'.[429] If it be countered that Muhammad was simply one of the many false prophets Christ warned of in a general sense, again the very historical and spiritual magnitude of Muhammad's movement excludes him from the general and plural warning of Christ. 'Moreover,' Schuon observes, 'it will be recalled that the Prophet in his doctrine has testified to the second coming of Christ without attributing to himself any glory, unless it be that of being the last Prophet of the [Abrahamic monotheistic] cycle... .'[430]

With this statement we can compare Seyyed Hossein Nasr when he writes that Islam is the only traditional religion which claims to be the final revelation, and that Muhammad 'announced that there would be no prophets after him and history has gone to prove his claim.'[431] Nasr goes on to qualify that although there is no Prophet after Muhammad, there is certainly ongoing inspiration that guides humanity as it looks forward, not to a new revelation or Prophet, but to the second coming of Jesus Christ.[432] Nasr claims that no religion previous to Islam claimed to be the final religion. This is historically accurate in the sense that Moses claimed a prophet would come after him (see *Deuteronomy* 18:18), and Christ promised the Paraclete would come and teach the world after Jesus's exaltation to God's right hand (see *John* chapters 14-16).

Schuon explains the concept of Muhammad as 'Seal of the Prophets' by noting that for Islam, 'the Word does not manifest itself in any particular man as such, but in the Prophetic function ... and above all in the revealed Books; and since ... Muhammad [is] the last representative of the Prophetic function, [he] recapitulates and synthesizes every aspect of this function and closes the cycle of manifestation of the Word... .'[433] Given that Christ's mission was chronologically prior to Muhammad, the Prophet necessarily incorporates Jesus's message into his own, and therefore the two cannot be said to be in essential contradiction to each other.

Christian theologians who simply assume that Islam is a 'false' religion would do well to meditate upon Gamaliel's rule, as enunciated in *Acts* 5:39, for discerning whether Christianity was of God: 'But if it be of God, you cannot overthrow it, lest perhaps you be found even to fight against God. And they consented to him.' Indeed, the church fathers universally consented to the rightness of Gamaliel's criterion, and assessed the continued existence of the church as a divine confirmation of his argument. But the same criterion can be applied to Islam, not to mention the continuation of Judaism after Christianity's historical emergence. From an Islamic perspective, the very prolonged and continuing existence also of Hinduism, Zoroastrianism, Buddhism, various Native religions and the like, demonstrates their origin in divine revelation, and like the church, they cannot be destroyed by the gates of hell, that is, by the forces of decay, dissolution or death. In view of the countless praises of Jesus in the Qur'an, which demonstrate that Islam receives Jesus as the Christ, Christian theologians should at the very least grant the applicability of the following gospel maxim to Islam: 'And whosoever shall receive me, receiveth not me, but him that sent me... . And John, answering, said: Master, we saw a certain man casting out devils in thy name, and we forbade him, because he followeth not with us. And Jesus said to him: Forbid him not; for he that is not against you, is for you' (*Luke* 9:48-50).

There is another startling biblical passage that has far-reaching implications for the thesis of the providential diversity of religions, a passage sorely neglected by Christian theologians for most of the last two millennia when the subject of non-Christian religions has arisen. The passage in question is *Isaiah* 44:28-45:1-14, which concerns the Persian king Cyrus the Great, a faithful Zoroastrian.[434] *Isaiah* 45:1 was used in the early church (see the *Letter of Barnabas* chapter 12) as a messianic prophecy by changing Κυρω to Κυριω, so that the Hebrew text, 'Thus saith the Lord to my anointed Cyrus,' became in Greek, 'Thus saith the Lord to my Christ the Lord.'[435] *Isaiah* 45:2, addressed to Cyrus, was similarly used in the early church (see the *Letter of Barnabas* 11:4, *Odes of Solomon* 17:8-11) as a prophecy of Christ's liberation of the souls in hell during his *descensus ad inferos*: 'I will go before thee, and will humble the great ones of the earth; I will break in pieces the gates of brass, and will burst the bars of iron.'[436] *Isaiah* 45:8's denomination of Cyrus as divine justice and salvation was adapted in the Catholic liturgy for Advent as a prophecy of Christ as 'the just one' who would 'rain down' from heaven, and the 'saviour' who would 'bud forth' from the 'opened earth'. The theological implications of a devout Zoroastrian king who made the faith of Zoroaster the official state religion of the Persian empire[437] serving as a symbol and type of the church's Messiah and Lord can simply not be ignored.

The first major implication to be drawn from the *Isaiah* Cyrus passage is that Cyrus's Zoroastrian God Ahura Mazda ('Lord of Wisdom') is equivalent to Israel's YHWH, for even though Cyrus worships Ahura Mazda, the *Isaiah* passage states that the Persian king is YHWH's shepherd (i.e., king; 44:28), anointed (i.e., Messiah; 45:1), justice (or 'just one'), and salvation (or 'saviour'; 45:8). Moreover, the nations that Cyrus conquers with God's assistance will honour and supplicate no one but Cyrus by confessing to the Persian king: 'Only with thee is God, and there is no God besides him.'

That YHWH says to Cyrus in *Isaiah* 45:5, 'thou hast not known me,' cannot in any way be construed as meaning that Cyrus does not know the true religion, or that Cyrus's God Ahura Mazda is not the true God. First of all, the passage never attacks the Zoroastrian religion; secondly, Cyrus never converted to Judaism, yet 45:14 clearly says that the true God is with Cyrus alone. Thirdly, from a traditional Catholic exegetical and liturgical perspective, Cyrus's 'ignorance' must ultimately be understood in a limited, accidental or extrinsic sense, for the entire *Isaiah* passage has been interpreted by the church in its patristic and liturgical heritage as referring prophetically to Christ, who is a manifestation of the very knowledge of God. The passage simply implies that Cyrus did not know God as source of political and military victory before God concretely revealed himself as such to Cyrus in or by means of the accomplishment, in history, of such victory. Cyrus's ignorance is no different from that which can be attributed prophetically to Israel itself under certain limited circumstances; it has to do not with ignorance of the truth, but with a fuller revelation of God to an individual already within a religion sanctioned by Heaven. And by implication, in the *Isaiah* Cyrus passage, both Zoroastrianism and Judaism would seem to be divinely sanctioned.

Support for our interpretation is not lacking in traditional Catholic sources. As early as 1915, Catholic authors recognized that *Isaiah* 44-45 implied the equivalence of the Zoroastrian Ahura Mazda and the Israelite YHWH.[438] Nicholas of Cusa in his *De pace fidei* writes that Zoroastrianism is a divinely revealed religion.[439] Zoroaster lived *ca.*1400–1200 BCE, whereas the Babylonian exile of the Jews occurred in the 6th century BCE.[440] Modern research sees Persian Zoroastrian influences in Jewish biblical literature composed after the Jewish exile to Babylon, where and when Judaism acquired much of its advanced angeology, demonology and apocalyptic theological themes in general.[441]

Isaiah 45:9-10, in condemning those who would question God's ways and sovereign choices by contesting Cyrus's messianic status, indeed the only 'pagan' ever to be called 'Messiah' in the Hebrew scriptures, suggests that for some it was scandalous to assert that a 'heathen' king could be the Messiah of God. This traditional biblical Jewish universalist inclusivism remains operative today, as witnessed by the following statement of Ruth Langer published in a recent interfaith edition of a major English-language Catholic theological journal. Langer comments on 'Christianity's teaching that its way is the universally true path to salvation': 'From a Jewish perspective, such an assertion is actually a limitation on God's omnipotence... . Judaism can understand other religions, and especially Christianity and Islam, also to be God's communications of divine will to the world.'[442]

The second major implication of the *Isaiah* 44-45 Cyrus passage becomes evident when we remember that the Zoroastrian Ahura Mazda is not a Semitic, but an Indo-European conception of God. Zoroastriansim can in one sense be historically viewed as a variant, or 'reform' of Hinduism as embodied in the ancient *Rigveda*. Despite various cultural and mythic differences, Ahura Mazda is essentially the equivalent of other chief deity conceptions belonging to additional Indo-European descent groups, such as the Greek Zeus, the Roman Jupiter, and the Scandinavian and Germanic Odin, etc. These are all merely culturally different versions or names of the same deity known as Ahura Mazda in Zoroastrianism, who is, as is implied in *Isaiah* 44-45, none other than YHWH. This is the essential import of *Isaiah* 45:5, according to which God declares to His Messiah Cyrus the Zoroastrian: 'I am YHWH, and there is none else: there is no God besides me.' Thus Ahura Mazda, and by logical associative extension, Zeus, Jupiter, Odin and further parallels, are in essence but culturally variant equivalents to YHWH.

The Sufis concede that as long as 'polytheism' is understood as a polymorphous affirmation of the divine unity, it can be reconciled with monotheism. The problem with polytheism arises when it is forgotten that the various 'gods' were created by the one supreme Creator, just as the angels are understood in Judaism, Christianity and Islam to have been created by God. If the angels or 'gods' are recognized as created entities, then the worship they receive is a relative, not an absolute worship; the latter is reserved for God alone. The same applies to sacred images. If, as in Catholicism and Eastern Orthodoxy, a statue or icon is honoured not *as such*, or as an end in itself, but as pointing beyond the physical object to the transcendent reality which it represents, then the use of sacred images, according to Christian theology, can be justified, and they cannot therefore be condemned *per se* or intrinsically.[443] If the purely symbolic status of images is forgotten, they become the 'idols' which prophets have traditionally censured. After these preliminary statements, we can understand how YHWH's Messiah Cyrus the Zoroastrian, although belonging to a religion which itself shuns the literal or absolute worship of idols, nevertheless after conquering Babylon in 539 BCE returned to their owners all the 'idols' which had been plundered and transported previously to Babylon by the vanquished authorities.[444]

From a Qur'anic perspective, because God sent messengers establishing religions among every people, the diversity of religions is divinely willed and therefore providential; indeed, Shi'i traditions enumerate 124,000 world prophets, of which 313 were Messengers who founded a religion.[445] As Schuon argues, if only one religion were true, 'the arguments put forward on behalf of this religion would not be so feeble, nor those of certain so-called "infidels" so powerful... .'[446] Similarly, 'that God could have allowed a religion that was merely the invention of a man [Muhammad] to conquer a part of humanity and to maintain itself for more than a thousand years in a quarter of the inhabited world ... , is contrary to the Laws of Divine Mercy... .'[447] As the same writer prefaces this passage, God's 'nature, as theology is far from being unaware, can be "terrible" but not monstrous.'[448]

Basing our exposition upon general Schuonian lines, we can survey the historical unfolding of the three Abrahamic religions and their complementary interconnectedness in the following manner. Judaism, generally speaking, is firstly an exoteric phenomenon – exoteric in a completely pejorative-free sense – in that it proclaimed the Unity of God in clear terms accessible to human reason, the Creator being logically and rationally deducible from the creation. In addition to the divine Unity, the exoteric doctrine of the future Messiah received increasing emphasis, but in the end excluded Jesus of Nazareth as the fulfillment of Messianic expectations. Judaism admittedly possessed an accompanying esoteric Kabbalah (literally, 'tradition') containing teachings on a polymorphous emanational expression of the divine Unity. The Kabbalah had ancient, especially apocalyptic roots, which attained formal fullness, however, only in the medieval period. By contrast, Christianity began as a religion that publicly proclaimed *esoteric* doctrines of divine Union (e.g., incarnation and trinity), while integrating the Jewish exoteric concept of the Messiah into the ecclesiastical doctrine of the divine triune union. Whereas Judaism proclaimed the divine Unity exoterically and the polymorphous emanational formulation of the divine Union esoterically, Christianity exoterically taught the esoteric doctrine of the triune divine Union. Admittedly, it was only after the early *lex arcani* was relaxed and then suspended in the church that Christianity later reformulated its esoteric mysteries of incarnation and trinity as publicly and rationally exposited dogmas. Lastly, in Islam, the exoteric doctrine of the divine Unity regains, as in Judaism, central place, while simultaneously integrating the Jewish doctrine of the Messiah by accepting the Christhood and Prophethood of Jesus of Nazareth, which were excluded in Judaism. In Islam, the doctrine of the 'polymorphous' divine Union in contrast to the 'simple' divine Unity is propounded by the Sufis at the esoteric, metaphysical level.

Thus, in Judaism, the exoteric divine Unity is central; in Christianity, the esoteric divine Union is predominant exoterically, the divine Unity secondary; in Islam, the exoteric divine Unity is restored to central significance, along with an exoteric acceptance of the prophet Jesus and his mother the Virgin Mary, the latter's son constituting a central inspiration for esoteric Sufi spirituality, in which Jesus is honoured as the Seal of Saints. In this way, Islam recapitulates in itself the messianism of Judaism along with strict Mosaic monotheism. At this point we should note that Jewish kabbalism, obeying an intuitive instinct, ascribes the origin of a polymorphous emanational affirmation of the divine Unity to Abraham. Aside from the question of historicity, the earliest classic exposition of the sefirot, *Sefer Yetzirah* (*The Book of Creation*), is attributed to Abraham.[449] Thus the Abrahamic exoteric proclamation of the divine Unity was accompanied by an Abrahamic esoteric polymorphous emanational tradition. In Judaism, under Moses, the exoteric declaration is maintained, while the esoteric polymorphous implications were increasingly developed with the passage of time. This development reached a climax, or was polarized as it were in Christianity, making the Jewish esoteric teaching of Union become, in a sense, 'exoteric' and primary, while simultaneously transposing the truth of Unity to the position of a secondary theological concern.

As Schuon astutely realized, it is at times necessary for the esoteric to become exoteric, in order to re-establish or maintain a certain spiritual equilibrium. The church's teaching on the polymorphous expression of divine Union, or trinitarian dogma, obviously spoke to the world to which the message was addressed. But after the establishment of the church's corrective equilibrium, with the rise of Islam the world saw what was exoteric in Christianity return in Islam to its 'primordial' Abrahamic state of the esoteric, and the church's secondary concern of the divine Unity regain a central emphasis, again as in the 'primordial' Abrahamic matrix. And given the fact that the preaching of the divine Unity entails an exoteric dogma accessible to unaided human reason, as opposed to the highly involved and philosophically complicated esoteric mystery of trinity,[450] which according to the church forever remains essentially beyond human reason, the swift spread of Islam after Muhammad, and again in our own day, is eminently comprehensible. This of course is not to deny that even the divine Unity entails mysteries which eons of human reflection could never fully articulate; but nevertheless, the concept of Unity being more primary than that of Union, the former is, though not 'self-evident', at least deducible by human reason without special revelation, in the sense that St. Paul says in his *Letter to the Romans* 1:20: 'For the invisible things of him from the creation of the world are clearly seen, being understood by the things that are made. His eternal power also and divinity: so that they are inexcusable.' This is an argument the Apostle to the Gentiles borrows from the Jewish *Book of Wisdom* chapter 13:1 and 5. Verse 1: 'But all men are vain, in whom there is not the knowledge of God: and who by these good things that are seen, could not understand him that is, neither by attending to the works have acknowledged who was the workman.' Verse 5: 'For by the greatness of the beauty, and of the creature, the creator of them may be seen, so as to be known thereby.'

Here we should further explicate the assertion that, even though at the beginning it was certainly not fully hidden, the esoteric in Christianity was nevertheless not publicly dogmatic before the suspension of the ancient *lex arcani*, which according to the general teaching of Dionysius had its justification not merely as a discretionary posture in a time of persecution, but also and most fundamentally as an indispensable property of an apophatically inclined negative theology, given that the absolute mysteries of faith remain beyond an exhaustive comprehension by human reason. Regarding the earliest period in the church, Karl Rahner notes, 'the NT authors, obeying an "instinct" which they feel no need to question, refuse to give a "rational" explanation to the mystery of the triune Father, Son, and Spirit.'[451] The New Testament authors, operating within a Semitic thought milieu, felt no need to explicate the triune mystery along Greek ontological lines. Dionysius, though admittedly employing Greek philosophy, was permeated with the sense of biblical, Semitic 'mystery' in his exploration of the trinity. The later church councils operated predominantly in the thought-world of Hellenism, not of biblical Semitism. As such, the council formulations could not but speak primarily to only a particular culture and mentality.

One might also consider the following point made by Hans Küng: 'Now it is no secret that neither Jews nor Muslims have been enlightened by the distinctions in God used by Christians in the doctrine of the Trinity (three persons, but one nature).'[452] Neither should we forget that the conciliar definitions were the result of the church engaging in dialogue with Hellenistic culture in an attempt to convince Greco-Roman humanity of the truth of Christianity by employing their native philosophical concepts. The councils were thus in a certain sense a sort of missionary outreach to the Greco-Roman world. History has amply demonstrated that the councils do not adequately clarify questions of christology and divine unity for a Jewish or Islamic perspective. We recall in this context an observation made by Frithjof Schuon: 'A typical feature of the monotheistic exoterisms is their dogmatization of theological speculations ... ; it would suffice in many a case to let the scriptural enunciations stand as they are, in a holy indetermination... .'[453] As the same author writes: 'The formal homogeneity of a religion requires not only truth but also errors – though these are only in the form – just as the world requires evil and as Divinity implies the mystery of creation by virtue of its infinity.'[454] To explain the various shortcomings or near-sightedness of councils and dogmas, theologians all too easily resort to assertions about a supposed spiritual 'blindness' on the part of non-Christians. We by no means imply that the church should abandon any of the doctrines revealed to her by heaven, representing as they do valid dogmas arrived at through centuries of philosophical investigation and intellective labour. What we suggest is that, just as the Catholic and Eastern Orthodox churches at certain points in history cancelled their mutual excommunications of each other, so the Great Church one day might find advisable a similar conciliatory move towards non-Pauline Jewish Christianity, a variant of Christian faith which in fact constitutes an archetypal bridge between Judaism and Islam.

If it be objected that the church's mission to Judaism was unsuccessful from the very beginning, as recorded in the *Book of Acts*, even at a time when she was still principally Jewish Christian culturally and theologically, then one need simply be reminded that the story of the failures of the early church with Judaism is only one side of the story. The *Book of Acts* also tells us that thousands of Jews entered the church in its early days, including countless priests. Of course, none of these Jews viewed their entering the church as a 'conversion' to a religion different than Judaism. The true friction between Christianity and Judaism began with Paul and his conflicts with the Jewish-Christian leadership of Jerusalem, which in turn led to the problem of the church's mission to Judaism. After these negative encounters Paul concluded that all Israel will be 'saved' (*Romans* 11:26) only at the eschaton; but then, of course, not even Christianity will exist as a world religion in the eschatological 'era'. Following the Pauline trajectory, the Great Church early on abandoned the mission to Judaism, in line with Paul's eschatological paradigm. Jewish Christianity, however, was in a far better position for dialogue with Judaism well past the first century CE. But its being stigmatized along with Jews by the Great Church led to the decline of Jewish Christianity, even though the latter did survive in various regions, and some elements of its heritage may still be found in various Islamic written sources, above all in various Jesus *ahadith*.

The later conciliar deliberations necessarily excluded the Semitic approach and understanding, because Jewish Christianity *en toto* had been so misunderstood as to be excommunicated from the 'Gentile' church. From this point of view, the 'ecumenical' aspect of the christological and trinitarian councils is seen to be somewhat truncated, and thus problematically relativized. Of course this does not mean that the councils were not authoritative; but it does imply that their articulations are not as effective in conveying its truths to non-Greco-Roman cultures. This does not necessarily have to be taken in any negative sense at all, for one could argue that, just as the early church saw no problem in simultaneously allowing Gentiles not to observe the Mosaic prescriptions and the Jewish Christians to maintain their Torah observance, so the later councils, almost completely dominated by Hellenistic thought, though valid for the Gentile Christians, should nevertheless not be thrust upon Jewish Christianity.

This is not to deny that there are universal concerns that either Gentile or Jewish Christianity could address at the conciliar level, it is only to maintain that the New Testament model of theological unity in diversity, not outward uniformity, remains a valid praxis model.

The above is not intended to imply that Judaism and Islam, the 'Semitic' Abrahamic variants (Semitic at least as to historical origins and the languages of their sacred scriptures), are not capable of philosophical and rational discourse. However, in these two religions the philosophical speculation regarding the nature of God remains, as in Dionysius, at the esoteric, metaphysical level, as in Kabbalism and Sufism, and not at the 'conciliar' or dogmatic level, and this despite the fact of the integration by Judaism and Islam of Greek philosophy (primarily Plato, Aristotle, Plotinus and Proclus). This esoteric approach is in agreement with the Semitic, biblical ethos of profound awe and reverential reserve in the face of the transcendent reality of the Divine Unity and Union.

It could rightly be said that the church basically presents esoteric doctrines in an exoteric mode, and that this trajectory was polarized with the abandonment of the ancient *lex arcani*, a somewhat questionable, even if perhaps necessary, development, given that the doctrines of incarnation and trinity remain mysteries of the faith even after their revelation by God. As Benedict XVI grants, Christians have taken these dogmas far too literally and without enough reserve. According to von Balthasar's articulation, Maximus the Confessor, for example, criticizes Jewish monotheism – which ironically was, after all, the faith of Christ himself – as static, while praising the 'dynamism' of Greek polytheism.[455] Though the Sufis have conceded that polytheism can be a legitimate polymorphous affirmation of the divine Unity, they do not criticize monotheism, but merely apply a generous *pia et modesta interpretatio* to polytheism under certain strict conditions. Therefore, Maximus's feeling that the trinity is a sort of synthesis of the 'static' monotheism of Judaism and the dynamism of polytheism remains disconcerting from the position of traditional monotheism. The possibility that such a formal spiritual disequilibrium could appear in a church father justifies Schuon's statement that Christianity cannot lay claim to the same centrality of the doctrine of the divine Unity as Islam can.[456] This should be evident in even a non-pejorative sense, given that in the church Union is stressed much more than Unity. Indeed, Christianity's focus on Union is the distinctive trait which distinguishes it from the other Abrahamic religions, constituting the church's very reason for existence.

In any event, to describe Jewish (or Islamic) monotheism as non-dynamic simply does not agree with the facts as reflected in the scriptures, theology and metaphysics of the Abrahamic faiths. In Judaism, the very fact that God creates implies a dynamic Divine Unity. This is the very function of personified Wisdom in the Hebrew scriptures, namely, to be the 'medium' of creation. Who could ever describe Philo's God as non-dynamic? Certainly the

Jewish Kabbalah also operates within the framework of a profoundly dynamic doctrine of monotheism. The Samaritan theologian Marqa's conception of God was as vitally dynamic as Philo's,[457] as the following statement indicates: 'In the Primordial Silence, Thou didst germinate (וטעה) words which generated creations. Thy powers are the fruit of Thy mind (Hymn I *vv.* 2-3).'[458] The Islamic understanding of monotheism is as non-static and dynamic as Judaism's.

The Sunni Islamic orthodox professions of faith speak of God's Word as an eternal, uncreated divine attribute. The distinctively Islamic semantic nuance of the Word as 'uncreated and eternal' could possibly semantically encompass the sense of the phrases that the Word was 'eternally created', or 'created in eternity, outside of time', so that the Word may nevertheless not be said in a certain sense to have been 'created'. The dialectical tension of 'created yet not created' cannot but fail to remind one of the church's teaching on the eternal generation of the Son, who is said to have been 'begotten, not made'. Even though the classical Islamic professions of faith had integrated Greek philosophical concepts, these Muslim creeds incorporated Greek thought along *functional* paradigms, so that the functional term 'eternally created' could possibly be equivalent to the ontic or ontological term 'begotten, not made'. But though the two phrases are equivalent, they cannot be reduced to each other or be made to exist undifferentiatedly in Islam and the church. To be sure, Islam allows the language of 'generation', yet only in metaphysical or esoteric mode, and not as exoteric dogma. For instance, the Sufi Fakhruddin 'Iraqi teaches, as William C. Chittick and Peter Lamborn Wilson summarize, that the Prophet as Logos 'is "generated" … at least in his external form… .' He is 'generated' in the sense of 'created', because 'he is a creature and not the Creator. And he is "all-comprehensive" because he embraces, quite literally, all things, from "God" to the tiniest atom.' Thus Muhammad is not to be completely identified with the Perfect Man as such, for strictly speaking, Muhammad is a 'manifestation' of the Perfect Man.[459] Such a qualification agrees in essence with Thomas Aquinas's insistence that the created human nature of Jesus cannot be simplistically or exhaustively identified with the eternal, uncreated divine attribute or 'person' of the Logos or 'Son'.

Thus the Sufis go so far as to associate the divine attribute of the Word with the person of Muhammad, so that they speak of the pre-existent *Nur Muhammadi* ('Muhammadan light') as the model from which God created the universe. Seyyed Hossein Nasr expresses this exalted view by distinguishing between the outward and inward realties of Muhammad: 'The Prophet is outwardly only a human being (*bashar*), but … [h]e is inwardly identified with the Logos and the Divine Intellect.'[460] Ibn al-'Arabi's philosophy contains a theology of God, Logos and creation that is every bit as dynamic as Philo and the Kabbalah, for Ibn al-'Arabi posits a 'First Entification' which he also calls the Perfect Man (or Universal Man), through which God creates the cosmos.[461]

If one counters that Philo does not represent 'normative' Judaism and that the Kabbalah represents only later, medieval Judaism, both contentions are questionable. The old distinction between 'Hellenistic' Judaism as divergent from 'normative' or even Palestinian Judaism, is untenable, and arose only after post-70 CE rabbinic Judaism distanced itself from certain 'mythic' (we do not use 'myth' in a pejorative sense) Jewish theological ideas emphasized by the church herself as a Jewish phenomenon.[462] As far as the Kabbalah is concerned, the last two generations of scholarship, represented mainly by Gershom Scholem and now Moshe Idel,[463] have established that its ultimate chronological roots are ancient, not medieval, and that it derives primarily from Jewish apocalyptic traditions and Jewish theosophical speculation, and not chiefly from Greek philosophy, though the latter was certainly integrated at various stages, often in more functional than ontic or ontological modes.

Some of the similarities between Greek philosophy and Jewish Kabbalah are to be traced back not to a direct borrowing by the Kabbalah from Greek philosophy, but rather to the fact that there was a mutual interpenetration between ancient Near Eastern culture (which would encompass the Semitic groups) and Indo-European descent groups (which would encompass the origins of later 'Greek' thought). Thus the latest scholarship correctly recognizes that some ideas that were formerly held to be Greek in origin are instead Near Eastern; in other instances, however, we cannot always sharply distinguish between ancient Near Eastern and Indo-European ideas. When we are faced with parallels between the Hebrew scriptures and Greek mythology – the *nephilim* of *Genesis* 6 and the Greek Titans (or even the equivalent Norse giants, the *Jötnar*), for instance – the Greek myth might be in part the result of influences from Near Eastern lore. Similarly, the later Greek idea of emanation to explain creation or the origin of the divine hypostases, may also be the result of a later distinct Greek reformulation of an originally ancient Near Eastern idea – an idea also found in Egyptian thought. Thus some of the most recent scholarship on the *Corpus Hermeticum* has moved away from the earlier thesis of a predominantly Hellenistic syncretistic philosophical matrix in favour of what the texts themselves claim, namely, a fundamentally Egyptian thought provenance. To counter that ancient Egypt was itself inundated with Greek philosophical influence once again misses the point that Greek culture and thought had been profoundly influenced by contact with Near Eastern ideas at an earlier stage. We have the situation where the Near Eastern *Epic of Gilgamesh* has very probably influenced Homer, and Homer may likely have influenced some passages of the Hebrew and Christian scriptures, though such influence would necessarily stem from archetypal forces rather than mere 'historical' influences. This is of course a subject plagued by the problems of indirect reconstruction, at times reaching back even to prehistoric eras, but the evidence is by no means negligible.[464]

To try to put some of the theological tensions between the three Abrahamic variants into a wider perspective, here we will offer a variety of speculative observations on the import of the trinitarian titles of Father, Son and Holy Spirit as *metaphorically* related to the ternary historical unfolding of Abrahamic monotheism. That the Father is emphasized in Judaism is clear enough. That the Son is the central emphasis of the church is equally as clear. The Son, as begotten, of course presupposes the Father as origin, as stressed in the Eastern Orthodox theology of divine paternal transcendence. But the Son also implies the Holy Spirit, and here it is important to realize that at the New Testament level the fullness of the Holy Spirit's mission in the world is reserved for the post-Son phase of history. That is, as taught in his farewell discourses (*Gospel of John* chapters 14-16), only after Christ's departure would the Holy Spirit be sent as the Paraclete to lead the church into the fullness of truth. We are not referring here to three different economies of salvation, but merely to three related yet distinct periods, manifestations and modes of a single divine salvific economy. What in any case cannot be denied is that from Christ's own perspective in history, the era of the Spirit was reserved for the future.

At this point, we can no longer avoid an investigation of Islam's claim that Muhammad was, in some sense at least, the Paraclete promised by Christ. Can this claim be taken realistically in any sense that would be acceptable to Christian theology of any stripe? Schuon remarks that Christ symbolically identified the historical destruction of Jerusalem with the eschatological last judgment, the result of the Messiah's 'synthetic' or 'essential and absolute' viewpoint. In regard to the subtle non-identitative relationship existing between the historical and eschatological events in question, Schuon posits a similar relationship existing between the heavenly descent of the Holy Spirit and the earthly coming of Muhammad. Both events 'embrace simultaneously ... all the modes of Paracletic manifestation, among others, therefore, the manifestation of the Prophet Muhammad, who was none other than the personification of the Paraclete or the cyclic manifestation of the latter; moreover, the Qur'an, like the appearance of the Holy Ghost at Pentecost, is called a "descent" (*tanzil*).'[465]

Elsewhere, Schuon reinforces his contention that the Paraclete is not to be identified exhaustively, or in every sense, with Muhammad, for 'the passages referring to the Paraclete must inevitably concern him – not exclusively but eminently... .'[466] Now, as long as the distinction between the Christly and Paracletic ages by no means presupposes two separate economies of salvation, Schuon's point, in common with Massignon's propositions, would not stand in contradiction to the Christian understanding of the unicity of the salvific economy. In any event, because according to Christ the complete truth will be revealed only *after* him by the Paraclete, in a certain sense we may say that Christ does not bring the definitive revelation, or possibly better, the definitive *articulative form* of revelation; that is reserved for the Paraclete; or alternatively, the definitive revealer of fully articulated truth is not Jesus but the Paraclete, who admittedly speaks in the name of Jesus, so that again we are not positing – indeed cannot posit – in this context two different salvific economies.

In the New Testament the promised Paraclete is the Holy Spirit, who descended 'publicly' upon the church, according to Luke's historicizing account, on the first Pentecost after Christ's exaltation to God's right hand; but according to John's gospel, the Spirit was in fact initially bestowed upon the church on the day of Christ's resurrection. Now, if the Paraclete's mission is to teach all truth, could not Christian theology concede that, in so far as Muhammad taught the truths of the divine Unity and the Christhood of Jesus of Nazareth, the Arabian Prophet participated – outside the visible structure of the church to be sure – in the Paracletic ministry? But perhaps we could go even beyond this merely minimal concession, by asserting that Muhammad's emphasis on the divine Unity offered a needed corrective to certain Christian theologians' disequilibrium in their exposition of the dogmas of incarnation and trinity. Muhammad's teaching, after all, preserves the truth of Jesus of Nazareth's created human nature and the truth of monotheism, and thus offers a corrective to those theologians who saw in Christ only a divine nature, and whose trinitarian theology was closer to tritheism than a validly triune or polymorphous affirmation of monotheism.

Recalling Schuon's view that even though Christ's promise of the Paraclete applies to Muhammad 'eminently', it nevertheless does not do so 'exclusively', we may interpret Schuon as implying that while the Prophet embraces or encompasses the Paracletic mission, he does not exhaust it; which is to say that Muhammad eminently fulfills the promise, but that there are others who share in the Paracletic mission, though not in the same way or in the same sense as Muhammad. But because the Prophet did not set himself up as a rival to Jesus, but rather presented himself as merely reaffirming Christ's message (the Paraclete, Christ said, 'will speak of me'), we may in a fuller sense assert that Muhammad participated in the Paracletic mission in a 'Christly' mode; 'Christly' as referring to the Messiah's chronologically anterior teaching activity. In fact, at a purely historical level, Muhammad's teaching 'eminently' accords with Christ's description of the Paraclete's 'convicting' message of 'sin, justice, and judgment' (*John* 16:8), as anyone will recognize who has even cursorily read the Qur'an with its constant dual theme of good news and judgment. One also thinks in this context of the Qur'an's consistently 'combative' tone, which at least on the direct level is fully understandable and indeed to be expected, given the intense historical and social conflicts that accompanied the Prophet's mission and career. In *John* 16:9 it is said, 'Of sin: because they believed not in me'; accordingly, one of Muhammad's central teachings is the condemnation of those who knowingly in bad faith reject Jesus as Messiah (not of course implying that all did so knowingly and in bad faith).

Here we should cite the Qur'anic prophecy of Jesus concerning the coming of Muhammad. Qur'an 61:6: 'And when Jesus son of Mary said: O Children of Israel! Lo! I am the messenger of Allah unto you, confirming that which was (revealed) before me in the Torah, and bringing good tidings of a messenger who cometh after me, whose name is the Praised One [= *Ahmad*].' Later Islamic theology was correct to situate this verse in relation to the sayings of Jesus concerning the promised Paraclete, though we do not imply that Muhammad had read the words as recorded in John's gospel. In any event, Islamic theologians claim that John's *parakletos* ('comforter') is a mistranslation or falsification of *paraklutos* ('praised one), the latter being equivalent to the Qur'an's 'Ahmad', one of Muhammad's names. In all fairness, it should be observed that there is no need to speak of mistranslation or corruption of scriptures here, for what we have instead is a perfectly legitimate practice of ancient Semitic wordplay that is most well known as a Jewish phenomenon (gematria and related techniques), but which is also present in Islam as arithmomancy and is called *'ilm al-huruf* and *hisab al-jummal*.[467] *Paraklutos* is, in other words, an inspired play on the word *Parakletos*, reflecting a 'prophetic' phenomenon also present in the New Testament, where we find verses from the Hebrew scriptures interpreted creatively and expansively as prophecies of the Messiah's birth, life and earthly ending. Some Old Testament verses are quoted so freely in the New Testament that in several instances scholars cannot agree among themselves when deciding upon which Hebrew verse a particular New Testament citation might be based.

As such, gematria and related procedures have a limited convincing value outside the faith community that formulates them, as history shows rather clearly in Christianity's non-acceptance of Qur'an 61:6's Christly prophecy of Muhammad, and in Judaism's non-acceptance of the New Testament's incorporation of Hebrew 'prophetic texts' as referring to events in Christ's life. To ascribe the rejection of such use of texts to bad faith and hardness of heart is psychologically unconvincing and theologically too convenient. Prophecy texts are not intended to function as 'proof texts' in isolation from the general theological justifications of a given religion. In other words, prophecy texts must be used along with other evidentiary considerations which usually assume their full function and force only when combined with additional elements of theology and metaphysics.

To return to the question of the Paraclete, *John* 15:26 and 27 closely associate the themes of Paraclete and bearing witness: 'But when the Paraclete cometh, whom I will send you from the Father, the Spirit of truth, who proceedeth from the Father, he shall give testimony (μαρτυρηοει) of me. And you shall give testimony (μαρτυρειτε), because you are with me from the beginning.' This thematic linking together of Paraclete and 'witness' is intriguing, because whereas the targum to *Job* 16:19 translates the Hebrew word for 'witness', *'ed*

(LXX, *martys*), as Aramaic *mesahda*, the same figure who witnesses for Job in heaven is translated in the Aramaic targum to *Job* in 16:20 and 33:23 by the Greek loan word *peraqlêta*, demonstrating that Paraclete and 'witness' were interchangeable concepts in early Jewish tradition.[468] To return at this point to John 16:14, 'to glorify' in biblical Hebrew would most likely be represented by כבד (*kabêd*), giving us at least a terminal phonetic similarity to the Hebrew word for 'witness', עד (*'êd*). The Johannine association of Paraclete = Witness and 'glorify', might thus qualify as a possible constellation for understanding Qur'an 61:6, despite the difference in John's Paraclete as actively glorifying another and the Qur'an's Ahmad as the one who is glorified or praised by others. Though we have no precise phonetic equivalent (in any case such is not required in gematria), there is an intriguing overlap in radicals and vowels in the Aramaic *mesahda* or *mshd'*, as the word appears in the prayer of Elchasai (*c.* 100 CE),[469] and 'Ahmad', not to mention the fuller form of 'Muhammad'.

In any event, Qur'an 61:6 does not say that the promised messenger will be called 'Muhammad', but 'Ahmad', which as Schuon says, is one of Muhammad's heavenly or spiritual names.[470] We therefore would appear not to have a prophecy directly concerning the historical advent of Muhammad, but a prophecy relating to his inward assimilation to the Logos in a Paracletic mode. A fluidity between Logos and Spirit-Paraclete is reflected in Paul's theology, where he writes that 'the Lord', who is the Logos, 'is the Spirit' (*2 Corinthians* 3:17). If we say that some Islamic exegetes have not sufficiently noted the 'spiritual' or 'inward' aspect of 'Ahmad', we must in fairness grant that in general, Christian theologians have not recognized the possibility of a human prophetic dimension in St. John's Paraclete. The name and reality of 'Ahmad' has an application that is both spiritual and human, or inward and outward (Paraclete/Ahmad and Muhammad); and the Paraclete denotes both the divine Holy Spirit and by extension the Spirit's prophetic messengers. We have already noted in this study that Eastern Orthodox Bishop George Khodr posits a reciprocal and secret prophetic bond between Christ and Muhammad. One could suggest that just as the Logos is not to be exhaustively identified with Jesus of Nazareth, so the Paraclete is not to be exhaustively identified with Muhammad; or positively stated, just as there is a profound unity between the Logos and Jesus, so there is a profound unity, along different lines of mode and manifestation, between the Paraclete and Muhammad. The Prophet of Islam manifests, but does not exhaust, the reality and mission of the Paraclete.

Regarding the variations between the messengers of the Abrahamic faiths, if we recall that Moses gave the Torah, which governed religious and social-legal life, we may then appreciate the significance of the fact that Christ did not deliver a law of such comprehensive detail. As Aquinas states in his *Summa theologiae* Part I. II, q. 108, art. 2:

[T]he New Law had to make only such prescriptions or prohibitions as are essential for the reception or right use of grace. And since we cannot of ourselves obtain grace, but through Christ alone, hence Christ of himself instituted the sacraments whereby we obtain grace.... .
The right use of grace is by means of works of charity. These, in so far as they are essential to virtue, pertain to the moral precepts, which also formed part of the Old Law. Hence, in this respect, the New Law had nothing to add as regards external action. The determination of these works in their relation to the divine worship, belongs to the ceremonial precepts of the Law; and, in relation to our neighbour, to the judicial precepts, as stated above. And therefore, since these determinations are not in themselves necessarily connected with inward grace wherein the Law consists, they do not come under a precept of the New Law, but are left to the decision of the people; when a matter relates strictly to us, the precept is left to an individual's own judgment; when a matter relates to the common good, the precept is left to superiors, temporal or spiritual.

Accordingly the New Law had no other external works to determine, by prescribing or forbidding, except the sacraments, and those moral precepts which have a necessary connection with virtue, for instance, that one must not kill, or steal, and so forth.[471]

In Part I. II, q. 107, art. 4, the angelic doctor pronounces similarly:

And in this respect the Old Law is a much heavier burden than the New: since the Old Law by its numerous ceremonies prescribed many more outward acts. The New Law, by contrast, in the teaching of Christ and the apostles, added very few precepts to those of the natural law; although after the apostolic era some laws were added by the fathers. But concerning these, Augustine warns that moderation should be observed, lest a Christian's life should become a burden again.[472] For Augustine says in reply to the queries of Januarius (*Ep.* lv) that, 'whereas God in His mercy wished the Christian religion to be a free religion, with only a small number of public sacraments, certain persons are now making it a slave's burden; so much so that the condition of the Jews was more tolerable. And the Jews were subject to the ordinances of the divine Law, and not to the presumptuous devices of man.

Not Christ, but the ecclesiastical authorities formed laws governing religious, and later, social-legal life; laws which they extrapolated from and based upon the Mosaic Law and the teaching of Christ. The fact that the main body of church law is an extrapolation rather than a direct gift of Christ may account for the constantly recurring disequilibrium in the church's history, involving legal casuistry and juridical extremism to the detriment of the spirit of the law. If one objects that casuistry also plagued Judaism in the time of Christ, even though Moses had directly bestowed the Law upon Judaism, one should not overlook the fact that historically Catholicism exceeded Judaism's 'legalism' both quantitatively and qualitatively. The church's thousands of canon law regulations (there were 2,414 in 1918) stand against the 613 'talmudic' laws, all of which were derived by the rabbis from the Torah, which the church also holds as sacred scripture.[473]

That Christ's teaching on divorce is not intended as an absolute social legislation (though it has implications for society), any more than his teaching on turning the other check cancels out 'an eye for an eye' in the social-legal realm, and was certainly not intended to abrogate the Mosaic law, is suggested by the church's own approval of the Pauline and Petrine marriage privileges, and the granting of annulments in general. Especially where royalty were concerned, the church was rather flexible throughout history in its ideas on marriage and divorce, usually in the interest of peace and social harmony, and this should not always be viewed a priori or per se as a manifestation of a hypocritical ecclesiastical double standard. Given the relative intentions and scope of Christ's 'social' teaching, it is understandable how Augustine could write in his treatise *On Faith and Works* ch. 19, that a woman who vows to remain faithful to her paramour might be granted baptism.[474]

Christ's divorce teaching certainly reflects and agrees with an ideal to be striven for, but being an 'ideal' which was only concretely existent in the protological Paradise, it will not be a concrete universal reality this side of the eschaton, when it will of course be manifested in a different operative mode (see *Luke* 20:35-36).

Indeed, at the level of praxis, the church not uncommonly has conceded dispensations, to be sure very discretely, to various local customs in missionary fields regarding not only divorce but polygamy as well. The fact is that in some cultures, entire social fabrics would have been destroyed, and entire peoples might have vanished had it not been for the limited allowances of divorce and polygamy, especially in warrior and nomadic societies. Again we note that the church has in practice at times relaxed her demands regarding polygamy in relation to Christian royalty. The case of Charlemegne is apropos here. Certainly polygamy was practiced by the Hebrew Patriarchs, so that its condemnation in later times must be seen as relative and not absolute.

One will note that the Qur'an does not strictly speaking command, but allows polygamy under certain conditions; indeed, the Qur'an cautions against, though not forbidding, having multiple wives. It is allowed in part as a social means of dealing with the poverty of orphans. Seyyed Hossein Nasr contends that 'Islam by legislating strict conditions for polygamy' greatly reduced the level of prostitution and poverty that otherwise would have existed in Arabian society.[475] As for divorce, though it is allowed, a *hadith* says that of all things allowed, divorce is the most hated by God.

In the end, we could summarize and say that Moses delivered a public law; Jesus delivered no such law, and the church was forced to form its own guidelines for a well-ordered society, with constant attendant disequilibrium; finally Muhammad synthesized the Mosaic and Christly approaches by giving a law covering not only religious life (as Christ did), but also public life (as Moses did). That Muhammad understood that the letter and the spirit of the law needed recognition may be deduced from the Qur'anic synthesis of the Mosaic and Christly teaching on revenge and forgiveness. A comparison of the following three texts will illustrate this aspect of the historically ternary nature of Abrahamic monotheism in the realm of ethics:

TORAH (*Exodus* 21:23-25): But if her death ensue thereupon he shall render life for life, Eye for eye, tooth for tooth, hand for hand, foot for foot, Burning for burning, wound for wound, stripe for stripe.

GOSPEL (*Matthew* 5:38-39): You have heard that it hath been said: An eye for an eye, and a tooth for a tooth. But I say to you not to resist evil: but if one strike thee on thy right cheek, turn to him also the other.

QUR'AN (Sura 5:45): And We prescribed for them [the Jews] therein [in the Torah]: The life for the life, and the eye for the eye, and the nose for the nose, and the ear for the ear, and the tooth for the tooth, and for wounds retaliation. But whoso forgoeth it (in the way of charity) it shall be expiation for him. Whoso judgeth not by that which Allah hath revealed: such are wrong-doers.

5:46: And We caused Jesus, son of Mary, to follow in their footsteps, confirming that which was (revealed) before him in the Torah, and We bestowed on him the Gospel wherein is guidance and a light, confirming that which was (revealed) before it in the Torah – a guidance and an admonition unto those who ward off (evil).

Here we see the synthetic approach of Islam, for what is stated as a thesis in the Torah, and then restated formally as an antithesis in the Gospel, is 'reconciled' by way of 'confirmatory' synthesis in the Qur'an. Just as Qur'an 5:46 states that the Gospel was a confirmation of the Torah, so 5:48 completes the cycle by declaring that the Qur'an is a confirmation of the earlier scriptures of Torah and Gospel. 5:48: 'And unto thee have We revealed the Scripture with the truth, confirming whatever Scripture was before it, and a watcher over it.' The aya ends by defining that 'For each [Jews, Christians, Muslims] We have appointed a divine law and a traced-out way. Had Allah willed He could have made you one community. But that He may try you by that which He hath given you (He hath made you as ye are). So vie one with another in good works. Unto Allah ye will all return, and He will then inform you of that wherein ye differ.' Here we have a profound explanation, already encountered in this study, of the providential diversity of religions and the guidelines for how each religion's members should respond to such diversity, namely, by a mutual competition in good works. As God 'will then inform you of that wherein ye differ' on the day of judgment, so St. Paul equivalently expresses in *1 Corinthians* 4:5: 'Therefore, judge not before the time: until the Lord come, who both will bring to light the hidden things of darkness and will make manifest the counsels of the hearts. And then shall every man have praise from God.'

The very fact of Muhammad's appearance *after* Christ, which at least historically justifies the Arabian Messenger's title of 'Seal of the Prophets', creates a certain theological tension between Islam and Christianity. If a Christian theologian recalls the Catholic distinction between the biblical canon and the deutero-canon, that is, between a primary and secondary canon, then could not one consider the parallel possibility of 'prophecy', or 'prophets', in contrast to 'deutero-prophecy', enabling one to refer to Muhammad, from a speculative Christian viewpoint at least, as a 'deutero-prophet', or even as *'the* deutero-Prophet', using the definite article in light of Muhammad's unique status as founder of the only post-Christian world religion revealed by Heaven, a religion that is not intended to replace, but to reaffirm the message of Christ? Since we have dealt with such tension already in this monograph, we will next examine how Frithjof Schuon has approached the problem of such Christian-Islamic tensions.

Displaying an impressive array of dialectical skills, Schuon argues that the mutual Christian and Islamic claims to revelational definitiveness by no means contradict each other in an absolute sense: 'Unquestionably, to say terminality is to say unique ... ; however, terminality can be defined according to different perspectives, and in this sense we shall say that if Christianity is the last word of God in the monotheistic cycle, it is so only in a certain respect, whereas Islam is in another.'[476] As Schuon elaborates: 'True terminality ... is not realized by any one religion as opposed to another, it is realized by esoterism in relation to all religion... .'[477]

Why should the church seek to convert Muslims to 'the faith of Christ' when the Islamic faith essentially coincides with that of the earliest Jewish Christians? This question is especially relevant in a time when Christian theologians concede that in the New Testament era uniformity of theological articulation not only did not exist, it was neither required nor even desirable; diversity of articulation of a single faith was moreover officially endorsed at the Council of Florence, when in 1439 an agreement was reached between the Catholic west and the Orthodox east, albeit temporarily, on the issue of the *filioque*. It can in any event be shown that Islamic christology profoundly overlaps with the New Testament True Prophet christology.[478] What is more, there can be little doubt that far more Muslims believe in the immaculate conception and virgin birth than do modern Christians in general. And if we view the trinitarian aspect of the great commission according to the 'economic' terms proposed in our discussion of Schuon's concept of the ternary nature of monotheism, then *Matthew* 28:19-20 takes on a surprisingly ecumenical character:[479] 'Going therefore, teach ye all nations: baptizing them in the name of the Father and of the Son and of the Holy Ghost. Teaching them to observe all things whatsoever I have commanded you. And behold I am with you all days, even to the consummation of the world.'

Here, Christ does not require or demand a teaching on the trinity along the lines of Greek ontology, but rather a baptism 'in the name', i.e., 'by the authority' of the Father, Son and Holy Spirit. And though even orthopraxis certainly involves issues of faith, Christ explicitly instructs the apostles to teach the world the *commandments* of Christ, which as the gospels of *Matthew* (22:37-40) and *John* (13:34) make clear, means above all the dual commandment to love God and one's neighbour, a two-fold commandment encompassing or fulfilling all other possible commandments. Consider Peter's speech in *Clementine Homilies* 17:7: 'Knowing therefore that we knew all that was spoken by him, and that we could supply the proofs, he sent us to the ignorant Gentiles to baptize them for remission of sins, and commanded us to teach them first. Of his commandments this is the first and great one, to fear the Lord God, and to serve Him only.' Indeed, Shem-Tob's Hebrew version of *Matthew* 28:19-20, in agreement with Eusebius, does not contain the trinitarian formula, but instead reads: 'Go and teach them to observe all things whatsoever I have commanded you to the consummation of the world.'[480] The teachings of Jesus certainly imply the 'economic' Father, Son and Holy Spirit, so that it does no good for opponents to argue that belief in the trinity must be a later ecclesiastical 'invention' since it *may* not have been in the original version of *Matthew*. Additionally, if one wishes to cite Karl Rahner, who correctly writes that modern exegesis does not consider *Matthew* 28:19-20 to be historically the words of Christ,[481] one must not at the same time avoid the question of *Matthew* 28's theological validity, which ultimately does not depend upon the issue of historicity but upon metaphysical truth.

The various gospel versions of the great commission direct that Christ's message be announced to all the world, or to every creature. The Qur'an agrees with the gospel in declaring that Jesus and Mary constitute a sign for all the worlds. Qur'an 21:91: 'And (remember) her who guarded her chastity: We breathed into her of Our spirit, and We made her and her son a sign for all the worlds.' Qur'an 21:107 similarly states that Muhammad is a mercy for all the worlds: 'We sent thee not save as a mercy for all the worlds.' Of course, from the Qur'anic perspective the message of Jesus and Muhammad, indeed, that of all previous prophets, was essentially the same, namely, the unity of God, with all that implies. Indeed, as the gospel is called a message of 'good tidings' requiring or presupposing a warning of repentance ('Repent and believe the good news,' *Mark* 1:15), so both Muhammad and the Qur'an are described as good tidings and a warning. The Qur'an is a 'Good tidings and a warning' (41:4) and Muhammad was commanded to preach: 'Serve none but Allah. Lo! I am unto you from Him a warner and a bringer of good tidings' (11:2). Admittedly, Qur'an 10:47 teaches that messengers are sent primarily to their own people: 'And for every nation there is a messenger.' But in one sense divine truth is relevant to the entire cosmos, and how could it not be?

Muhammad's and Jesus's message is not the annunciation of a 'religion' in the sense of a 'separate' historical or sociological 'organization', but in the sense of a human collectivity uniting under heavenly impulse to follow the primordial universal truth ultimately transcending all religions, though necessarily present in them at the particular or formal level. Christ instructs his apostles to go into all the world to preach the truth, not a 'religion', especially not a religion opposed to or supplanting Judaism. The same paradigm applies to Muhammad, for in so far as his message is the same as Christ's, the Arabian Prophet's body of followers can in no way be legitimately opposed to the other divinely revealed religions.

On another level, in view of the necessarily limited character of the formal appearance of supraformal Truth, the Truth as announced will be applicable fully only to a particular 'humanity', though the essence, in view of its absolute universality, will providentially manifest itself also outside the 'visible' structures of any given revealed religion. Accordingly, Christ never demanded the Gentiles whom he praised for their great faith to adopt Judaism; neither did he tell his apostles to command those who were doing good in Christ's name, yet not following after the apostles, to join their 'group', for they were already followers of Christ in an essential sense.[482] Neither was the Samaritan woman at the well, to whom Christ said, 'Salvation is of the Jews' (*John* 4:22), instructed to become a Jew.[483] Christ merely pointed out, from the viewpoint of Jewish orthodoxy, elements in the Samaritan praxis incompatible with Judaism, such as worshipping on Mount Gerazim, which, moreover, since the essence of worship is unlocalized 'in spirit and in truth' (*John* 4:24), was ultimately not absolutely irreconcilable with the essence of divine worship. This of course does not cancel out the importance for Judaism of those divinely revealed forms of ritual and belief wherein they differed from the Samaritans. To say, 'Salvation is of the Jews,' also may have been an assertion that the Messiah would come from among the Jews, and not from among the Samaritans. Yet the Samaritans believed in the coming of the *Taheb*, the Prophet like Moses who was to come, and so again their beliefs overlapped in essence with those of Judaism as regards messianic hopes.

The interplay of the universality of supraformal Truth and the particularity of formal truth is central to Schuon's dialectical concept of the 'relatively absolute'. From this spiritual point of view, such 'absolutist' texts as *John* 14:6 and *Acts* 4:12 assume a certain relativity. When Christ preaches that 'no man cometh to the Father, but by me' (*John* 14:6), he is not implying that only Christians can be saved, for while the words imply uniqueness they do not necessarily require exclusivity. Catholic theologians have posited theologies such as that of the 'anonymous Christian' (Karl Rahner), and the Catholic Church has traditionally taught that salvation extends beyond the visible boundaries of the church.[484] From an ecumenical perspective, it must be conceded that the Rahnerian and traditional Catholic paradigms, the latter of which is ably represented by the thought of Jean Cardinal Daniélou,[485] are both primarily 'negative', at least in the sense that the non-Christian religions are viewed in a positive light only in so far as they invisibly partake of or reflect the church's invisible 'Spirit' of Christ. This is of course a perfectly legitimate and even necessary stance to maintain within a dogmatic, exoteric framework. Catholic theologians have yet to integrate seriously the essentially positive paradigm of Cardinal Nicolas of Cusa's treatise *De pace fidei*, which presents the diversity of religions positively as providential, and their respective founders as divine messengers sent to preach a common message of divine unity, albeit in culturally diverse modes and formalizations. This posture startlingly agrees with that of the Qur'an, and enables us to understand that every messenger of God rightly proclaims that he is, for the people and age being addressed, the only way to God and the only name (i.e., 'authority') by which salvation is possible (see *Acts* 4:12).[486]

From an exoteric viewpoint it is admittedly difficult to understand how the three Abrahamic religions could have a single divine origin. Some Sufis have seen in the following Islamic *hadith* of Jesus a mystical parable illustrating the common source of the diverse religions by means of the story of Christ drawing forth clothes of different colours from a single container of dye.[487] This 'esoteric' story will provide a fitting closure to our investigations into the transcendent religious unity and the ternary nature and development within history of Abrahamic monotheism:

'Ata' said: 'When Mary had taken Jesus from the school, she handed him over to various trades, and the last to which she entrusted him was to the dyers; so she handed him over to their chief that he might learn from him. Now the man had various clothes with him, and he had to go on a journey, so he said to Jesus, "You have learned this trade, and I am going on a journey from which I shall not return for ten days. These clothes are of different colours, and I have marked every one of them with the colour with which it is to be dyed, so I want you to be finished with them when I return." Then he went out. Jesus (Peace be upon him!) prepared one receptacle with one colour and put all the

clothes in it and said to them, "Be, by God's permission, according
to what is expected of you." Then the dyer came, and all the clothes
were in one receptacle, so he said, "O Jesus, what have you done?" He
replied, "I have finished them." He said, "Where are they?" He replied,
"In the receptacle." He said, "All of them?" He replied, "Yes." He said,
"How are they all in one receptacle? You have spoiled those clothes."
He replied, "Rise and look." So he arose, and Jesus took out a yellow
garment and a green garment and a red garment until he had taken them
out according to the colours which he desired. Then the dyer began to
wonder, and he knew that that was from God (Great and glorious is
He!). Then the dyer said to the people, "Come and look at what Jesus
(Peace be upon him!) has done." So he and his companions, and they
were the disciples, believed on him; and God (Great and glorious is
He!) knows best.'[488]

NOTES

1 We do not say 'sect', for to argue that Christianity is a mere 'sect' of Judaism would be to imply that is was derived from Judaism in a solely historical and outward or extrinsic sense. This would be a denial that Christianity emerged from the same transcendent archetype, that is, the primordial Abrahamic archetype, from which Judaism itself originally emerged. As our discussion below concerning transcendent religious archetypes will clarify, the 'Christian' anti-Islamic argument that claims Islam and its mysticism reflect mere historical derivatives of the forms of Judaism and 'heretical' Christianity encountered by Muhammad in Arabia, is not only false in that it fails to recognize that Islam is descended from the same transcendent Abrahamic religious archetype as Judaism and Christianity, but also in that the 'historical' argument can just as easily be turned on its own head and directed against Judaism (as supposedly derived from Near Eastern paganism) and Christianity (as reputedly being nothing but a syncretistic mix of Judaism and 'sacramental' mystery religions).

2 *Acts* 15:5 portrays 'the Pharisees that believed' as a powerful influence in the Jerusalem church. A quite notable Essene factor in the early church can be deduced from the fact of Christianity's preservation of religious literature that was esteemed in Christ's time principally among the Essenes, such as the *Book of Enoch*, which is quoted as authentic and authoritative in *Jude* 14. The *Book of Enoch* is only one example from among a plethora of extra-canonical works circulated among or composed by Essenes yet preserved only in the church.

3 See David Flusser, *Das Christentum – eine jüdische Religion?* (Munich: Kösel, 1990).

4 Daniel Boyarin, 'The Gospel of the *Memra*: Jewish Binitarianism and the Prologue of John,' *Harvard Theological Review* 94 no. 3 (2001), 246. Though one must approach his articulations with some caution, Boyarin rightly observes that 'Judaism is, from the very beginning, from its very origins, a Hellenistic form of culture.' (ibid.). As Boyarin reminds us, 'Hellenism' is defined as a 'creative synthesis of Greek and "Eastern" culture and thought …' (ibid., 251).

5 See Frithjof Schuon, *The Transcendent Unity of Religions*. Translated by Peter Townsend (New York: Harper Torchbooks, 1975), 89.

6 Ibid.

7 Ibid., 93.

8 Ibid.

9 Ibid., 94.

10 Ibid., 106.

11 Ibid., 118-19.

12 See *Romans* 11:16-18, 24, 28-29.

13 *The Holy Qur'an*. Text, Translation and Commentary by Abdullah Yusuf Ali. Facsimile of 1938 edition. Fourth U.S. edition (Elmhurst, NY: Tahrike Tarsile Qur'an, Inc., 2002), 46, note 107.

14 See Eusebius, *Ecclesiatical History*, 2.23 and Josephus, *Jewish Antiquities* 20.9.1.

15 Roelof van den Broek has clarified that Eusebius's list of the 15 earliest Jerusalem bishops from James the Just to Judas contains too many names for such a short period of time, for the last thirteen would have reigned from 107 to 135 CE. The solution is that twelve of these 'bishops' were actually James's 'fellow workers', who 'reigned' simultaneously and not in succession, constituting a sort of parallel to Christ and his band of twelve disciples, which is fitting in view of the fact that James was, according to early ecclesiastical traditions, appointed as 'successor' to Christ in the church. See Roelof van den Broek, 'Der Brief des Jakobus an Quadratus und das Problem der judenchristlichen Bischöfe von Jerusalem (Eusebius, *HE* IV, 5, 1-3),' in T. Baarda, A. Hilhorst, G. P. Luttikhuizen, A. S. van der Woude (eds.), *Text and Testimony. Essays on New Testament and Apocryphal Literature in Honour of A. F. J. Klijn* (Kampen: Uitgeversmaatschappij J. H. Kok, 1988), 56-65.

16 The above outline is based upon Hans Küng, *Christianity: Essence, History, and Future* (NY: Continuum, 1999), 98-99.

17 Hans Joachim Schoeps, *Theologie und Geschichte des Judenchristentums* (Tübingen: Verlag J. C. B. Mohr/Paul Siebeck, 1949). Hereafter cited as Schoeps, *Geschichte*.

18 In the discussion that follows, it should be borne in mind that we are not arguing for a simple identification of the later Ebionites known to the church fathers with the original Jewish Christians of the Jerusalem church under James, Jesus's 'brother'. Nor are we overlooking the fact that there were several distinct ancient Jewish-Christian groups besides the Ebionites. We are, with Schoeps, asserting a line of continuity between the early Jerusalem church and later Ebionites, that is, the latter were the literal physical and spiritual descendents of the Jerusalem church members. The Jewish Christians certainly do not represent merely a later 're-Judaization' of Christianity. New Testament scholars tend to argue for such a 're-Judaization' theory because of the disturbing theological consequences that would emerge should the Ebionites turn out to have been related to the original Christians of Jerusalem. For a typical example of the 're-Judaization' theory, see E. Bammel and C. F. D. Moule (eds.), *Jesus and the Politics of His Days* (Cambridge: Cambridge University Press, 1984). In the later Ebionite groups, there were admittedly not only theological and ritual continuities with the primitive community under James, but also discontinuities and certain ideological disequilibria. But the same may be said of the Gentile 'Great Church' in relation to the original thought of St. Paul, the 'Apostle to the Gentiles'. The original followers of Jesus called themselves in Hebrew, *Ebionim*, that is, the *Poor Ones*. Not only spiritual poverty (i.e., humility), but material poverty was also implied in the title, reflecting the early Jerusalem church's practice of voluntary community of goods (see *Acts* 4:34). This title, often overlooked in the New Testament by modern readers, very likely occurs as a technical term for the Jerusalem Jewish Christians under James in *Romans* 15:26 ('the poor saints in Jerusalem', i.e., 'the holy *Ebionim* in Jerusalem') and *Galatians* 2:10 (James, Cephas and John of Jerusalem instruct Paul and his attendants that they 'should be mindful of the poor', i.e., of the *Ebionim* in Jerusalem). The title *Ebionim* is to be traced back to Christ's sayings on poverty recorded in *Matthew* 5:3, 11:5, *Luke* 4:18, 6:20. See Hans Joachim Schoeps, *Jewish Christianity. Factional Disputes in the Early Church*. Translated by Douglas R. A. Hare (Philadelphia: Fortress Press, 1964), 11. Hereafter cited as Schoeps, *JwCh*.

19 See Schoeps, *JwCh.*, 137.

20 Consider the following observations from Frithjof Schuon, *Dimensions of Islam*. Tr.

by P. N. Townsend (Lahore, Pakistan: Suhail Acadamy, 1999): '[T]here nevertheless exists a certain connection between the Revelation and the ethnic genius which is its vehicle,' 15; 'Revelation must take account of pre-existing tendencies,' 22; 'The Bible would be much more comprehensible ... if one did not ignore rabbinical exegesis,' 54. We cite further F. Schuon's comment that 'it is not to be forgotten that the Koran presupposes not only the Biblical texts but also the Arab and Talmudic traditions; and sometimes these traditions more so than the Bible.' *From the Divine to the Human. Survey of Metaphysics and Epistemology*. Tr. by Gustavo Polit and Deborah Lambert (Bloomington, Indiana: World Wisdom Books, 1982), 132.

21 Ibid., 138.

22 Schoeps, *Geschichte*, 335-36, note 5. This, of course, does not imply that Muhammad *displaces* Jesus in Islam, for Jesus is included in the list of seven principal pre-Islamic prophets found throughout the Qur'an. The point is that the symbolic number seven is so essential that it must be maintained in both systems; the actual individual prophets who make up the seven may be fluid and subject to change without by any means impairing the overall structural symbolism. The same may be said, with some qualifications, regarding the identity of the eighth Prophet as cumulative Ogdoad within both systems. Though the Talmud tractate *Baba Batra* 15b also names seven prophets sent to the nations (see Schoeps, *Geschichte*, 338), the Islamic version agrees more with the specifically Ebionite Jewish-Christian nuance of the concept.

23 Schoeps, *Geschichte*, 335.

24 Cited in ibid., 337, note 2.

25 *Verus propheta ab initio mundi per saeculum currens* ('the True Prophet, from the beginning of the world hastening through the age'). This is in fact a quotation of *Micah* 5:1: *et egressus eius ab initio a diebus aeternitatis* ('and his going forth is from the beginning, from the days of eternity'). The Latin words *aeternitatis, saeculum,* and *mundi* are all semantically equivalent and reflect the Hebrew word *olam. Micah* 5:4 (Vulgate 5:5), then foretells the coming of 'seven shepherds and eight principal men' ('septem pastores et octo primates homines'). In his version, the Ebionite Symmachus translated the eight 'principal men' as eight 'Christs', understood as a reference to the multiple manifestations of the True Prophet. Cf. Schoeps, *JwCh*, 72 and Schoeps, *Geschichte*, 105.

26 Schoeps, *JwCh*, 70-71. Cf. also Schoeps, *Geschichte*, 105-09. The Clementine theology here is quite biblical, for in *Wisdom* 10-11 there is also a succession of seven representatives of pre-existent Wisdom beginning with Adam, followed by Noah, Abraham, Lot, Jacob, Joseph and Moses. Each of these seven has an evil opposite, in accord with the idea of the syzygy in the Clementine literature.

27 Mohammad Ali Amir-Moezzi, *The Divine Guide in Early Shi'ism. The Sources of Esotericism in Islam*. Translated from the French by David Streight (Albany, NY: SUNY, 1994), 42.

28 Note the close association of resting and reigning, which we also find joined together in the *Letter to the Hebrews*, the *Gospel of the Hebrews* and the *Gospel of Thomas*. The resemblance of this Ebionite Clementine passage to the *hadith* of Muhammad just cited above is stunning. Furthermore, the reference to 'mercy' is reminiscent of the Qur'anic proclamation regarding Muhammad as a mercy to all the worlds (21:107; Jesus and Mary are 'a sign to all the worlds' according to 21:91).

29 Schoeps, *JwCh*, 71, note 16.

30 Frithjof Schuon, *Spiritual Perspectives and Human Facts*. Translated by P. N. Townsend (Pates Manor, Bedfont, Middlesex: Perennial Books, 1987), 57.

31 Ibid.

32 Ibid., 216.

33 See Jean Daniélou, *The Theology of Jewish Christianity*. Translated and edited by John A. Baker (London: Darton, Longman & Todd; Chicago: Henry Regnery Co., 1964), 309.

34 Compare the exegesis found in John Overton, *Inquiry into the Truth and Use of the Book of Enoch, as to its Prophecies, Visions, and Account of Fallen Angels* (London: Simpkin and Marshall, 1822), 76.

35 Frithjof Schuon, *Spiritual Perspectives and Human Facts*, 58.

36 See Jarl Fossum, 'Jewish-Christian Christology and Jewish Mysticism,' *Vigiliae Christianae* 37 (1983), 279; emphasis in the original. Both Fossum and Daniélou refer to the following work, which we have consulted, for their explication of *Wisdom* 10:1-2: A. Dupont-Sommer, 'Adam. "Père du Monde" dans la *Sagesse de Solomon* 10, 1.2,' *Revue de l'histoire des religions* 119 (1939), 182-203.

37 Cited in Reynold A. Nicholson, *The Mystics of Islam* (London: Penguin Arkana, 1989), 105.

38 See ibid., 87-88.

39 Cf. Schoeps, *JwCh*, 138-39.

40 Schoeps, *Geschichte*, 336.

41 Schoeps, *JwCh*, 67, 68; italics in the original.

42 Compare Qur'an 3:80: 'And he commanded you not that ye should take the angels and the prophets for lords.'

43 Alexander Roberts, James Donaldson (eds.), *The Ante-Nicene Fathers*, vol. 8 (Grand Rapids, Michigan: Wm. B. Eerdmans. American Edition, undated), 271.

44 It should be pointed out that the above Ebionite passage has doctrinal parallels in St. Paul's *Epistle to the Romans* 2:12-15, 25-26. For an example of toleration from the Jewish side, consider the following interesting account from Schoeps: 'Similarly, ... Resh Laqish, one of the Palestinian Amoraim who flourished around 250, declared that the fire of hell has no power over the *poshei Israel* [apostates from Israel, i.e., the Ebionites] since they are, "like a pomegranate" (*Song of Sol.* 4:3), full of good works (*Erubin* 19a; *Hagigah* 27a).' See Schoeps, *JwCh*, 106.

45 See *The Holy Qur'an*. Text, Translation and Commentary by Abdullah Yusuf Ali. Facsimile of 1938 edition. Fourth U.S. edition, page 33, note 76.

46 See 'Abdullah Yusuf 'Ali, *The Meaning of the Holy Qur'an*. New Edition with Revised Translation and Commentary (Brentwood, Maryland: Amana Corporation, 1411 AH/1991 A.C.), 33, note 76.

47 Schoeps, *JwCh*, 93.

48 Ibid., 69.

49 Ibid., 94.

50 See ibid., 84.

51 See Frithjof Schuon, *The Transcendent Unity of Religions*, 39-43.

52 The following Ebionite positions are supported in various degrees by their doctrine of the falsification of scripture: Moses did not write the entire Torah (Schoeps, *JwCh*, 96-97); sacrifices were not a part of the original Torah, for they were added only after the Torah was lost and then restored after much later scribal activity (see Schoeps, *JwCh*, 82-84; 118-19; see *Amos* 5:2; *Jeremiah* 7:22; *Hosea* 6:6; *Mark* 12:33, *Matthew* 9:13); the building of the Temple was not unconditionally commanded by God in the scriptures (Schoeps, *JwCh*, 84-87; see 2 *Samuel* 7; *Acts* 7:44-50); the establishment of the Israelite monarchy was not commanded by God as his most perfect will (Schoeps *JwCh*, 84-87; see *Hosea* 8:4). Since the later Ebionites rejected sacrifices as repugnant to God, they did not interpret the death of Christ as a sacrificial atonement as did Paul. Similarly, Islam finds the idea of an atoning sacrifice of Christ on the cross as strange. Even Maimonides grants that the Jewish scriptural injunctions on sacrifices involved a 'divine ruse', or 'gracious ruse'. See Shlomo Pines, '*Some Traits of Christian Theological Writing in Relation to Moslem Kalam and to Jewish Thought*,' Proceedings of the Israel Academy of Sciences and Humanities, vol. 5, no. 4 (Jerusalem, 1973), 107-09 [3-5]. The Ebionites may have found biblical support for their idea of falsified scriptures in *Jeremiah* 8:8, *Ezekiel* 13:9, 20:25 (see Schoeps, *JwCh*, 78); certainly they found support in their interpretation of Christ's sayings in *Matthew* 15:9 and 13. Islamic *ahadith* of Jesus's sayings at times reveal an ambiguity concerning the temple which is Ebionite in tone: 'The disciples said to the Messiah (Peace be upon him!), "Look at this mosque, how beautiful it is!" Then he said, "My people, my people, verily I say unto you, God will not leave one stone of this mosque standing on another, but will destroy it for the sins of its people. Verily God does not pay any heed to gold, or silver, or these stones which charm you. The things dearest to God (Exalted is He!) are the pure hearts. With them God preserves the earth, and with them He destroys it if they are otherwise."' See James Robson, *Christ in Islam* (London: John Murray, 1929), 47. 'The Messiah (God bless him and grant him peace!) said, "The world is a bridge, so pass over it and do not inhabit it." And some people said to him, "O prophet of God, if you would only order us to build a house in which we might worship God!" He replied, "Go and build a house on water." They said, "How will a building stand on water?" He replied, "And how will worship stand along with love of this world?"' See ibid., 71.

53 Frithjof Schuon mentions 'a subordinate degree of inspiration (*ilqa ar-Rahmaniyah*)' and a higher one, *nafas ar-Ruh*, parallel to the Hindu *smriti* and *shruti*. The 'derived and secondary inspiration' is generally applicable to the New Testament epistles as opposed to the 'higher' level found in the gospels. However, both degrees are sometimes found together in the epistles, especially in 1 *Corinthians* chapter 7 (see Frithjof Schuon, *The Transcendent Unity of Religions*, 113 and 125-26). From a Catholic perspective, Schuon's argumentation makes sense if we take his two categories of inspiration as analogous to the idea of the primary and secondary (deutero-canonical) scriptural canons, a quite orthodox Roman Catholic distinction. Furthermore, Catholicism recognizes that certain parts of the Bible address more historically contingent matters and concerns than do other sections.

54 Schoeps, *Geschichte*, 337.

55 On the question of falsification of Jewish scriptures, see Scott Walker Hahn, John Sietze Bergsma, 'What Laws Were "Not Good"? A Canonical Approach to the Theological Problem of Ezekiel 20:25-26,' *Journal of Biblical Studies* vol. 123, no. 2 (2004), 201-18.

56 On difficulties and paradoxes in sacred scriptures in general, see Frithjof Schuon, *Form and Substance in the Religions* (Bloomington, Indiana: World Wisdom Books, 2002), 165-79.

57 See Schoeps, *JwCh*, 139.

58 Ibid.

59 Schoeps, *JwCh*, 139-40.

60 See Schoeps, *Geschichte*, 341, note 4.

61 Ibid., 340. The following Islamic *hadith* of Jesus seems to reflect the Ebionite Eucharistic use of bread and water: 'This is the meaning of the Messiah, son of Mary (Peace be upon them!), when he had water in his right hand and bread in his left hand, "This is my father and this is my mother."' As the commentary reveals, this Eucharist, though without wine, was interpreted as in the Great Church, as signs of the divine life and spiritual fecundity: 'He made the water father, and he made the food mother, because the water of the earth is in the place of the semen with relation to the woman. This (the earth) brings forth from this (water), and this (woman) becomes pregnant from this (semen).' See Robson, 90.

62 For a recent critical evaluation of the different ancient Jewish-Christian gospels, see Dieter Lührmann, *Die apokryph gewordenen Evangelien.Studien zu neuen Texten und neuen Fragen* (Leiden/Boston: Brill, 2004), 229-58.

63 Schoeps, *JwCh*, 71.

64 See Michael D. Goulder, *Paul and the Competing Mission in Corinth* (Peabody, Massachusetts: Hendrickson Publishers, Inc., 2001), especially 92-110.

65 Schoeps, *Geschichte*, 338-39.

66 Ibid., 340.

67 Ibid., 341.

68 Schoeps, *JwCh*, 32.

69 Ibid., 140.

70 Schoeps, *Geschichte*, 336.

71 Frithjof Schuon, *The Transcendent Unity of Religions* (Wheaton, Illinois: Quest, 1984), 31.

72 Schoeps, *JwCh*, 140. To offer more precision on the question of historical influences between various religions, we offer the following insight of F. Schuon, which illuminates the question incisively: 'In a general manner, intertraditional influences are always possible under certain conditions, but without any syncretism. Unquestionably Buddhism and Islam had an influence on Hinduism, not of course by adding new elements to it, but by favouring or determining the blossoming of pre-existing elements.' *The Essential Frithjof Schuon*. Ed. By Seyyed Hossein Nasr (World Wisdom: Bloomington, Indiana, 2005), 102. This clarifies the relationship between Jewish Christianity and Islam far better than any theory of 'historical borrowing'.

73 John Toland, *Nazarenus: or, Jewish, Gentile, and Mahometan Christianity* (London: J. Brown, J. Roberts, and J. Brotherton, 1718).

74 For example, see Shlomo Pines, *The Jewish Christians of the Early Centuries of Christianity according to a New Source*. The Israel Academy of Sciences and Humanities Proceedings, vol. 2, no. 13 (1966), 70-71.

75 Toland, *Nazarenus*, v.

76 Ibid., vi.

77 Ibid., viii.

78 Ibid., xiv.

79 Ibid., 5.

80 Ibid. Rather than speaking of Islamic doctrines having their rise from Christianity, we must insist that similarities in Islamic and Christian theology are the result of archetypal forces; even when historical 'influences' play a role, the reality of assimilation would be caused and guided by the inner laws of celestial religious archetypes, which is to say that core religious values and ideas always determine the processes involved in integrating outer historical influences shared between the religions.

81 Ibid., 24.

82 See ibid., 28. Jerome mentions the Jewish-Christian 'Nazareans' who were unopposed to St. Paul; from precisely such a Jewish-Christian community came the apocryphal *Letter of James to Quadratus,* which describes St. Paul as a 'co-worker' of St. James. See Roelof van den Broek, 'Der Brief des Jakobus an Quadratus und das Problem der judenchristlichen Bischöfe von Jerusalem (Eusebius, HE IV, 5, 1-3),' in T. Baarda, A. Hilhorst, G. P. Luttikhuizen, A. S. van der Woude (eds.), *Text and Testimony. Essays on New Testament and Apocryphal Literature in Honour of A. F. J. Klijn*, 57-58.

83 See ibid., 31.

84 Ibid., 36.

85 Ibid.

86 Ibid.

87 Ibid., 37.

88 Ibid., 37-38.

89 Ibid., 39.

90 'Till all things be fulfilled', that is, 'till all history is finished'. The phrase is merely a poetic repetition of the phrase occurring previously in the same sentence: 'till heaven and earth pass'. The Law will endure as long as creation. The patristic interpretation that all things [of the Law] were fulfilled by Christ, so that no one need observe the Law any longer, cannot easily or fully be reconciled with the clear statement that the Law will not pass 'till heaven and earth pass'. Nevertheless, there is a certain relative validity to the fathers' argument, given that their main burden was quite rightly to assert that Gentiles are not bound by the Levitical precepts, but only by the Noachide laws as set down in *Acts* 15.

91 Ibid., 42.

92 Ibid.

93 Ibid., 44.

94 Ibid., 45.

95 Ibid., 48.

96 Ibid., 53; see *Galatians* 4:10, *Colossians* 2:16.

97 Ibid., 55.

98 Ibid., 56.

99 Ibid. Of course, from Toland's inclusive framework, Jews embracing Christ would by no means understand themselves to be forsaking Judaism, that is, 'converting' to a different religion in the modern pejorative sense of the word.

100 Ibid., 57.

101 Ibid., 58.

102 Ibid., 59.

103 Ibid.

104 Ibid.

105 Ibid., 62-63.

106 Ibid., 65.

107 Ibid., 67-68.

108 Ibid., 76.

109 We of course recognize that there was a variety of Jewish-Christian written gospels in the early church, e.g., the *Gospel of the Hebrews,* the *Gospel of the Ebionites,* the *Gospel of the Nazoreans* (or Nazarenes), etc. Even the titles of such gospels are a subject of scholarly debate. While not at all wishing to overlook various groups' real differences, we nevertheless feel justified in speaking of a Jewish or Hebrew Gospel, given the overlapping and common traits shared by the multiplicity of ancient Jewish-Christian groups and their written gospels.

110 Ibid., 78-79. A recent philological study published by Cambridge University Press strongly suggests that the *Gospel of the Ebionites* was one of Luke's sources, and was not secondarily derived from Matthew or any other of the canonical gospels. See James R. Edwards, '*The Gospel of the Ebionites and the Gospel of Luke,*' *New Testament Studies* 48 (2002), 568-86. For a contrary view, see Andrew Gregory, 'Prior or Posterior? The Gospel of the Ebionites and the Gospel of Luke,' *New Testament Studies* 51 (2005), 344-60.

111 Toland, *Nazarenus,* 79-80.

112 See ibid., 84-85.

113 See Schoeps, 451.

114 Gilles Quispel convincingly interprets the conflict between Paul and Peter at Galatia as being motivated in part by the fears of James and Peter over the threat of persecution of the nascent church by Jewish Zealot terrorists in the explosive years leading up to 70 CE. The Zealots were all too eager to find any potential signs of supposed religious or political 'compromise' in any Jewish group of the time. Though he was at first incensed by Peter's and James's policy at Galatia, Quispel argues that later Paul must have recognized the wisdom of their pragmatism, given the alarming developments in Jerusalem that later degenerated into military conflict with Roman forces. See Gilles Quispel, '*Paul and Gnosis: a Personal View,*' in Roelof van den Broek and Cis van Heertum (eds.), *From Poimandres to Jacob Böhme: Gnosis, Hermetism and the Christian Tradition* (Amsterdam: Bibliotheca Philosophica Hermetica, 2000), 271-302, especially 276-79.

115 See also Christ's comment in *John* 15:27.

116 We have generally, though not slavishly followed Michael D. Goulder's reconstruction of the events at Corinth, as found in his *Paul and the Competing Mission at Corinth*. Goulder does not, however, refer to Paul's allusions in *Galatians* to *Matthew* 16, though he does recognize the connection between 1 *Corinthians* 3 and *Matthew* 16. See also Schoeps, *Geschichte*, 445-51.

117 On the subject of the Islamic 'schism' as the consequence of extrinsic political and intrinsic archetypal realities, see the chapter 'Seeds of a Divergence' in Frithjof Schuon, *Islam and the Perennial Philosophy*. Translated by J. Peter Hobson (World of Islam Festival Publishing Company Ltd., 1976), 91-110.

118 See Schoeps, *Geschichte*, 450.

119 See ibid., 259.

120 See ibid., 134-35.

121 Frithjof Schuon, *From the Divine to the Human*, 123-25.

122 Hans Küng, *Christianity: Essence, History, and Future*, 107.

123 Quoted in Charles A. Gieschen, *Angelomorphic Christology. Antecedents and Early Evidence* (Leiden/Boston/Köln: Brill, 1998), 304. Gieschen does not point out the parallels to Muhammad's titles.

124 As Jean Daniélou observes, there is nothing inherently unorthodox in applying angelic imagery to Christ; the Bible itself does so not infrequently. What would be unorthodox from a Catholic perspective would be the attribution to Christ, not of angelic imagery, but of angelic ontological status in a strict sense. See Jean Daniélou, *The Theology of Jewish Christianity*, 117-46. On the Jewish-Christian view of Gabriel as the Spirit, see the section titled, 'The Spirit and Gabriel,' in ibid., 127-31. On the subject of 'angel' christology in the New Testament and the early church, see Charles A. Gieschen, *Angelomorphic Christology. Antecedents and Early Evidence*.

125 Hans Küng, *Christianity: Essence, History, and Future*, 108. Again, in this context one must always guard against a purely historicist outlook.

126 John Toland, *Nazarenus*, 20.

127 Ibid., 84-85.

128 See Raymond Brown, *The Anchor Bible. The Gospel according to John* I-XII (Garden City, NY: Doubleday, 1983), 519-24.

129 See the discussion and references in Edward Schillebeeckx, *Jesus. An Experiment in Christology*. Translated by Hubert Hoskins (NY: Seabury Press, 1979), 98-99.

130 Frithjof Schuon, *The Transcendent Unity of Religions*, 33-34. Consider the following Qur'anic passages, 2:136 and 3:84, both of which end with the following comment on God's prophets, including Jesus: 'We make no distinction between any of them, and unto Him we have surrendered.' 4:150-52: 'Lo! those who disbelieve in Allah and His messengers, and seek to make distinction between Allah and His messengers, and say: We believe in some and disbelieve in others, and seek to choose a way in between; Such are disbelievers in truth. ... But those who believe in Allah and His messengers and make no distinctions between any of them, unto them Allah will give their wages; and Allah is ever Forgiving, Merciful.' By contrast, 2:252-53 proclaims: 'These are the portents of Allah which We recite unto thee (Muhammad) with truth, and lo! thou art of the number of (Our) messengers; Of those messengers, some of whom We have caused to excel others, and of whom there are some unto whom Allah spake,

while some of them He exalted (above others) in degree; and We gave Jesus, son of Mary, clear proofs (of Allah's sovereignty) and We supported him with the holy Spirit.' Schuon refers to some of these verses in his *Christianity/Islam. Essays on Esoteric Ecumenism.* Translated by Gustavo Polit (Bloomington, Indiana: World Wisdom Books, 1985), 159-60, where he also explains concerning Muhammad's pre-eminent position in Islam as 'the best' of the prophets: '"The best" refers to the Logos' and not to a man, but if we define the Logos as the 'Muhammadan Light', 'it is because Muhammad proceeds from it' (160). Accordingly, '"the best" is Muhammad inasmuch as he manifests or personifies the Logos; but in this respect, every other "Messenger" (*Rasul*) is equally "the best." Thirdly, "the best" is Muhammad inasmuch as he alone ... manifests the whole Logos, the other Messengers manifesting it only in part ... but as much can be said, of course, of every other Messenger within the framework of his own Message. Fourthly, Muhammad is "the best" inasmuch as he represents a quality of Islam by which it surpasses the other religions; but every integral religion necessarily possesses such an unequalable quality, lacking which it would not exist' (ibid., 160-61).

131 Frithjof Schuon, *The Transcendent Unity of Religions*, 34.

132 Quoted in Frithjof Schuon, *Spiritual Perspectives and Human Facts*, 84.

133 Frithjof Schuon, *Dimensions of Islam.* Translated by P. N. Townsend (London: George Allen and Unwin, 1970), 68.

134 Frithjof Schuon, *Christianity/Islam. Essays on Esoteric Ecumenism*, 58-59.

135 Ibid., 59

136 Quoted in Mir Valiuddin, *Love of God. A Sufic Approach* (Farnham, Surrey, England: Sufi Publishing Co., 1972), 73. It should be noted, however, that the Sufis also utter anti-Christian criticisms, which usually do not find their way into popular Western editions of Sufi poetry anthologies, editions which also tend to play down the specifically Islamic identity and Muhammadan devotional elements in Sufism. On Rumi's anti-Christian remarks, see the chapter titled, 'Christianity as Portrayed by Jalal Al-Din Rumi,' in Lloyd V. J. Ridgeon, *Crescents on the Cross. Islamic Visions of Christianity* (Oxford: Oxford University Press, 1999), 32-64. On some of Ibn al-'Arabi's anti-Jewish and anti-Christian comments, see Mahmoud al-Ghorab, 'Muhyiddin Ibn al-'Arabi amidst Religions (*adyan*) and Schools of Thought (*madhahib*),' in Stephen Hirtenstein and Michael Tiernan (eds.), *Muhyiddin Ibn 'Arabi. Commemorative Volume* (Element Books, Shaftesbury, 1993), 200-27. Naturally these negative comments by Rumi and al-'Arabi do not cancel out or contradict their positive statements concerning the providential diversity of religions; they serve, among other things, to stress the quite concrete differences existing in the spiritual nuances of the various religions.

137 See Hans Küng, Josef van Ess, Heinrich von Stietencron, Heinz Bechert, Peter Heinegg, *Christianity and World Religions. Paths to Dialogue* (Maryknoll, NY: Orbis, 1993), 126.

138 Cf. Margaret Smith, *Studies in Early Mysticism in the Near and Middle East* (Oxford: Oneworld Publications, 1995), 103-52. Although some of Smith's conclusions are questionable, she does present undeniable records of Islamic-Christian contacts in early Islam.

139 See Hans Küng, *Christianity and World Religions. Paths to Dialogue*, 125.

140 See Moshe Idel, Bernard McGinn (eds.), *Mystical Union in Judaism, Christianity, and Islam: An Ecumenical Dialogue* (NY: Continuum, 1989, 1996).

141 On the doctrine of the Eternal Imam, see the comprehensive essay by Henry Corbin,

'*Divine Epiphany and Spiritual Birth in Ismailian Gnosis,*' in Man and Transformation. Papers from the Eranos Yearbooks. Bollingen Series XXX, vol. 5 (NY: Pantheon Books, 1964), 69-160, especially 127-40. Even though Corbin points out that this doctrine, which he writes on with obvious enthusiasm and sympathy, is 'far from Islamic orthodoxy' (see 136), for our purposes we need merely note that, historically viewed, as eccentric as the doctrine may be for exoteric Islam, it nevertheless developed historically from and within the borders of the Islamic faith.

142 Frithjof Schuon, *Understanding Islam*. Translated by D. M. Matheson (London: George Allen & Unwin, 1976), 98.

143 See Matthias Joseph Scheeben, *The Mysteries of Christianity*. Tr. by Cyril Vollert (St. Louis, Missouri: B. Herder, 1947).

144 See Karl Rahner's comment on Jesus Christ in his article on the 'Incarnation', that 'he possesses a human, sensible and spiritual soul (Denziger 13, 25, 111a, 148, 216, 255, 283, 290, 480, 710), created, not eternally pre-existent (D 204).' Karl Rahner, ed., *Encyclopedia of Theology. The Concise Sacramentum Mundi* (NY: Crossroad, 1991), 694.

145 Seyyed Hossein Nasr, *Islamic Life and Thought* (Albany, NY: State University of New York Press, 1981), 209.

146 See ibid., 209-10.

147 Henry Corbin, translated by Ralph Manheim, *Creative Imagination in the Sufism of Ibn 'Arabi*. Bollingen Series XCI (Princeton, NJ: Princeton University Press, 1981), 313, note 65. Compare Frithjof Schuon's following formulation: 'It is important to emphasize that when Christ says, "I am the Way, the Truth, and the Life," this is absolutely true of the Divine Word ("Christ"), and relatively true of its human manifestation ("Jesus"); an absolute truth cannot in fact be limited to a relative being. Jesus is God, but God is not Jesus; Christianity is Divine, but God is not a Christian.' Frithjof Schuon, *The Transcendent Unity of Religions*, 26.

148 Quoted in Seyyed Hossein Nasr, *Islamic Life and Thought*, 196.

149 Quoted in Martin Lings, *A Sufi Saint of the Twentieth Century. Shaikh Ahmad al-'Alawi* (Berkeley and Los Angeles: University of California Press, 1973), 150.

150 Seyyed Hossein Nasr, *Sufi Essays*. Second edition (Albany, NY: State University of New York Press, 1991), 135, note 14.

151 See Bruce Chilton, *Judaic Approaches to the Gospel* (Atlanta, Georgia: Scholars Press, 1994), 184-201. The 'contradictory' interpretation of *John* 1:17 proffered by Edward Schillebeeckx in his monograph, *Christ. The Experience of Jesus as Lord*, (New York: Seabury Press, 1980) 352-72, is typical of misguided ideological and anti-historical exegesis. It is ironic that Schillebeeckx recognizes that the Johannine prologue speaks not only of Christ as Logos manifestation, but also of Moses and John the Baptist as such. Schillebeeckx, however, confines this meaning in the prologue strictly to its pre-canonical stage, thus missing the parallel to *Hebrews* 1:1-3's gradual and increasing historical unfolding of Logos manifestations, as we discuss in depth below.

152 The less literal rendering of 'dwelt *among* us' in *John* 1:14 somewhat weakens the force of the Greek statement, which stresses that the Logos became fully human, that is, became 'man', not 'a man', though the latter is of course involved in the process.

153 This theological orientation agrees in several respects with primitive christology as

found in the *Shepherd of Hermas*, Similitude 5:6. We give here J. B. Lightfoot's version: 'The Holy Pre-existent Spirit, which created the whole creation, God made to dwell in flesh that He desired. This flesh, therefore, in which the Holy Spirit dwelt, was subject unto the Spirit, walking honourably in holiness and purity, without in any way defiling the Spirit. When then it had lived honourably in chastity ... , He chose it as a partner with the Holy Spirit... . He therefore took the son as adviser and the glorious angels also, that this flesh too, having served the Spirit unblameably, might have some place of sojourn... ' This in turn agrees with the 'manifestational' christology of *2 Clement* 14, again given according to Lightfoot: 'For she [the church] was spiritual, as our Jesus also was spiritual, but was manifested in the last days that He might save us. Now the Church, being spiritual, was manifested in the flesh of Christ... .' In this text, Jesus, which really refers to the *Logos*, was pre-existent 'from the beginning' of creation, but was 'manifested' in the eschaton in Jesus. But Clement then states that the pre-existent church was also 'manifested in the flesh of Christ'. It would seem that the pre-existent church is somehow equivalent to the pre-existent Logos, which would make a certain kind of sense from the Pauline perspective, which sees the church as the '*body* of Christ'. For Clement, therefore, both the 'spirit' and 'body' of Christ are pre-existent. He seems to imply that the 'body' in which the Logos would be clothed in eschatological manifestation is the church, which was created at the beginning of the world for the purpose of the later 'incarnation'. After Christ's exodus from the earth, his 'body' remains behind as the church. Clement's comment that 'Jesus was spiritual', really refers to the pre-existent Logos as 'spirit', in agreement with Hermas's designation of the Logos as the 'holy pre-existent spirit'. Both authors speak of the Logos's 'manifestation' taking place 'in the flesh of Christ'. Like *John* 1:14, this is a Jewish 'tabernacling' incarnational christology. Whatever else may be said of these texts, they should certainly not be criticized for lacking a later post-Nicene articulatory dogmatic precision.

154 On the functional christology of Jewish Christianity in general and of *John* 1:14 in particular, see Edward Schillebeeckx, *Jesus. An Experiment in Christology*, 457, 553, 556-57.

155 'Abd Allah ibn Abi Zaid, al-Quairuwani, *Risala. A Maliki Shariah Text*. Translated by Bello Muhammad Daura (Zaria: Northern Nigerian Publishing Co., 1983).

156 See Arthur Jeffery (ed.), *A Reader on Islam* ('S-Gravenhage: Mouton & Co., 1962), 333-34.

157 Translated by Hamid Algar, Professor of Persian and Islamic Studies, University of California, Berkeley (published in the journal *Al-Bayan* 1980) from *The Heritage of Islamic Literature*; also available online at: http://ccat.sas.upenn.edu/~bvon/pages/fiqh.html.

158 See Arthur Jeffery (ed.), *A Reader on Islam*, 348.

159 Gershom Scholem, *On the Mystical Shape of the Godhead. Basic Concepts in the Kabbalah* (NY: Schocken Books, 1991), 148, 147.

160 Ibid., 152-53.

161 Ibid., 154.

162 Ibid., 155.

163 Hans Küng makes a connection between the Jewish concept of the *Shekhinah* dwelling in the temple and the incarnation of the Logos: 'And why should not God's presence, *Shekhinah*, for once take its abode in an individual human being instead of a temple ... ?' Hans Küng, *Judaism. Between Yesterday and Tomorrow* (New York: Crossroad, 1992), 384. Küng, however, does not note that this very possibility was acknowledged in ancient Judaism.

164 Alexander Broadie, *A Samaritan Philosophy* (Leiden: E. J. Brill, 1981), 71.

165 The parallel to the Islamic doctrine of the sinlessness of the prophets is suggestive.

166 *The Works of Philo*. Complete and Unabridged. New Updated Edition. Translated by C. D. Yonge (Hendrickson Publishers, 1993), 331, modified. This revised Yonge edition of Philo's works should always be compared with the critical Greek text found in the Loeb classical library version.

167 See Crispin H. T. Fletcher-Louis, *All the Glory of Adam. Liturgical Anthropology in the Dead Sea Scrolls* (Leiden/Boston/Köln: Brill, 2002), 56-87, especially 69-74. Therefore, as Boyarin notes, what separates Judaism from Christianity is not the worship of the Logos embodied in a human, but rather the identification of that embodiment as Jesus of Nazareth. See Boyarin, 256, note 54.

168 Ibid., 72-75. On page 74 Fletcher-Louis details the convincing evidence that for *Sirach*, the high priest Simon is assimilated to the pre-existent Wisdom 'incarnate'. *Sirach* 24:8-11 applies to Wisdom the images and themes of the holy tent, taking root, cedar in Lebanon, cypress, rosebushes, olive tree, growth beside water, and incense. These are all paralleled by images of Simon in *Sirach* 50:5, 8-9, 10, and 12, where we encounter the themes of the sanctuary, a rooted shoot, cedar in Lebanon, cypress, roses, olive tree, growth beside water, and incense. For an exploration of Jewish-Christian 'kabod' christology, see Jarl Fossum, 'Jewish-Christian Christology and Jewish Mysticism,' *Vigiliae Christianae* 37 (1983), 260-87.

169 Quoted in Boyarin, 278.

170 Richard Bauckham, *God Crucified: Monotheism and Christology in the New Testament* (Grand Rapids, Michigan: Eerdmans, 1998).

171 See the following studies in general: ibid.; Crispin H. T. Fletcher-Louis, *All the Glory of Adam. Liturgical Anthropology in the Dead Sea Scrolls*; Darrell D. Hannah, 'The Throne of His Glory,' *Zeitschrift für die Neutestamentliche Wissenschaft und die Kunde der älteren Kirche* 94, no. 1/2 (2003), 68-96; Charles A. Gieschen, 'The Divine Name in Ante-Nicene Christology,' *Vigiliae Christianae* 57, no. 2 (2003), 115-58.

172 See Crispin H. T. Fletcher-Louis, *All the Glory of Adam. Liturgical Anthropology in the Dead Sea Scrolls*, 85.

173 See Reynold A. Nicholson, *The Mystics of Islam*, 149ff. As Frithjof Schuon explains: "Man cannot become 'God'; the servant cannot change into the Lord; but there is something in the servant that can – not without the Lord's grace – surpass the axis 'servant-Lord' or 'subject-object' and realize the absolute Self." *Dimensions of Islam*, 46.

174 Darrell D. Hannah, "The Throne of His Glory," 77.

175 This position may be acceptable to Christian theology in two senses: either it can be understood with reference to Christ's created human nature, or to the Logos's status of being eternally 'begotten' by the Father who is neither begotten, as is the Son, nor who proceeds, as does the Spirit, from any other divine 'person'.

176 Hannah, 71.

177 Ibid., 89.

178 For the sake of completeness, we add that Aquinas in *Summa Theologiae* 3. Q23 Art 2-5 explains that according to Christian theology, Christ's humanity is adored, viewed in itself,

with *dulia*, whereas with a view to its hypostatic union with the divine nature, Christ's humanity is adored with *latria*.

179 Ibid., 93.

180 Quoted in Eusebius of Caesarea, *Preparation for the Gospel*. Translated by E.H. Gifford, vol. 3, part 2 (Oxford: Clarendon, 1903). I have modified Gifford's text in light of Eusebius's original and R. G. Robertson's translation and notes in James H. Charlesworth (ed.), *The Old Testament Pseudepigrapha*, vol. 2 (NY: Doubleday, 1985), 803-19.

181 Hannah, 94, quoting Bauckham.

182 The Islamic equivalent of the idea of having a share in God's throne, or divine authority, is found in the Qur'anic teaching on Adam as God's caliph upon earth. We might add here that in the Christian scriptures the term 'Son of God' with reference to Christ is used in a strictly metaphorical sense of 'enthronement'. In the Hebrew scriptures, the enthronement of a king of Israel was metaphorically called his divine birth, so that in *Psalm* 2:7 we read of the enthroned king: 'You are my son, this day have I begotten you,' and similarly in *Psalm* 110:3: 'From the womb, before the daystar, have I begotten you.' *Acts* 13:33 applies *Psalm* 2:7 to the resurrection of Jesus when he was enthroned at God's right hand; *Romans* 1:4 says that Jesus was made the Son of God at his resurrection, which again coincides with his enthronement.

183 See Gilles Quispel, 'Paul and Gnosis: a Personal View,' 298.

184 See James H. Charlesworth (ed.), *The Old Testament Pseudepigrapha*, vol. 1 (NY: Doubleday, 1983), 934.

185 Cited in ibid., 157-58.

186 Of course, given the nature of the human mind, it was inevitable for the church to explore the ontological implications of the New Testament with regard to christology and trinity. Yet, as Karl Rahner notes, an overemphasis on the immanent trinity has led to an obscuration of the 'economic' trinity, and to such a point that the subject of the trinity is an issue that little concerns the average Christian in the concrete situation of life in the modern world. See Rahner's entry, 'Trinity,' *Encyclopedia of Theology*, 1765-66.

187 See Wilson B. Bishai, 'A Possible Coptic Source for a Qur'anic Text,' *Journal of the American Oriental Society* 91 (1971), 125-28.

188 We say 'is' an angel in functional terms; that is, angelic in the strict sense that a created status is attributed to the humanity of Christ. After all, he is described here as the 'Son of *Man*'. See the discussion of *Apocalypse* 14 and 15 in R. H. Charles, *A Critical and Exegetical Commentary on the Revelation of St. John*, vol. 1. The International Critical Commentary (NY: Charles Scribner's Sons, 1920), lii-liii. Not understanding that the 'high' christology of the *Apocalypse* refers to the humanity of Christ, Charles was forced to argue that *Apocalypse* 14:14ff., which speaks of Christ as an angel, was an interpolation to the text.

189 Quoted in Eusebius of Caesarea, *Preparation for the Gospel*. Translated by E.H. Gifford, vol. 3, part 2 (Oxford: Clarendon, 1903). I have substantially emended the text in light of Eusebius's original and based upon M. Lafargue's critical footnotes in James H. Charlesworth, *The Old Testament Pseudepigrapha*, vol. 2, 799-800.

190 See James H. Charlesworth, *The Old Testament Pseudepigrapha*, vol. 2, 800.

191 The verses concerning universal rule over heaven, earth and ocean, applied to Moses in

the longer recension, are applied to God ('Zeus') in the shorter recension of this Orphic hymn. See ibid., 800-01. This makes the longer recension's application of these verses to a mortal all the more startling, and fundamentally suggests that often the common modern understanding of ancient Jewish monotheism might be somewhat truncated and incomplete.

192 Boyarin, 271, note 107.

193 'As for the Spirit (al-Ruh in Arabic), it may be said to be at the border between the Divine and created orders.' Seyyed Hossein Nasr, *The Garden of Truth. The Vision and Promise of Sufism, Islam's Mystical Tradition* (New York: HarperOne, 2007), 50. 'The *Logos* is the "Spirit" (*Ruh*), of which it has been said that it is neither created nor uncreated... .' Frithjof Schuon, *Sufism: Veil and Quintessence.* Ed. by James S. Cutsinger (Bloomington, Indiana: World Wisdom Books, 2006), 105.

194 Quoted in Gershom Scholem, *On the Mystical Shape of the Godhead*, 155.

195 See Boyarin, 249.

196 Quoted in ibid., 250.

197 Ibid., 251.

198 Broadie, 38.

199 Ibid., 40-41.

200 Ibid., 41.

201 Ibid., 42.

202 Ibid., 70.

203 Ibid., 73.

204 Ibid., 79.

205 Ibid. We should be careful when interpreting Philonic statements on the Logos that seem structurally parallel to Catholic articulations, for Philo also says that the entire cosmos emanates from God and shares in the very nature of God (see *De Opficio Mundi* v 22). And if for Philo the Logos is somehow quasi-uncreated and immortal, then so is the human mind not named with 'a title resembling any created entity' (see *De Plantatione* v 18). Regarding the philosophical idea of emanation, its most distant parallels lie not in Greek philosophy, but in Egyptian mythology. See Gilles Quispel, 'The Original Doctrine of Valentinus the Gnostic,' in Roelof van den Broek and Cis van Heertum (eds.), *From Poimandres to Jacob Böhme: Gnosis, Hermetism and the Christian Tradition*, 244. Similarly, the idea of hypostatic *nous* and *logos* creating the cosmos is already paralleled in the Egyptian mythology of Hu and Thoth, the 'lord of life'. See Peter Kingsley, 'Poimandres: The Etymology of the Name and the Origins of the Hermetica,' in ibid., 64. In Babylonian mythology, personified Wisdom and Word dwelt with the creator Ea. See W. O. E. Oesterly, *The Books of the Apocrypha. Their Origin, Teaching and Contents* (London: Robert Scott, 1915), 231-32. The Egyptian and Babylonian conceptions remind one of the early ante-Nicene patristic doctrine of God creating the universe with his two hands, Word and Wisdom, that is, the Logos and Holy Spirit.

206 See Goulder's following works: 'Ignatius' Docetists,' *Vigiliae Christianae* 33 (1999), 16-30; 'A Poor Man's Christology,' *New Testament Studies* 45 (1999), 332-48; 'Hebrews and the Ebionites,' *New Testament Studies* 49 (2003), 393-406; *Paul and the Competing Mission in Corinth*, 197-221.

207 See Edward Schillebeeckx, *Jesus. An Experiment in Christology*, 443, 475-76, 495.

208 *The Ante-Nicene Fathers*, vol. 8, 315.

209 This can be a perfectly orthodox statement for Christian theology, for Peter is essentially denying the identity of the Son with the Father.

210 Ibid., 316. Simon's formulation is also found in Iranaeus's *Proof of the Apostolic Preaching*, but with another meaning. Peter's refutation of the claim is therefore not an argument against Iranaeus, but against the very Gnosticism that Iranaeus himself combated.

211 Ibid. 'Same substance' must not necessarily be read as a quotation of the Nicene formulation. Peter might be quoting heretical Gnosticism, not Nicaea. This would imply that by a 'coincidence' Nicaea adopted a terminology that had been in earlier use, with a different sense than in Gnosticism. When the Great Church began using the very same terminology which Jewish Christianity had earlier encountered in certain forms of Gnosticism, Jewish Christians could not but have been shocked and rejected the new articulation, at least for themselves. In any event, in the text above, by denying that the generated Wisdom (= Son) is of the 'same substance' as the Father, Peter only intends to deny that the Logos is a different god than the God of the Jews. Again, we must remember that for Jewish Christians the term 'God' always refers, in typical biblical fashion, exclusively to the Father.

212 Ibid.

213 See Jarl Fossum, 'Jewish-Christian Christology and Jewish Mysticism,' 269-72, where Fossum discusses the Ebionite doctrine of True Prophet succession, beginning with Adam, as evidence that the church fathers have misunderstood the Ebionite doctrine as mere 'adoptionism', in the sense of a man having no inward connection with the eternal Logos.

214 An interesting Islamic *hadith* of Jesus possibly seems to reflect an Islamic concession that the 'popular' Christian understanding of Jesus's divinity had at least a certain amount of overlap with the truth in it, if understood metaphysically: 'I saw in a book that Jesus (Blessing and peace be upon him!) passed a man who was making donkey-saddles and saying in his worship, "O Lord, if I knew where thine ass is on which thou ridest, I would make a saddle for it and inlay it with jewels." Then the Messiah shook him and said, "Woe to you! Has God (Exalted is He!) an ass?" Then God (Exalted is He!) revealed to Jesus (Blessing and peace be upon him!), "Leave the man alone, for he has glorified Me according to his ability"' (Robson, 125-26).

215 Frithjof Schuon, *Christianity/Islam. Essays on Esoteric Ecumenism*, 166.

216 See *Fakhruddin 'Iraqi. Divine Flashes*. Translation and introduction by William C. Chittick and Peter Lamborn Wilson (NY/Mahwah, New Jersey: Paulist Press, 1982), 15. This is related to the Sufi teaching on the two statements of the Islamic profession of faith, namely, 'There is no god but God, and Muhammad is His Messenger.' The first statement, implying the absoluteness of the *Ipsum Esse*, relativizes the contingent. The second statement, about God's 'Messenger', relativizes or neutralizes the former relativization by establishing a link between the creature and the Creator, so that entified being is related to *Ipsum Esse*. The latter, as origin of the former, and as that without which entified being would dissolve into the absolute nothingness of non-being, is in a sense inseparably of the *essence* of contingent beings. That is, created being presupposes and requires the creative 'action' of uncreated Being.

217 In a related vein of thought, we could say that immortality is not a 'natural' property

of the soul, but one that is bestowed entirely by God. This situation lies behind the traditions known in early Christianity, inherited from Judaism, of an 'annihilation' of the wicked rather than of their eternal punishment in hell.

218 Seyyed Hossein Nasr, *The Heart of Islam. Enduring Values for Humanity* (San Francisco, California: Harper, 2002), 23.

219 F. Buhl, 'Koran,' in *The Encyclopaedia of Islam*, vol. 2, E–K (Leyden: Brill, 1927), 1076.

220 Louis Massignon, 'Nur Muhammadi,' in *The Encyclopaedia of Islam*, vol. 3, L–R (Leiden: Brill, 1936), 961.

221 Frithjof Schuon, *Understanding Islam*, 44.

222 Compare the following beautifully intriguing Islamic *hadith* of Jesus: 'In the Gospel [there is written], "I am the prince of life and the ways of truth; whoever believes in me and dies, has not died a death but has only lived a life"' (Robson, 56).

223 To Qur'an 5:46 and 48 we could also add 4:136 and 150-51, which we have already had occasion to mention: 'O ye who believe! Believe in Allah and His messenger [Muhammad] and the Scripture which He hath revealed unto His messenger, and the Scripture which He revealed aforetime.... Lo! those who disbelieve in Allah and His messengers, and seek to make distinction between Allah and His messengers, and say: We believe in some and disbelieve in others, and seek to choose a way in between; Such are disbelievers in truth....'

224 *Nicholas of Cusa's De Pace Fidei and Cribatio Alkorani.* Translation and Analysis by Jasper Hopkins. 2nd ed. (Minneapolis: Arthur J. Banning Press, 1994), 669. My explanatory glosses in brackets; contents in parentheses by Hopkins.

225 Jacob Neusner, *Rabbinic Literature & the New Testament. What We Cannot Show, We Do Not Know* (Valley Forge, Pennsylvania: Trinity Press International, 1994), 183.

226 We say 'interestingly', because Michael Goulder has recently argued that the *Epistle to the Hebrews* presupposes the Great Church's unique incarnational theology and is a polemical treatise combating the Ebionite angelic 'possessionist' or adoptionist christology. See Michael Goulder, 'Hebrews and the Ebionites,' in *New Testament Studies* 49 (2003), 393-406. Goulder is overstating his case by attributing the later explicit theological understanding of incarnation to Paul, a concept which in the apostle's time could have existed only in an implicit sense. Moreover, in light of Charles A. Gieschen's recent study, *Angelomorphic Christology. Antecedents and Early Evidence*, it would appear that the conceptual distance between Ebionitism's 'angelic' christology and the New Testament's ideas on Christ is not as wide as Goulder supposes. Gieschen's work demonstrates that from an early Jewish perspective, to describe Christ in angelic terms is to honour him and not at all to denigrate him. Such an angelomorphic approach therefore represents not a 'low' but a 'high christology', especially in view of the application of angelomorphic imagery to God in the Hebrew scriptures and intertestamental literature. From a certain metaphorical viewpoint, we could say that to speak of the earthly Christ in functional terms (leaving aside the question of ontology for the moment), implies that he would thus constitute the intermediary 'angelic' link between the human and divine realms, the angelic being the connective middle link between the two polarities. Compare Dionysius's *The Celestial Hierarchy*, chapter 4, where it is taught that the angelic elevates humanity to the divine. To use Arabic terms, we could say that the human world, *nasut*, is linked to the divine world, *lahut*, by means of the angelic world, or *malakut*. This is how the Semitic frame of

reference of the early Jewish Christians enabled them to recognize in Christ what the Gentile church later called the hypostatic union. The Ebionites could not call Jesus 'God', since for them that was reserved as a biblical designation for the Father; Christ was a man, but not a 'mere' man, in virtue of his intimate relationship with the Father. This 'something' beyond 'mere' humanity was in typical early Jewish fashion designated 'angelic'. Goulder perhaps erred in assuming the Ebionites' angelic christology was more ontological than functional, though in the latter there also inhere ontological implications.

227 This is the revised Latin text found in Robertus Weber (ed.), *Biblia Sacra: iuxta Vulgatam versionem*. Editio altera emendata, tomus II (Stuttgart: Württembergische Bibelanstalt, 1975), 1843.

228 Compare *1 Peter* 1:11, which says of the ancient prophets that 'the Spirit of Christ [was] in them.' We would maintain that here the 'spirit of Christ' is a title for the Logos, as it appears to be also in the *Shepherd of Hermas* Similitude 5:6 and in *2 Clement* 14.

229 See Daniel Boyarin, 'The Gospel of the *Memra*: Jewish Binitarianism and the Prologue of John,' 265.

230 See ibid., 276.

231 See Edward Schillebeeckx, *Christ. The Experience of Jesus as Lord*. Translated by John Bowden (NY: Crossroad, 1981), 359-62.

232 Boyarin, 280.

233 Ibid., 283.

234 See Thomas F. O'Meara, 'Christian Theology and Extraterrestrial Intelligent Life,' *Theological Studies* 60 (1999), 12.

235 Ibid., 13.

236 Peter C. Phan, 'Multiple Religious Belonging,' *Theological Studies* 64 (2003), 500-01.

237 See ibid., note 14.

238 Article on 'Incarnation' in *Encyclopedia of Theology*, 695.

239 O'Meara, 13.

240 Cited in ibid. In view of the importance of the Aquinas passage cited above by O'Meara, we give here the Latin text, quoted more fully: 'Respondeo dicendum quod id quod potest in unum et non in amplius, habet potentiam limitatam ad unum. Potentia autem divinae personae est infinita, nec potest limitari ad aliquid creatum. Unde non est dicendum quod persona divina ita assumpserit unam naturam humanam quod non potuerit assumere aliam. Videretur enim ex hoc sequi quod personalitas divinae naturae esset ita comprehensa per unam humanam naturam quod ad eius personalitatem alia assumi non possit. Quod est impossibile, non enim increatum a creato comprehendi potest. Patet ergo quod, sive consideremus personam divinam secundum virtutem, quae est principium unionis; sive secundum suam personalitatem, quae est terminus unionis, oportet dicere quod persona divina, praeter naturam humanam quam assumpsit possit aliam numero naturam humanam assumere.'

241 Frithjof Schuon, *Christianity/Islam. Essays on Esoteric Ecumenism*, 127, note 10.

242 Phan, 502.

243 See ibid., 503.

244 Frithjof Schuon, *The Transcendent Unity of Religions*, 104.

245 Frithjof Schuon, *Understanding Islam*, 90.

246 Ibid., note 2.

247 Ibid., 91.

248 Frithjof Schuon, *The Transcendent Unity of Religions*, 116.

249 Frithjof Schuon, *Treasures of Buddhism* (Bloomington, Indiana: World Woisdom Books, 1993), 106.

250 According to Gilles Quispel, one of the greatest authorities on the subject, the *Gospel of Thomas* saw its final redaction ante 140 CE, and was composed by combining two earlier sources at the disposal of the redactor, namely, a Jewish-Christian gospel written *c.*50 CE in Jerusalem, and an Encratite gospel written *c.*100 CE in Alexandria. See Gilles Quispel, 'Gnosis and Alchemy: the Tabula Smaragdina,' in Roelof van den Broek and Cis van Heertum (eds.), *From Poimandres to Jacob Böhme: Gnosis, Hermetism and the Christian Tradition*, 321, 331.

251 See M. R. James, *The Apocryphal New Testament* (Oxford: Clarendon Press, 1924), 5.

252 Jean Daniélou, *The Theology of Jewish Christianity*, 202.

253 See ibid., 203-04.

254 J. E. Hanauer, *The Holy Land. Myths and Legends* (London, Senate, 1996), 3.

255 Seyyed Hossein Nasr, *Ideals and Realities of Islam* (NY: Frederick A. Praeger, 1967), 53.

256 To state that Semitic biblical thought is primarily functional, metaphorical and concrete, and the Hellenistic substantial and abstract, is not to create an absolute oppositional contrariety between the two; for while biblical thought, being mythic (we use the term in its etymological, and not its modern pejorative sense), is primarily universal, synthetic and concentric, and Hellenistic predominantly particular, discursive and linear, nevertheless, the two cognitive modes of intuitive synthesis and discursive *argumentatio* are present in both, and operate in mutual support. The situation is simply that mythic thought concentrates upon the overall picture at hand, whereas philosophical thought concentrates upon the static constituent and active constitutive parts of the whole. Yet in absolute terms, synthetic thought presupposes discursive cognitive activity, and conversely, discursive thought presupposes, admittedly in a different mode and degree, synthetic cognitive activity. The importance for trinitarian dogma of functional thought as opposed to 'substantial' thought has been recognized by Joseph Cardinal Ratzinger, now Pope Benedict XVI, though he rightly sees an overlap between function and substance. See Joseph Cardinal Ratzinger, *Introduction to Christianity*. Translated by J. R. Foster (San Francisco, CA: Ignatius Press, 1990), 124-25, 131-37, 169-71. On the subject at hand in relation to Islam and the subject of the trinity, see the chapter, 'Alternations in Semitic Monotheism' in Frithjof Schuon, *Christianity/Islam*, 119-48.

257 According to Frithjof Schuon, while Islam is the final possible exoteric world religion, Sikhism is the final possible esoterism; see his *Understanding Islam*, 48. The veneration Sikhs show toward copies of their sacred scriptures demonstrates that they hold their scriptures to be the hypostatic embodiment of the divine Word.

258 Frithjof Schuon, *Dimensions of Islam*, 63.

259 Frithjof Schuon, *Form and Substance in the Religions*. Translated by Mark Perry and Jean-Ierre LaFouge (Bloomington, Indiana: World Wisdom Books, 2002), 231.

260 Ibid., 232.

261 Frithjof Schuon, *In the Face of the Absolute*, 113-14.

262 On the symbolism of Jesus's marriage, other Islamic texts clarify that he will be rewarded virgins, or houris of paradise, mentioned frequently in the Qur'an. Even according to Islamic theology, the houris can on one level be interpreted in an allegorical sense, and so should not *per se* offend Christian sensibilities. The symbolism of the houris is, in any event, fitting and congruent with the New Testament symbolism of Jesus and the church as the bride of Christ. The latter symbolism is, after all, ultimately based on the primordial man and woman Adam and Eve, the very image of 'marriage'.

263 Arthur Jeffery (ed.), *A Reader on Islam*, 597.

264 Ibid.

265 Robson, 66.

266 Cited in Robson, 87-89. Emphases added. We suspect that these traditions are not secondary, but preserve Jewish-Christian traditions independent of the canonical gospel accounts. The above account is derived from the *Rasa'il Ikhwan al-Safa*; see Ian Richard Netton, *Muslim Neoplatonists. An Introduction to the Thought of the Brethren of Purity (Ikhwan al-Safa)* (Edinburgh: Edinburgh University Press, 1991), 58ff.

267 See *Summa theologiae* 3, q3, a7 and *Sententiarum* lib. 3, d1, q2, a5.

268 See *Summa theologiae* 3, q2, a2.

269 *Summa theologiae* 3, q46, a12.

270 See Frithjof Schuon, *The Transcendent Unity of Religions*, 128.

271 See J. Dudley Woodberry, Osman Zümrüt, Mustafa Köylü, eds., *Muslim and Christian Reflections on Peace. Divine and Human Dimensions* (Lanham, Maryland: University Press of America, 2005), 40.

272 See ibid., 40-41. Frithjof Schuon, *In the Face of the Absolute*, 25.

273 Frithjof Schuon, *In the Face of the Absolute*, 25.

274 Frithjof Schuon, *Islam and the Perennial Philosophy*, 36-37.

275 Robson, 40. See Qur'an 3:55, Pickthall translation: '(And remember) when Allah said: O Jesus! Lo! I am gathering thee and causing thee to ascend unto Me, and am cleansing thee of those who disbelieve and am setting those who follow thee above those who disbelieve until the Day of Resurrection. Then unto Me ye will (all) return, and I shall judge between you as to that wherein ye used to differ.'

276 Edward Schillebeeckx, *Christ. The Experience of Jesus as Lord*, 356.

277 Seyyed Hossein Nasr, *Islamic Life and Thought*, 210.

278 Henry Corbin, 'Divine Epiphany and Spiritual Birth in Ismailian Gnosis,' 69.

279 Quoted in ibid., 70.

280 See ibid., 131.

281 Seyyed Hossein Nasr, 'Comments on a Few Theological Issues in the Islamic-Christian Dialogue,' in Yvonne Yazbeck Haddad and Wadi Zaidan Haddad (eds.), *Christian-Muslim Encounters* (Gainesville, Florida: University Press of Florida, 1995), 464.

282 See Daniélou, 249-50.

283 M. R. James, *The Apocryphal New Testament*, 503.

284 Daniélou, 242.

285 Ibid., 242-43.

286 See the references in Edward Schillebeeckx, *Jesus. An Experiment in Christology*, 343 and 705, note 61, for the 40 days motif in the Hebrew scriptures, and especially in *4 Esdras* and *2 Baruch*. In the former, Ezra spends 40 days rewriting the lost scriptures and is then, according to Arabic, Armenian, Ethiopic and Syriac versions, caught up alive to heaven. In *2 Baruch*, Jeremiah's secretary spends his last 40 days on earth teaching the people before he is assumed to heaven alive. Both will be reserved in heaven or paradise with others like them, apparently referring to Elijah and Enoch, and so it may be implied that Ezra and Baruch will return to earth, like Elijah and Enoch, at the end of time in the messianic age. The Lukan parallel to Christ's 40-day period of post-resurrectional teaching before his ascension, which is accompanied by a promise of the second coming at the end of time, is self-evident and needs no comment.

287 Daniélou, 252-53.

288 See ibid., 253.

289 See ibid., 257.

290 See Raymond Brown, 1012.

291 Ibid., 1013.

292 See ibid.

293 Ibid.

294 Ibid.

295 Ibid., 1014.

296 See ibid.

297 Cited in M. R. James, *The Apocryphal New Testament*, 8.

298 'My power, my power' does not denote a Gnostic provenance. On the contrary, 'Power', like 'Heaven', is a Semitic reverential evasive synonym for 'God', and indicates a Jewish-Christian origin for the *Gospel of Peter*.

299 See Daniélou, 267, 246.

300 Ibid., 253.

301 See Daniélou, 234, 243.

302 See M. E. Boismard, *L'évangile de l'enfance (Luc 1-2) selon le Proto-Luc* (Paris: Gabalda, 1997).

303 See [William Hone, ed.], *The Apocryphal New Testament* (London: William Hone, 1820), 73. This particular translation of the *Gospel of Nicodemus* was made from the version published by Johann Jacob Grynæus in his *Monumenta S. Patrum Orthodoxographa*, vol. i, tom ii. (Basiliae: Per Henrichum Petri, 1555; 1569), beginning on p. 643 (see W. Hone, 63). All manuscripts (Galba, Harley, Sion, etc.) of the Middle English version of *Nicodemus* (lines 685-724) also quite clearly place the resurrection of the saints on Good Friday before Christ's burial. See *William Henry*

Hulme (ed.), The Middle-English Harrowing of Hell and Gospel of Nicodemus. Now first edited from all the known manuscripts, with introduction and glossary (London: Early English Text Society by K. Paul, Trench, Trübner & Co., 1907), 67-69. There are a number of older and modern critical editions available for the *Gospel of Nicodemus*, a work which is typified by a very fluid text, many versions of which omit all mention of the Good Friday resurrection of the saints. The scene may or may not have been removed for theological reasons. See Achim Masser and Max Stiller (eds.), *Das Evangelium Nicodemi in spätmittelalterlicher deutscher Prosa: Texte* (Heidelberg: C. Winter, 1987); Hak Chin Kim (ed), *The Gospel of Nicodemus; Gesta Salvatoris; edited from the Codex Einsidlensis, Einsiedeln Stiftsbibliothek, MS 326* (Toronto: Centre for Medieval Studies by the Pontifical Institute of Medieval Studies, 1973); C. William Marx and Jeanne F. Drennan (eds.), *The Middle English Prose Complaint of our Lady and Gospel of Nicodemus: ed. from Cambridge, Magdalene College, MS Pepys 2498* (Heidelberg: C. Winter Universitätsverlag, 1987); James E. Cross and Dennis Brearly (eds.), *Two Old English apocrypha and their manuscript source: The Gospel of Nichodemus and the Avenging of the Saviour* (Cambridge/New York: Cambridge University Press, 1996). See also: Gaston Bruno Paulin and Alphonse Bos (eds.), *Trois versions rimées de l'Evangile de Nicodème par Chrétien, André de Coutances, et un anonyme, publiées d'après les manuscrits de Florence et de Londres par Gaston Paris & Alphonse Bos* (Paris: Firmin Didot et cie, 1885); Johann Georg Hohman and Philip Kegel, *Das Evangelium Nicodemus* (Reading, Pennsylvania: C.A. Bruckman, 1819); *Nicodemus. His Gospel* (1646; imprint of a Bodleian Library manuscript).

304 See Allan Menzies (ed.), *The Ante-Nicene Fathers*, vol. 10, 123.

305 George Howard, *Hebrew Gospel of Matthew* (Georgia: Mercer University Press, 1995), 147. The origin of medieval Jewish scholar Shem-Tob's Hebrew version of *Matthew* is still under debate by scholars, who remain deeply divided on the issue of whether or not it represents a translation from Latin or perhaps Spanish into Hebrew, or preserves, to some extent at least, a pre-canonical Hebrew edition of the Greek *Gospel of Matthew*.

306 Daniélou, 252.

307 See Anton Baumstark, *Comparative Liturgy* (London: A.R. Mowbray & Co. Limited, 1958), 174.

308 Edward Schillebeeckx has demonstrated that the three days motif is a standard one referring to 'the decisive day', and this is the standard opinion of exegetes. As such, the phrase 'after three days', or 'the third day' occurs dozens of times in the Hebrew scriptures, and is used 'without any chronological qualification.... . The third day is not, therefore, a focal point of time but of salvation.' Edward Schillebeeckx, *Jesus. An Experiment in Christology*, 529 and 725, note 27. The same author shows that the 'three day' motif in the resurrection accounts cannot possibly have a literal chronological content; see ibid., 528 and 725-26, note 33.

309 Kenneth L. Waters' recent attempt to interpret the resurrection of the saints in *Matthew* 27 not as a description of Good Friday events, but as an eschatological prophecy exhibiting literary traits of time and event compression, is simply the latest manifestation of theologians' unwillingness to grapple with the paradigm-shaking implications of the subject at hand. See Kenneth L. Waters, SR., 'Matthew 27:52-53 as Apocalyptic Apostrophe: Temporal-Spatial Collapse in the Gospel of Matthew,' *Journal of Biblical Literature* 122, no. 3 (Fall 2003), 489-515. Neither does Raymond Brown confront the implications of a Good Friday ascension in his commentary on the *Gospel of John*, but tries to preserve a distinction, along the interpretative lines of P. Benoit, between two distinct categories of ascension. See Raymond Brown, *The*

Anchor Bible. The Gospel according to John XIII-XXI, 1012-16.

310 *Or. Res. I*, cited in Jean Daniélou, *The Theology of Jewish Christianity*, 290.

311 Frithjof Schuon, *The Transcendent Unity of Religions*, 120.

312 Ibid., 121.

313 Ibid.

314 Ibid.

315 Ibid., 119-20.

316 Frithjof Schuon, *Understanding Islam*, 20-21.

317 Claus Schedl, *Muhammad und Jesus. Die christologisch relevanten Texte des Korans neu übersetztund erklärt* (Wien, Freiburg, Basel: Herder, 1978), 469.

318 Ibid.

319 Ibid.

320 Ibid.

321 See ibid., 476-79.

322 Ibid., 479.

323 Frithjof Schuon, *The Transcendent Unity of Religions*, 26.

324 Quoted in David A. Kerr, '"He Walked in the Path of the Prophets": Toward Christian Theological Recognition of the Prophethood of Muhammad,' in Yvonne Yazbeck Haddadd and Wadi Zaidan Haddad (eds.), *Christian-Muslim Encounters* (Jacksonville, Florida: University Press of Florida, 1995), 434.

325 See Hans Küng, *Christianity and World Religions*, 21. Küng observes that if Christians can speak of ordinary and extraordinary means of salvation, why could the church not also posit ordinary and extraordinary prophets? See ibid., 23-24.

326 See Daniel J. Sahas, '"Holosphyros"? A Byzantine Perception of "The God of Muhammad,"' in Yvonne Yazbeck Haddadd and Wadi Zaidan Haddad (eds.), *Christian-Muslim Encounters*, 109.

327 'Vatican Council and Papal Statements on Islam,' Jesuit Social Justice Center: http://www.uniya.org.au/education/interfaith_statements.html.

328 *Nicholas of Cusa's De Pace Fidei and Cribatio Alkorani*. Translated by Jaspar Hopkins, 10.

329 Ernst Cassirer, *The Individual and the Cosmos in Renaissance Philosophy*. Translated by Mario Domandi (New York/Evanston: Harper & Row, 1963), 28, 30-31.

330 Ibid., 30.

331 Ibid., 32.

332 Ibid., 36.

333 Frithjof Schuon, *In the Face of the Absolute* (Bloomington, Indiana: World Wisdom Books, 1994), 29.

334 *Nicholas of Cusa's De Pace Fidei and Cribatio Alkorani*. Translated by Jaspar Hopkins, 17.

335 Ibid., 19-20.

336 Ibid., 21. See Karl Rahner's statement, 'In this humanity (not in virtue of it), Jesus

Christ is the natural Son of the Father ... .' 'Incarnation,' *Encyclopedia of Theology*, 694.

337 Unfortunately, under the influence of subsequent political events, Nicholas of Cusa's rather generous attitude of 1453 towards Islam later hardened and polarized somewhat by the time he wrote his polemical treatise *Cribatio Alkorani* in 1460-1461. Still, the later work, though it contains some misinterpretations of the Qur'an, nevertheless also correctly deconstructs a variety of unjust misrepresentations of Islam which several earlier Catholic authors had fallen into.

338 Frithjof Schuon, *Understanding Islam*, 54.

339 Hopkins, 13.

340 Frithjof Schuon, *The Transcendent Unity of Religions*, 102.

341 Ibid., 23.

342 Frithjof Schuon, *Understanding Islam*, 22.

343 Frithjof Schuon, *The Transcendent Unity of Religions*, 92.

344 Robson, 93.

345 Though Jewish Christianity quite legitimately also speaks of the Holy Spirit as 'Mother', it understands the formula 'Father, Mother, Son' in a different and more orthodox Jewish monotheistic sense than in some forms of Gnosticism. Space does not allow us to comment upon the legitimate forms of Gnosis which also existed in Jewish Christianity. When it comes to Jewish Christianity, there are a number of factors that render it difficult to make sharp distinctions in every case between such reified terms as 'Christian,' 'Jewish,' 'Jewish Christian' and 'Gnostic.' Additionally, that there are valid esoteric elements in Gnosticism and docetism has been argued by Henry Corbin throughout his 'Divine Epiphany and Spiritual Birth in Ismailian Gnosis.' Therefore, when we speak of heretical Gnostics, this is not to imply that all gnostics were heretics, for traditional religions have all endorsed legitimate expressions of gnosis. Paul may call the Holy Spirit the 'Mother' in *Ephesians* 5:31, quoting *Genesis* 2:24, according to the interpretation and translation of Gilles Quispel, with additional explanatory comments in brackets added by the present author: 'Therefore shall [the Divine] Anthropos [Christ/Logos] leave his Father [God] and Mother [the Holy Spirit], and shall cleave unto his spouse [the church]. And the two shall become one flesh [for the church is the *body* of Christ].' See Gilles Quispel, 'Paul and Gnosis: a Personal View,' 294. Even if Paul himself did not mean what Quispel proposes, there can be little doubt that *Ephesians* 5:31 was understood so by *2 Clement* 14.

346 See Epiphanius, *Panarion* 78.13.

347 See Louis Gardet, *Mohammedanism*. Twentieth Century Encyclopedia of Catholicism, vol. 143 (NY: Hawthorn Books, 1961), 38.

348 See David A. Kerr, '"He Walked in the Path of the Prophets": Toward Christian Theological Recognition of the Prophethood of Muhammad,' 429.

349 Ibid.

350 Ibid., 430.

351 Ibid.

352 The bibliographic information is supplied in ibid., 428 and 443, note 19.

353 Ibid., 430.

354 See ibid., 430-31.

355 Ibid., 431.

356 Ibid., 432.

357 See ibid.

358 See ibid.

359 See ibid., 432-33.

360 Ibid., 433.

361 Ibid., 435.

362 Ibid., 437.

363 See ibid., 438.

364 See ibid., 439-40.

365 Ibid., 441. Consider the following astute remark of Louis Gardet: 'For a Christian it is perhaps more important first to see the religions as they are and as they want to be than to make a judgment about them.' Louis Gardet, *Islam* (Cologne: J. P. Bechem, 1968), 353.

366 Seyyed Hossein Nasr, *Sufi Essays*, 136.

367 Ibid., 140.

368 Frithjof Schuon, *The Transcendent Unity of Religions*, 139.

369 Seyyed Hossein Nasr, *Religion and the Order of Nature* (NY/Oxford: Oxford University Press, 1996), 13.

370 Ibid.

371 Michael A. Sells (ed.), *Early Islamic Mysticism. Sufi, Qur'an, Mi'raj, Poetic and Theological Writings. The Classics of Western Spirituality* series (NY/Mahwah, New Jersey: Paulist Press, 1996), 1.

372 Ibid.

373 See ibid., 17.

374 See David Martin, 'The Return to "The One" in the Philosophy of Najm Al-Din Al-Kubra,' in Parviz Morewedge (ed.), *Neoplatonism and Islamic Thought* (Albany, NY: State University of New York, 1992), 212.

375 Seyyed Hossein Nasr, *Sufi Essays*, 134.

376 Seyyed Hossein Nasr, *Ideals and Realities of Islam*, 37.

377 Frithjof Schuon, *The Transcendent Unity of Religions*, 102.

378 Seyyed Hossein Nasr, *Traditional Islam in the Modern World*, (NY: State University of New York, 1994), 258. It should be added that de Foucald, being a child of his times, naturally shared some of the then prevailing notions concerning the spiritual poverty of Islam and certain ideas on proselytism. But Nasr's comments nevertheless shed light on the particular spiritual nuance given to such ideas by de Foucald.

379 Some ancient manuscripts omit the Trinitarian formula.

380 For a general introduction to the Targums in relation to the Gospels, see Martin

McNamara, *Targum and Testament. Aramaic Paraphrases of the Hebrew Bible: A Light on the New Testament* (Grand Rapids, Michigan: William B. Eerdmans Publishing Co., 1972).

381 Fernand Prat, S. J., *The Theology of Saint Paul.* Vol. 2. Translated by John L. Stoddard (London: Burns Oates and Washbourne, 1942), 353, 357.

382 *The Holy Qur'an.* Text, Translation and Commentary by Abdullah Yusuf Ali. Facsimile of 1938 edition. Fourth U.S. edition, ix-x.

383 See William C. Chittick, *Imaginal Worlds. Ibn al-'Arabi and the Problem of Religious Diversity* (New York: State University of New York Press, 1994), 123-60.

384 Frithjof Schuon, *Christianity/Islam. Essays on Esoteric Ecumenism*, 102.

385 See Frithjof Schuon, *The Transcendent Unity of Religions*, 1-6; 31-56; 118-38.

386 On the question of whether any religion can communicate the entirety of truth, consider the following reflections of Avery Dulles, writing from a Catholic perspective, when he points out concerning dogma, that it is not identical to revelation, does not possess 'conceptual objectivity', is not immutable, and is not universal. See Avery Dulles, *The Survival of Dogma* (Garden City, New York: Doubleday Image, 1973), 158. Furthermore, dogmas are not 'capable of exactly circumscribing the content they affirm' (ibid., 160). Dogma is provisional and metaphorical (ibid., 161). Neither are dogmas 'descriptive or scientific statements' (ibid.). We may say that the eternal Truth implied by a dogma can only be imperfectly expressed in the human language in which the dogma is formulated. This fact and limitation applies to all world religions. As Dulles observes, faith and dogma are not identical (ibid., 167); thus unity of faith does not necessarily require unity of dogma. Again, dogmas affirm immutable truths in mutable and imperfect language (see ibid., 194). But the providential power of dogma to refer adequately to supraformal Truth should not be lost sight of. Frithjof Schuon compares dogmas to arteries in the body (see *The Transcendent Unity of Religions*, 140). In the same work, he discusses the positive nature and function of dogma by observing that 'a dogma is both a limited idea and an unlimited symbol at one and the same time' (7).

387 See Frithjof Schuon's essay, 'Form and Substance in the Religions,' in his *Christianity/Islam. Essays on Esoteric Ecumenism*, 87-108.

388 See ibid., 99.

389 Hans Urs von Balthasar, *Mysterium Paschale. The Mystery of Easter* (San Francisco, California: Ignatius Press, 1990), 247.

390 Ibid., 235.

391 Ibid., 236.

392 Ibid., 245.

393 See ibid.

394 Ibid., 246. The same points may be applied to the subject of Jesus's 'crucifixion'.

395 Ibid.

396 Ibid., 247.

397 Ibid., 248.

398 On the question of the possibility of 'natural' knowledge of God in relation to revelation, see Vincent Potter, S.J., 'Revelation and "Natural" Knowledge of God,' in Parviz

Morewedge (ed.), *Neoplatonism and Islamic Thought*, 247-57. In our view, Potter is correct to judge that the positing of transcendence and immanence as an 'either-or' scenario is fundamentally misguided. There must be at least some degree of natural knowledge of God in order to recognize revelation as divine in origin. As Potter writes: 'It will not do either to say that the Revelation is self-authenticating since this merely puts the same problem at another step removed.' Ibid., 251.

399 Ibid., 121-22

400 See ibid., 124.

401 Ibid., 130.

402 Ibid., 122.

403 To label Dionysius 'Pseudo' is at times a convenient maneuver by certain scholars to simply avoid the question, unrelated to historical authorship, of the theological authenticity of the writings in question. Our own personal view is that the author believed he was inspired by the spirit of the historical Dionysius and was therefore fully justified, from an ancient mystical perspective, in assuming that identity. The same may be said of much of the ancient so-called pseudepigraphical writings, which should not be considered 'forgeries' in the modern pejorative sense. Some of the ancient pseudepigrapha are held as sacred by the Catholic Church, e.g., the *Wisdom of Solomon*. We could also mention *Jude* 14's quotation of *1 Enoch*. One theory of Dionysius is that of Frothingham published in 1886, namely, that his teacher Hierotheus was the Syrian gnostic Stephen bar Sudhaili. A single precious manuscript of the *Book of Hierotheus on the Hidden Mysteries of the Divinity* lives at the British Museum. For references, see David Martin, 'The Return to "The One" in the Philosophy of Najm Al-Din Al-Kubra,' in Parviz Morewedge (ed.), *Neoplatonism and Islamic Thought*, 211 and 240, note 1. However, the identification of Hierotheus with Stephen bar Sudhaili has been contested. Consult the discussion in Irénée Hausherr, 'De doctrina spirituali christianorum orientalium,' *Orientalia Christiana* 30 (1933): 175-211.

404 Joseph Cardinal Ratzinger, *Introduction to Christianity*, 114.

405 Ibid., 117.

406 Ibid., 122.

407 Ibid.

408 Karl Rahner, ed., article, 'Trinity,' *Encyclopedia of Theology*, 1757.

409 See Frithjof Schuon, *The Transcendent Unity of Religions*, 1-6.

410 Ibid., 3.

411 Ibid.

412 We say 'supraformal' in reflection of Aristotle's dictum that 'the whole is of necessity prior to the part' (*Politics* I 1253a), which is certainly related to, even if not identical with, Plato's concept of the archetype.

413 Frithjof Schuon, *The Transcendent Unity of Religions*, 99.

414 Ibid., 24.

415 Frithjof Schuon, *Dimensions of Islam*, 66.

416 Article, 'Incarnation,' *Encyclopedia of Theology*, 694.

417 Ibid., 691.

418 Frithjof Schuon, *Dimensions of Islam*, 66-67.

419 See Frithjof Schuon, *The Transcendent Unity of Religions*, 86. On page 28 of the same work, Schuon offers a working metaphor for 'relative absoluteness': '[W]ould anyone speaking of the sun seriously contend that the placing of the definite article before the word "sun" was tantamount to denying the existence of other suns in space?' The implication is that there is a multiplicity of 'religious' solar systems created, or revealed, by God.

420 See Karl Rahner, *The Spirit in the Church* (NY: Seabury Press, 1979), 100-01.

421 Frithjof Schuon, *Gnosis. Divine Wisdom*. Translated by G. E. H. Palmer (Pates Manor, Bedfont, Middlesex: Perennial Books, 1990), 30, 37.

422 See ibid., 91.

423 Ibid.

424 Ibid.

425 'Colouring' refers to the process of dyeing by the immersion of cloth in a vat.

426 As Schuon notes (see *The Transcendent Unity of Religions*, 122), Muhammad's approach and method of argumentation in these verses regarding Judaism and Christianity is paralleled by St. Paul's argumentation regarding Judaism in *Romans* 2:25-29.

427 See Frithjof Schuon, *Dimensions of Islam*, 69.

428 Cited in ibid., 68-69, note 1.

429 Frithjof Schuon, *The Transcendent Unity of Religions*, 108-09.

430 Ibid., 109-10.

431 Seyyed Hossein Nasr, *Ideals and Realities of Islam*, 35.

432 See ibid., 36.

433 Frithjof Schuon, *The Transcendent Unity of Religions*, 115.

434 Cyrus ruled the Persian empire 550–530 BCE. After conquering Babylon in 538, he allowed the exiled Jews of Babylon to return home and rebuild the holy city of Jerusalem and its temple. In 539, Cyrus returned all sacred images ('idols') that had had been captured and transferred to Babylon to their rightful owners from whom they had been plundered.

435 See the discussion in Daniélou, *The Theology of Jewish Christianity*, 93.

436 See ibid., 245.

437 See Mary Boyce (ed.), *Textual Sources for the Study of Zoroastrianism* (Chicago, Ill.: University of Chicago Press, 1990), 22.

438 See A. Frhr. v. Ow, *Brahma-Wodan. Indogermanische Zusammenhänge* (Regensburg: G. J. Manz, 1915), 39.

439 See Samuel Zinner, *Christianity and Islam: Essays on Ontology and Archetype* (London: Matheson Trust, 2011), 126.

440 See Mary Boyce (ed.), *Textual Sources for the Study of Zoroastrianism*, 11-12.

441 As Mary Boyce remarks, Judaism, Christianity and Islam 'all ... owe great debts to the Iranian religion'. Ibid., 12. Consider the following observation by Frithjof Schuon on interreligious 'influences': 'Moreover it is not excluded in metaphysics that one doctrine

should borrow dialectical keys from another ... ; since ... they are possible, there is no reason for not admitting that they have taken place. There is no doubt that Neoplatonism played such a part in relation to the esoterisms of Semitic origin.' Frithjof Schuon, *Spiritual Perspectives and Human Facts*, 76. In the same passage, Schuon explains that the presence of kabbalistic traditions in Christian mysticism is explained by Christianity's origin in Judaism.

442 Ruth Langer, 'Jewish Understandings of the Religious Other,' *Theological Studies* 64 (2003), 277.

443 Consider Frithjof Schuon's following assertion: 'If the religion of these "misbelievers" [polytheists] is false ... , why have Sufis declared that God can be present ... in the temples of idolaters? ... [F]rom the point of view of some Sufi, it was not Apollo who was false but the way he was regarded.' *Understanding Islam*, 55-56. We may also note that Cardinal Nicolas of Cusa liberally grants in his *De pace fidei* treatise that polytheists ultimately worship the one, true God.

444 *Asclepius* asserts that sacred images which are understood to be symbols should not be called 'idols'. See *Corpus Hermeticum* XVII.

445 See Henry Corbin, 'Divine Epiphany and Spiritual Birth in Ismailian Gnosis,' 78.

446 Frithjof Schuon, *The Transcendent Unity of Religions*, 14.

447 Ibid., 20.

448 Ibid., 19.

449 For a traditional translation and commentary, see Aryeh Kaplan, *Sefer Yetzirah in Theory and Practice* (York Beach, Maine: Samuel Weiser, Inc., 1997). For a modern critical approach, see David R. Blumenthal, *Understanding Jewish Mysticism. A Source Reader. The Merkabah Tradition and the Zoharic Tradition* (New York: Ktav Publishing House, Inc., 1978), 15-44. Kaplan takes the Abrahamic origin of the *Sefer Yetzirah* seriously. Simo Parpola of the University of Helsinki, while not ascribing the *Sefer Yetzirah* to Abraham, nevertheless historically situates its basic ideas in the time of Abraham. See Simo Parpola, 'The Assyrian Tree of Life: Tracing the Origins of Jewish Monotheism and Greek Philosophy,' *Journal of Near Eastern Studies* 52 no. 3 (July 1993), 161-208.

450 We emphasize again that not in a literal sense, but in a metaphysical sense there is a correspondence between the Christian dogma of trinity and Logos, Jewish kabbalistic sefirotic emanationism (each *sefirah* is a Logos corresponding to the ten words or commands of creation in *Genesis* 1) and *Adam Kadmon*, Islamic philosophical emanationism, the Sufi doctrine of the *Nur Muhammadi* (Light of Muhammad), and the Shi'i idea of the eternal Imam. The exoteric explication of these esoteric ideas is providentially excluded, or at the very least strictly guarded, in Judaism and Islam.

451 See article, 'Trinity,' *Encyclopedia of Theology*, 1756.

452 Hans Küng, *Judaism. Beyond Yesterday and Tomorrow*, 374.

453 Frithjof Schuon, *In the Face of the Absolute*, 24-25.

454 Frithjof Schuon, *Spiritual Perspectives and Human Facts*, 73.

455 See Ratzinger, *Introduction to Christianity*, 84-85, note 13.

456 See Frithjof Schuon, *The Transcendent Unity of Religions*, 103.

457 For a comparison of Marqa with Aristotle and Philo on the subject of the Logos and the divine attributes, see Alexander Broadie, *A Samaritan Philosophy. A Study of the Hellenistic Cultural Ethos of the Memar Marqah* (Leiden: E. J. Brill, 1981). See especially the chapters on 'The Oneness of God' (23-33) and 'The Powers of God' (54-87). Michael Goulder argues that Marqa propounds a doctrine of divine hypostases; see Michael Goulder, 'Two Roots of the Christian Myth,' in John Hick (ed.), *The Myth of God Incarnate* (Philadelphia: The Westminster Press, 1977), 68-71.

458 Quoted in Alexander Broadie, *A Samaritan Philosophy. A Study of the Hellenistic Cultural Ethos of the Memar Marqah*, 79.

459 See *Fakhruddin 'Iraqi. Divine Flashes*. Translation and introduction by William C. Chittick and Peter Lamborn Wilson, 6-22, especially 11-12.

460 Seyyed Hossein Nasr, *Ideals and Realities of Islam*, 88.

461 See *Fakhruddin 'Iraqi. Divine Flashes*, 6-22.

462 See Daniel Boyarin, 'The Gospel of the *Memra*: Jewish Binitarianism and the Prologue of John,' 243-84.

463 See Moshe Idel, *Kabbalah. New Perspectives* (New Haven and London: Yale University Press, 1988).

464 On the ancient Near Eastern elements of the Kabbalah, see Simo Parpola, 'The Assyrian Tree of Life: Tracing the Origins of Jewish Monotheism and Greek Philosophy,' *Journal of Near Eastern Studies* 52 no. 3 (July 1993), 161-208. For the mutual influences between Near Eastern and Indo-European culture and thought, see Simon Pulleyn, *Homer. Iliad Book One*. Edited with an Introduction, Translation, and Commentary (Oxford/New York: Oxford University Press, 2000), 11-15; Trevor Bryce, *Life and Society in the Hittite World* (Oxford/New York: Oxford University Press, 2002), 257-68; Stephanie Dalley, *Myths from Mesopotamia. Creation, the Flood, Gilgamesh, and Others* (Oxford/New York: Oxford University Press, 2000), 47-49; Walter Burkert, *Greek Religion* (Cambridge, Mass.: Harvard University Press, 1985), 18-19; Thomas V. Gamkrelidze and Vjaceslav V. Ivanov, *Indo-European and the Indo-Europeans*. 2 vols. (Berlin/New York: Mouton de Gruyter, 1995). For recent scholarship on the predominantly Egyptian intellective ambient of the *Corpus Hermeticum*, see Peter Kingsley, 'Poimandres: The Etymology of the Name and the Origins of the Hermetica,' in Roelof van den Broek and Cis van Heertum (eds.), *From Poimandres to Jacob Böhme: Gnosis, Hermetism and the Christian Tradition*, 41-76. Gilles Quispel emphasizes more the mutual interplay between Greek and Egyptian influences in the *Corpus Hermeticum*. See Gilles Quispel, 'Reincarnation and Magic in Asclepius,' in ibid., 168-231. However, when on page 212 Quispel argues that the theme of ascensional apotheosis is Hellenistic in origin, and not Hebrew, he overlooks the Jewish scriptural evidence of the enthroned king of Israel's transformation into the 'begotten Son of YHWH', who is worshipped along with God. Also unmentioned is *1 Enoch*'s vision of Enoch's ascent and apotheosis, which would seem to have been influenced not by Hellenistic but Zoroastrian thought. *1 Enoch* is much older than the text of *3 Enoch*, a work which Quispel does quote. But a primary Hellenistic influence in *3 Enoch* also seems a questionable and unnecessary theory. Finally, neither does Quispel allude to the ancient Near Eastern extra-biblical concept of royal divinization.

465 Frithjof Schuon, *The Transcendent Unity of Religions*, 28.

466 Ibid., 108.

467 On Islamic gematria, see Mohammad Ali Amir-Moezzi, *The Divine Guide in Early Shi'ism* (Albany, NY: State University of New York Press, 1994), 95, 105-08. We should address the fact that in Christianity, as opposed to Judaism and Islam, there is no developed system of theological gematria. As Seyyed Hossein Nasr explains, in 'incarnational' religions such as Christianity there is no sacred language: 'In such traditions there is no sacred language because the body or external form of the founder itself is the external form of the Word of God. For example, in Christianity, Christ himself is the Word of God and it does not matter whether one celebrates mass in Greek, Latin or for that matter Arabic or Persian to be able to participate in the "blood and body" of Christ. Latin in the Catholic church is a liturgical language not a sacred one.' Seyyed Hossein Nasr, *Ideals and Realities of Islam*, 45. Nasr's point is an observation based purely on a simple comparative model of world religions. The so-called avataric religions do not possess sacred languages; only religions of an 'incarnate' Book seem to possess a sacred language. This is precisely why the church did not develop a theology based on letter and gematria symbolism as did Judaism and Islam. This is of course not to denigrate religions with sacred languages, but merely to point out that certain authors who describe the church and Latin as an institution and a sacred language which parallel Judaism and Hebrew are confusing (i.e., fusing together) religious categories that are providentially designed to remain separate. Of course, gematria is not completely unknown in Christianity, but it has never been a dominant mode of theological exegesis as it is in Judaism, at least not in Pauline Christianity.

468 See Jarl Fossum, 'Jewish-Christian Christology and Jewish Mysticism,' 275.

469 See ibid. for the prayer in full, which in translations runs: 'I [the prophet Elchasai] am witness over you on the day of judgment.' Muhammad as witness to and preacher of the day of judgment, one of the most central of the Qur'anic themes, comes naturally to mind.

470 See Frithjof Schuon, *Dimensions of Islam*, 79-80. Here Schuon writes that in Qur'an 61:6, 'Ahmad' refers esoterically to 'the transcendent and immanent Logos, and thus the "inward Prophet" ... ; it [the immanent Logos] is the Divine Spirit... . [T]he name "Ahmad" is the "heavenly name" of the Prophet; ... it is thus a question not so much of an earthly reality as of its heavenly root... .' (page 80).

471 *The Summa Theologica*. Translated by Fathers of the English Dominican Province (Benziger Bros. edition, 1947). Modified translation. I am grateful to Dr. Michael Ewbank for this reference.

472 'A burden again', that is, as under the Torah's Levitical precepts.

473 See Hans Küng, *Christianity and World Religions*, 62. It is not correct to call Islamic *ahadith* 'commandments' or 'laws', though as Küng observes, the *ahadith*, which in the various collections run into the thousands, are often 'the basis for rendering legal decisions' (ibid.).

474 See St. Augustine, *On Faith and Works*. Translated and annotated by Gregory J. Lombardo (New York/Mahwah, New Jersey, 1988), 43.

475 See Seyyed Hossein Nasr, *Muhammad: Man of God* (Chicago, Illinois: KAZI Publications, 1995), 19.

476 Frithjof Schuon, *Christianity/Islam. Essays on Esoteric Ecumenism*, 175.

477 Ibid., 178.

478 Compare Schoeps' description of the Ebionite conception of the True Prophet in his *Jewish Christianity*, 68-73, 126-27, with Schillebeeckx's description of the New Testament's 'Prophet' christology in his *Jesus. An Experiment in Christology*, 475-99.

479 In this context, see Frithjof Schuon, *The Transcendent Unity of Religions*, 93 (see Schuon's footnote at the bottom of the page marked with an asterisk).

480 'To the consummation of the world', or more literally, 'always', or 'for ever'.

481 See Rahner's article, 'Trinity,' *The Encyclopedia of Theology*, 1755.

482 *John* 4:22: 'You adore that which you know not: we adore that which we know. For salvation is of the Jews.' Here Christ concedes that the Samaritans do worship the true God; he only criticizes, understandably from a Jewish perspective, their praxis of not worshipping according to such knowledge.

483 Christ's condemnation of proselytism in *Matthew* 23:15, 'Woe to you, scribes and Pharisees, hypocrites, because you go round about the sea and the land to make one proselyte. And when he is made, you make him the child of hell twofold more than yourselves,' should always be kept in mind by the church as it strives to fulfill Christ's directive to teach the nations his commandment of love. Christ's never having given an example of demanding pagans and Samaritans to convert to Judaism should lead theologians to ponder deeply just what is involved in Christ's great commission directive to the apostles.

484 For some Catholic attempts at grappling with the issue of salvation outside the church, see Avery Dulles, *Models of Revelation* (New York, NY: Doubleday Publishing, 1985) and Hans Küng, *On Being a Christian* (Garden City, NY: Image Books, 1984), 89-116.

485 See James Fredericks, 'The Catholic Church and the Other Religious Paths: Rejecting Nothing That Is True and Holy,' *Theological Studies* 64 (2003), 227-33.

486 Antonie Wessels, after a discussion of *John* 14:6 and *Acts* 4:12, emphasizes the importance of several scriptural passages implying salvation beyond the visible boundaries of either Judaism or Christianity. The Canaanite Melchizedek blessed the monotheist Abraham (*Genesis* 14:18-20); Christ extended salvation to a Canaanite woman (*Matthew* 15:21-28) and to a Roman centurion (*Matthew* 8:5-13), and of neither did he require a conversion to Judaism (Wessels does not make this last point); Peter in *Acts* 10:9-29, 24-36, teaches that God shows no partiality to either Jew, Christian or pagan. Other 'pagans' praised in Judaism or Christianity are Rahab the prostitute, Ruth the Moabite, and Cyrus the Persian king. See Antonie Wessels, 'Some Biblical Considerations Relevant to the Encounter Between Traditions,' in Yvonne Yazbeck Haddad and Wadi Zaidan Haddad (eds.), *Christian-Muslim Encounters*, 54-64.

487 Cf. Qur'an 2:138: 'We take our colour [i.e., immersion] from Allah, and who is better than Allah at colouring?'

488 Robson, 33-34.

BIBLIOGRAPHY

Ali, Abdullah Yusuf, *The Holy Qur'an*. Text, Translation and Commentary by Abdullah Yusuf Ali. Facsimile of 1938 edition. Fourth U.S. edition, Elmhurst, New York: Tahrike Tarsile Qur'an, Inc., 2002.

Ali, Abdullah Yusuf, *The Meaning of the Holy Qur'án*. New Edition with Revised Translation and Commentary, Brentwood, Maryland: Amana Corporation, 1411 AH/1991 A.C.

Amir-Moezzi, Mohammad Ali, *The Divine Guide in Early Shi'ism*, Albany, NY: State University of New York Press, 1994.

Augustine, Saint, *On Faith and Works*, tr. and annotated by Gregory J. Lombardo, New York/Mahwah, New Jersey, 1988.

von Balthasar, Hans Urs, *Mysterium Paschale. The Mystery of Easter*, San Francisco, California: Ignatius Press, 1990.

Bauckham, Richard, *God Crucified: Monotheism and Christology in the New Testament*, Grand Rapids, Michigan: Eerdmans, 1998.

Baumstark, Anton, *Comparative Liturgy*, London: A.R. Mowbray & Co. Limited, 1958.

Bishai, Wilson B., "A Possible Coptic Source for a Qur'anic Text," *Journal of the American Oriental Society* 91, 1971, 125-28.

Blumenthal, David R., *Understanding Jewish Mysticism. A Source Reader. The Merkabah Tradition and the Zoharic Tradition*, New York: Ktav Publishing House, Inc., 1978.

Boismard M.E. , *L'évangile de l'enfance (Luc 1-2) selon le Proto-Luc*, Paris: Gabalda, 1997.

Boyarin, Daniel, "The Gospel of the *Memra*: Jewish Binitarianism and the Prologue of John," *Harvard Theological Review* 94 no. 3, 2001, 243-84.

Boyce, Mary, ed., *Textual Sources for the Study of Zoroastrianism*, Chicago, Ill.: University of Chicago Press, 1990.

Broadie, Alexander, *A Samaritan Philosophy. A Study of the Hellenistic Cultural Ethos of the Memar Marqah*, Leiden: E. J. Brill, 1981.

van den Broek, Roelof, "Der Brief des Jakobus an Quadratus und das Problem der judenchristlichen Bischöfe von Jerusalem (Eusebius, HE IV, 5, 1-3), in T. Baarda, A. Hilhorst, G. P. Luttikhuizen, A. S. van der Woude, eds., *Text and Testimony. Essays on New Testament and Apocryphal Literature in Honour of A. F. J. Klijn*, Kampen:

Uitgeversmaatschappij J. H. Kok, 1988, 56-65.

Brown, Raymond, *The Anchor Bible. The Gospel according to John I-XII*, Garden City, New York: Doubleday, 1983.

Bryce, Trevor, *Life and Society in the Hittite World*, Oxford/New York: Oxford University Press, 2002.

Burkert, Walter, *Greek Religion*, Cambridge, Mass.: Harvard University Press, 1985.

Cassirer, Ernst, *The Individual and the Cosmos in Renaissance Philosophy*, tr. by Mario Domandi, New York/Evanston: Harper & Row, 1963.

Charles, R. H., *A Critical and Exegetical Commentary on the Revelation of St. John*, vol. 1. The International Critical Commentary, New York: Charles Scribner's Sons, 1920.

Charlesworth, James H., ed., *The Old Testament Pseudepigrapha,* vol. 1, New York: Doubleday, 1983.

_____, ed., *The Old Testament Pseudepigrapha*, vol. 2, New York: Doubleday, 1985.

Chilton, Bruce, *Judaic Approaches to the Gospels*, Atlanta, Georgia, Scholars Press, 1994.

Chittick, William C., *Imaginal Worlds. Ibn al-'Arabi and the Problem of Religious Diversity*, New York: State University of New York Press,1994.

Corbin, Henry, *Creative Imagination in the Sufism of Ibn 'Arabî*, tr. by Ralph Manheim, Bollingen Series XCI, Princeton, NJ: Princeton University Press, 1981.

_____, "Divine Epiphany and Spiritual Birth in Ismailian Gnosis," in *Man and Transformation*. Papers from the Eranos Yearbooks.Bollingen Series XXX, vol. 5, New York: Pantheon Books, 1964, 69-160.

Cusa, Nicholas of, *Nicholas of Cusa's De Pace Fidei and Cribatio Alkorani*. Translation and Analysis by Jasper Hopkins. 2nd ed., Minneapolis: Arthur J. Banning Press, 1994.

Dalley, Stephanie, *Myths from Mesopotamia. Creation, the Flood, Gilgamesh, and Others*, Oxford/New York: Oxford University Press, 2000.

Daniélou, Jean, *The Theology of Jewish Christianity*, tr. and edited by John A. Baker, London: Darton, Longman & Todd; Chicago: Henry Regnery Co., 1964.

Dulles, Avery, *Models of Revelation*, New York, NY: Doubleday Publishing, 1985.

_____, *The Survival of Dogma*, Garden City, New York: Doubleday Image, 1973.

Dupont-Sommer, A., "Adam. 'Père du Monde' dans la *Sagesse de Solomon* 10, 1.2," *Revue de l'histoire des religions* 119, 1939, 182-203.

Edwards, James R., "The *Gospel of the Ebionites* and the Gospel of Luke," *New Testament Studies* 48, 2002, 568-86.

Eusebius of Caesarea, *Preparation for the Gospel*, tr. by E.H. Gifford, vol. 3 part

2, Oxford: Clarendon, 1903.

Fletcher-Louis, Crispin H. T., *All the Glory of Adam. Liturgical Anthropology in the Dead Sea Scrolls*, Leiden/Boston/Köln: Brill, 2002.

Flusser, David, *Das Christentum – eine jüdische Religion?* Munich: Kösel, 1990.

Fossum, Jarl, "Jewish-Christian Christology and Jewish Mysticism," *Vigiliae Christianae* 37, 1983, 260-87.

Fredericks, James, "The Catholic Church and the Other Religious Paths: Rejecting Nothing That Is True and Holy," *Theological Studies* 64, 2003, 227-33.

Gamkrelidze, Thomas V. and Ivanov, Vjaceslav V., *Indo-European and the Indo-Europeans*. 2 vols., Berlin/New York: Mouton de Gruyter, 1995.

Gardet, Louis, *Islam*, Cologne: J. P. Bechem, 1968.

_____, *Mohammedanism*. Twentieth Century Encyclopedia of Catholicism, vol. 143, New York: Hawthorn Books, 1961.

Gieschen, Charles A., *Angelomorphic Christology. Antecedents and Early Evidence*, Leiden/Boston/Köln: Brill, 1998.

_____, "The Divine Name in Ante-Nicene Christology," *Vigiliae Christianae* 57 no. 2, 2003, 115-58.

al-Ghorab, Mahmoud, "Muhyiddin Ibn al-'Arabi amidst Religions (*adyân*) and Schools of Thought (*madhâhib*)," in Stephen Hirtenstein and Michael Tiernan, eds., *Muhyiddin Ibn 'Arabi. Commemorative Volume*, Element Books, Shaftesbury, 1993, 200-27.

Goulder, Michael D., "Hebrews and the Ebionites," *New Testament Studies* 49, 2003, 393-406.

_____, "Ignatius' Docetists," *Vigiliae Christianae* 33, 1999, 16-30.

_____, *Paul and the Competing Mission in Corinth*, Peabody, Massachusetts: Hendrickson Publishers, Inc., 2001.

_____, "A Poor Man's Christology," *New Testament Studies* 45, 1999, 332-48.

Gregory, Andrew, "Prior or Posterior? The *Gospel of the Ebionites* and the Gospel of Luke," *New Testament Studies* 51, 2005, 344-60.

Haddad, Yvonne Yazbeck and Haddad, Wadi Zaidan, eds., *Christian-Muslim Encounters*, Gainesville, Florida: University Press of Florida, 1995.

Hanauer, J. E., *The Holy Land. Myths and Legends*, London, Senate, 1996.

Hannah, Darrell D., "The Throne of His Glory," *Zeitschrift für die Neutestamentliche Wissenschaft und die Kunde der älteren Kirche* 94 no. 1/2, 2003, 68-96.

Hausherr, Irénée, "De doctrina spirituali christianorum orientalium," *Orientalia Christiana* 30, 1933, 175-211.

Hick, John, ed., *The Myth of God Incarnate*, Philadelphia: The Westminster Press, 1977.

Homer, *Iliad Book One*. Edited with an Introduction, Translation, and Commentary by Simon Pulleyn, Oxford/New York: Oxford

University Press, 2000.

Howard, George, *Hebrew Gospel of Matthew*, Georgia: Mercer University Press, 1995.

Idel, Moshe, *Kabbalah. New Perspectives*, New Haven and London: Yale University Press, 1988.

_____, Bernard McGinn, Bernard, eds., *Mystical Union in Judaism, Christianity, and Islam: An Ecumenical Dialogue*, New York: Continuum, 1989, 1996.

'Iraqi, Fakhruddin, *Divine Flashes*. Translation and introduction by William C. Chittick and Peter Lamborn Wilson, New York/Mahwah, New Jersey: Paulist Press, 1982.

James, M. R., *The Apocryphal New Testament*, Oxford: Clarendon Press, 1924.

Jeffery, Arthur, ed., *A Reader on Islam*, 'S-Gravenhage: Mouton & Co., 1962.

Kaplan, Aryeh, *Sefer Yetzirah in Theory and Practice*, York Beach, Maine: Samuel Weiser, Inc., 1997.

Küng, Hans, *Christianity: Essence, History, and Future*, New York:Continuum, 1999.

_____, van Ess, Josef; von Stietencron, Heinrich, Bechert, Heinz; Heinegg, Peter, eds., *Christianity and World Religions. Paths to Dialogue*, New York: Orbis, 1993.

_____, *On Being a Christian*, Garden City, New York: Image Books, 1984.

_____, *Judaism. Between Yesterday and Tomorrow*, New York: Crossroad, 1992.

Langer, Ruth, "Jewish Understandings of the Religious Other," *Theological Studies* 64, 2003, 255-77.

Lightfoot, J. B., *The Apostolic Fathers*, Grand Rapids, Michigan: Baker Book House, 1974.

Lings, Martin, *A Sufi Saint of the Twentieth Century. Shaikh Ahmad al-'Alawî*, Berkeley and Los Angeles: University of California Press, 1973.

Lührmann, Dieter, *Die apokryph gewordenen Evangelien. Studien zu neuen Texten und neuen Fragen*, Leiden/Boston: Brill, 2004.

Massignon, Louis, "Nur Muhammadi," in *The Encyclopaedia of Islam*, vol. 3, L-R, Leiden: Brill, 1936, 961.

McNamara, Martin, *Targum and Testament. Aramaic Paraphrases of the Hebrew Bible: A Light on the New Testament*, Grand Rapids, Michigan: William B. Eerdmans Publishing Co., 1972.

Morewedge, Parviz, ed., *Neoplatonism and Islamic Thought*, Albany, New York: State University of New York, 1992.

Nasr, Seyyed Hossein, *The Garden of Truth. The Vision and Promise of Sufism, Islam's Mystical Tradition*, New York: HarperOne, 2007.

_____, *The Heart of Islam. Enduring Values for Humanity*, San Francisco, California: HarperSanFrancisco, 2002.

_____, *Ideals and Realities of Islam*, New York: Frederick A. Praeger, 1967.

_____, *Islamic Life and Thought*, Albany, New York: State University of New

York Press, 1981.

_____, *Muhammad: Man of God*, Chicago, Illinois: KAZI Publications, 1995.

_____, *Religion and the Order of Nature*, New York/Oxford: Oxford University Press, 1996.

_____, *Sufi Essays*, 2nd ed., Albany, New York: State University of New York Press, 1991.

_____, *Traditional Islam in the Modern World*, New York: State University of New York, 1994.

Netton, Ian Richard, *Muslim Neoplatonists. An Introduction to the Thought of the Brethren of Purity (Ikhwan al-Safa)*, Edinburgh:Edinburgh University Press, 1991.

Neusner, Jacob, *Rabbinic Literature & the New Testament. What We Cannot Show, We Do Not Know*, Valley Forge, Pennsylvania:Trinity Press International, 1994.

Oesterly, W. O. E., *The Books of the Apocrypha. Their Origin, Teaching and Contents*, London: Robert Scott, 1915.

O'Meara, Thomas F., "Christian Theology and Extraterrestrial Intelligent Life," *Theological Studies* 60, 1999, 103-123.

Overton, John, *Inquiry into the Truth and Use of the Book of Enoch, as to its Prophecies, Visions, and Account of Fallen Angels*, London: Simpkin and Marshall, 1822.

v. Ow, A. Frhr., *Brahma-Wodan. Indogermanische Zusammenhänge*, Regensburg: G. J. Manz, 1915.

Parpola, Simo, "The Assyrian Tree of Life: Tracing the Origins of Jewish Monotheism and Greek Philosophy," *Journal of Near Eastern Studies* 52 no. 3, July 1993, 161-208.

Phan, Peter C., "Multiple Religious Belonging," *Theological Studies* 64, 2003, 495-519.

Philo, *The Works of Philo*. Complete and Unabridged. New Updated Edition, tr. by C. D. Yonge, Hendrickson Publishers, 1993.

Pines, Shlomo, *Some Traits of Christian Theological Writing in Relation to Moslem Kalâm and to Jewish Thought*. Proceedings of the Israel Academy of Sciences and Humanities, vol. 5 no. 4, Jerusalem, 1973.

Prat, S. J. Fernand, *The Theology of Saint Paul*. Vol. 2, tr. by John L. Stoddard, London: Burns Oates and Washbourne, 1942.

Quispel, Gilles, "Paul and Gnosis: a Personal View," in Roelof van den Broek and Cis van Heertum, eds., *From Poimandres to Jacob Böhme: Gnosis, Hermetism and the Christian Tradition*, Amsterdam: Bibliotheca Philosophica Hermetica, 2000, 271-302.

Rahner, Karl, ed., *Encyclopedia of Theology. The Concise Sacramentum Mundi*, New York: Crossroad, 1991.

_____, *The Spirit in the Church*, New York: Seabury Press, 1979.

Ratzinger, Joseph Cardinal, *Introduction to Christianity*, tr. by J. R. Foster, San Francisco, CA: Ignatius Press, 1990.

Ridgeon, Lloyd V. J., *Crescents on the Cross. Islamic Visions of Christianity*, Oxford: Oxford University Press, 1999.

Roberts, Alexander and Donaldson, James, eds., *The Ante-Nicene Fathers*, vol. 8, Grand Rapids, Michigan: Wm. B. Eerdmans. American Edition, undated.

Robson, James, *Christ in Islam*, London: John Murray, 1929.

Schedl, Claus, *Muhammad und Jesus. Die christologisch relevanten Texte des Korans neu übersetzt und erklärt*, Wien, Freiburg, Basel:Herder, 1978.

Scheeben, Matthias Joseph, *The Mysteries of Christianity*, tr. by Cyril Vollert, St. Louis. Missouri: B. Herder, 1947.

Schillebeeckx, Edward, *Christ. The Experience of Jesus as Lord*, tr. by John Bowden, New York: Crossroad, 1981.

_____, *Jesus. An Experiment in Christology*, tr. by Hubert Hoskins, New York: Seabury Press, 1979.

Schoeps, Hans Joachim, *Jewish Christianity. Factional Disputes in the Early Church*, tr. by Douglas R. A. Hare, Philadelphia: Fortress Press, 1964.

_____, *Theologie und Geschichte des Judenchristentums*, Tübingen:Verlag J. C. B. Mohr/Paul Siebeck, 1949.

Schuon, Frithjof, *Christianity/Islam. Essays on Esoteric Ecumenism*, tr. by Gustavo Polit, Bloomington, Indiana: World Wisdom Books, 1985.

_____, *Dimensions of Islam*, tr. by P. N. Townsend, London: George Allen and Unwin, 1970.

_____, *The Essential Frithjof Schuon*, ed. by Seyyed Hossein Nasr, World Wisdom Books: Bloomington, Indiana, 2005, 102.

_____, *Form and Substance in the Religions*, Bloomington, Indiana: World Wisdom Books, 2002.

_____, *From the Divine to the Human. Survey of Metaphysics and Epistemology*, tr. by Gustavo Polit and Deborah Lambert, Bloomington, Indiana: World Wisdom Books, 1982.

_____, *The Fullness of God. Frithjof Schuon on Christianity*, ed. by James S. Cutsinger, Bloomington, Indiana: World Wisdom Books, 2004.

_____, *Gnosis: Divine Wisdom*, tr. from the French by G. E. H. Palmer, Pates Manor, Bedfont, Middlesex: Perennial Books, 1990.

_____, *In the Face of the Absolute*, Bloomington, Indiana: World Wisdom Books, 1994.

_____, *Islam and the Perennial Philosophy*, tr. by J. Peter Hobson, World of Islam Festival Publishing Co., 1976.

_____, *Spiritual Perspectives and Human Facts*, tr. by P. N. Townsend, Pates Manor, Bedfont, Middlesex: Perennial Books, 1987.

_____, *Sufism: Veil and Quintessence*, ed. by James S. Cutsinger, Bloominton,

Indiana: World Wisdom Books, 2006.

_____, *The Transcendent Unity of Religions*, tr. by Peter Townsend, New York: Harper & Row, 1975.

_____, *Treasures of Buddhism*, Bloomington, Indiana: World Wisdom Books, 1993

_____, *Understanding Islam*, tr. by D. M. Matheson, London: George Allen & Unwin, 1976.

Sells, Michael A., ed., *Early Islamic Mysticism. Sufi, Qur'an, Mi'raj, Poetic and Theological Writings. The Classics of Western Spirituality* series, New York/Mahwah, New Jersey: Paulist Press, 1996.

Toland, John, *Nazarenus: or, Jewish, Gentile, and Mahometan Christianity*, London: J. Brown, J. Roberts, and J. Brotherton, 1718.

Valiuddin, Mir, *Love of God. A Sufic Approach*, Farnham, Surrey, England: Sufi Publishing Co., 1972.

Waters, SR., Kenneth L., "Matthew 27:52-53 as Apocalyptic Apostrophe: Temporal-Spatial Collapse in the Gospel of Matthew," *Journal of Biblical Literature* 122 no. 3, Fall 2003, 489-515.

Weber, Robertus, ed., *Biblia Sacra: iuxta Vulgatam versionem. Editio altera emendata*, tomus II, Stuttgart: Württembergische Bibelanstalt, 1975.

Zinner, Samuel, *Christianity and Islam*, London: Matheson Trust, 2011.

INDEX